JOHN TAYLOR'S VILLAGE STORIES

VOLUME 5

SIMPSON
& WOUGHTON

JOHN A TAYLOR

i

JOHN TAYLOR'S VILLAGE STORIES
5 SIMPSON & WOUGHTON

Published by Magic Flute Publishing Ltd. 2022
ISBN 978-1-915166-09-8

Copyright © John A. Taylor

John A. Taylor has asserted his right under the Copyright, Designs and Patents Act 1988 to be identified as the author of this work.

All rights reserved. No part of this publication may be reproduced, stored in a retrieval system, or transmitted in any form or by any means, electronic, mechanical, photocopying, recording or otherwise, without the prior permission of the copyright owner.

Magic Flute Publishing Limited
231 Swanwick Lane
Southampton SO31 7GT
www.magicflutepublishing.com

A catalogue description of this book is available from the British Library

MAGIC FLUTE
PUBLISHING

CONTENTS

ACKNOWLEDGEMENTS

The staff of Milton Keynes Central library
'Village Memories' by Ouida Rice
Royal Horticultural Society
Michael Day
Rebekah Taylor
Sally Mason
Peter Barnes
Eric Gates
Clive Birch
Mick Shaw

FURTHER READING

Additional aspects of the past have already been fully researched in the following sources.

Charles Warren of Simpson House

In 2019 at Simpson the present occupant of Simpson House, Eric Gates, gave a talk entitled 'Charles Warren & the Lost Inheritance.' This encapsulated his extensive research into the man and the House, and a transcript is available.

The Plough

Researched by Paul Cox, the story of the pub through the ages is copiously told on the website www.mkheritage.org.uk. In additional information, until his tragic death in 1741 a Simpson man had a roadside hut, or stall, for the sale of ale and other liquors opposite where the Denbigh Hall inn would be.

(In 1844 there were three pubs: The Plough, kept by Richard Hazlewood; the New Inn, kept by J.S Bodley; and the Lion and the Lamb, kept by William Webb, who had served his apprenticeship to a tallow chandler.)

WW2

Several personnel involved with the Bletchley Park code breaking were billeted at Simpson. Their stories were researched by the

Simpson History Group, and displayed on information boards at an exhibition in 2015 on September 12th. In 1950 the Old Bakehouse in the village became the family home of Brigadier J.C.H. Mead, a distinguished soldier who had seen extensive wartime service in France, including the Dunkirk evacuation, India and Burma, where he was awarded the DSO. He retired from the Army in the summer of 1959. Ironically, having survived countless actions during the war, he was killed riding with the Whaddon Chase Hunt in 1959 on Saturday, December 12th. His horse failed to clear a fence and he was thrown off, breaking his neck. He left a widow, two sons and a daughter. (The premises were refurbished in 1976.)

Warren Royal Dawson

Having lived at Simpson for 23 years, at the age of 70 in the Birthday Honours of 1959 Warren Royal Dawson received the OBE for services to historical research. He published 20 volumes on various historical subjects, and his life story is variously told on Internet sites. Locally an obituary appeared in the Bletchley Gazette of May 10th 1968. Additionally a reminiscence was included in the copy of October 25th 1974.

SIMPSON

Above: An old photograph of the village.
Below: A modern plan of the present village layout.

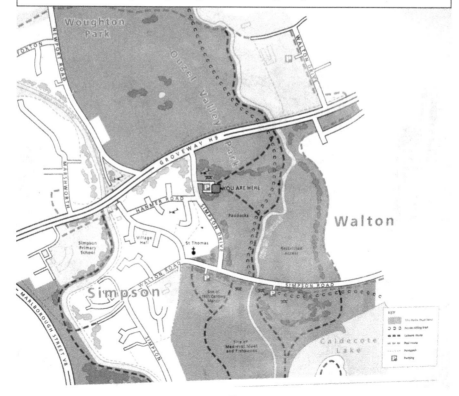

THE EARLY HISTORY OF SIMPSON[A]

LORDS OF THE MANORS AND LANDOWNERS

Queen Edith, wife of Edward the Confessor, held Simpson before the Conquest, and since she managed to retain possession until her death, in 1075, presumably connived with William to find such favour. Apparently the locals were made of sterner stuff, for their resistance to the invaders resulted in a devastation of the village. A second, although less significant landowner at Simpson, was Lewin Oaura, who, having held lands at the village before 1066, managed to retain around one and a half hides after Harold's defeat. An indication that perhaps he had also bent with the winds of fortune. At her death, the Queen's manor of nine hides found grant to the Bishop of Coutances, who also locally held that of 'Etone' (Bletchley). Then before the mid 13th century Simpson had been acquired by Geoffrey de Cauz. Probably through marriage the powerful de Grey family came by the estate, with John de Grey mentioned as lord in 1254. By his son, Reginald, first Baron Wilton, in 1307 the manor passed with those of Bletchley and Stoke Hammond to his second son Roger. By 1551 due to the spendthrift ways of Richard de Grey, son of George, the second Earl of Kent, the manor had been purchased by Thomas Pigott. Then to be sold in 1578 by his son, also Thomas, to Thomas and William Cranwell. In 1622 Thomas Cranwell put the manor up as part security for a debt of £165 to one Robert Dixon. However he forgetfully omitted to mention that the manor had been previously mortgaged to Sir Arthur Wilmot. Needless to say Robert was non too pleased when he found out! A legal action consequently brought about settlements of the manor, such that by 1631 Arthur Warren held sole possession. Meanwhile during the past decades the Hatch family had been busily acquiring various village holdings, and now feathered their nest by gaining the Simpson manor. Thomas of the family married Dorothy, daughter of John Spencer, from Windsor, and their offspring, Spencer, duly inherited the manor. By Spencer, to include an entourage of his mother and his wife, the estate passed in 1683 to a resident of Coventry, John Walden. He died six years

---

A Reproduced from the book *Cows Before Concrete*, based on a local newspaper series published in 1980.

later and eventually at the onset of the 18th century the interest was acquired by Susan, daughter of his brother, Thomas. She married Job Hanmer in 1717 and their son, Walden, succeeded on Job's death in 1739. Walden would be a school fellow of the celebrated Bletchley diarist William Cole, and following education at Eton and Oxford he progressed to the Inns of Court, eventually practising as a councillor in Bucks. He made his home in the village of Broughton but his mother continued to reside in Simpson at Simpson Place, as the manorial home. By Walden, created a baronet in 1774, the first attempt to enclose the village was made in 1762. However the other landowners, including John Goodman, as the second largest, had other ideas and successfully defeated the plan. Only after eight years of petty bickering did the move go through, with Walden acquiring, mostly along the Ouzel banks, some 288 acres, and John Goodman and his son a combined 185 acres. Walden died in 1783 to be succeeded by his son Sir Thomas, who in 1806 then sold off the manor house plus some 200 acres of land. The purchaser was Charles Pinfold, by whom the house was demolished and the ancient manor farm lands, formerly in the tenure of one Thomas Cumberland, let to William Sipthorp as tenant. He held the tenancy of the Manor Farm at Walton (the village where he lived and died) and by his namesake son the estate was purchased prior to 1860, when the house tenancy expired William then moved to Simpson where he lies buried in the churchyard. John, his son, inherited the property and rebuilt the frontage of the village 'Manor Farm.' The name reflected the social aspirations of his wife, who together with her husband assumed the airs and privileges of Lord and Lady of the Manor, despite no manor having existed at the village for many generations. In fact the manorial rights had ceased in the early 19th century although the parish still paid 4s 6d a year to Lord Carrington, of Gayhurst, at his Newport Pagnell court. William Sipthorp had shared the position of a principal landowner with such worthies as the Rev. T. W. Hanmer, Miss Pinfold, of Walton Hall, and Gregory Odell Clarke, of Fenny Stratford. Also Charles Warren, who in 1823 built Simpson House on the site of the Goodman's ancient farmhouse. In fact his wife, Leonora, was a member of the Goodman family, and her death in 1841 predeceased that of her husband by 31 years. By all accounts the

House had fine grounds occupying the site of the previous cottages of farm labourers, with rock gardens and a fountain. Alterations to the House took place during and after Warren's lifetime, and indeed beneath the dining room floor remained a 25ft deep well. Interestingly with the installation of a new pump this found a re-use in 1942, filling a water tank as an emergency war measure. After the death of his wife in 1841 Warren had remarried, and after his death in 1872 his widow gained occupancy of the house for life. Following her decease the house was sold to Octavius Berrell of London for £1,250. He later sold it to Thomas Kench and his wife. They then held possession until their deaths, which strangely occurred within hours of each other. Early tenants of the House would include a widow, Mrs. Maria Annie Pitt, with her two daughters. Also her 'dandy of diminutive size' son, who having unfortunately put Ada Maud White in the family way absconded during the paternity trial, and was never heard of again. Since then the old House variously found military use as a first aid post, ARP Centre and Home Guard Quartermasters stores during World War II. With the arrival of the new city it then provided within the former grounds a site for several new houses, and within the House accommodation for quantity surveyors of Milton Keynes Development Corporation. By the end of the 19th century the principal landowners of the village were John Sipthorp, Francis Farnborough, and Miss Pinfold of Walton Hall. In the early 20th century the Sipthorps retained this status and shared the position of landowner with Dr. Vaughan Harley, MD, as the new occupant of Walton Hall. Then by the outbreak of World War II, Hugh Sipthorp, previously in residence at the 'Oaks,' occupied the 'Mount', and with Thomas Sipthorp of Rectory Farm, held most of the land.

GROWTH & TRADES

The name Simpson derives from early times, when a Saxon named Sigewine founded his settlement, or 'tun,' within the area. Thereby this became 'Sigewines tun,' condensed to Simpson. Presumably his Saxon successors took exception to the Norman takeover, for their resistance to the invaders led to a ravaging of the village. However they perhaps spared the water mill on the Ouzel, for it was valued by the Domesday Survey at 10s a year. Throughout the ensuing centuries farming long remained of importance, with a compaction of the lands into large separate fields by 'Enclosure' in 1770. Many dwellings survive from that century, with several evident along the course of the old village main street. This once formed a section of the Bletchley to Newport Pagnell road but has since been dislocated and bypassed through a web of new road layouts. Apart from the creation of new fields the three enclosure commissioners further brought into being 'Groveway', laid down to connect the village with the Watling Street at a point near 'Denbigh Hall'. For the affected landowners one benefit of enclosure was the abolition of tiresome tithes, originally one tenth of produce and cattle payable to the rector for his upkeep. Replacing this burden each landowner instead gave up a proportion of their acreage, which, totalling some 240, were positioned mostly along Groveway, and provided compensation for the rector. However as a reminder of the previous system at Rectory Farm evidence has been discovered of a 17th century tithe barn. Also several 13th or 14th century pits which, since one contained traces of wattle work, might have been used for storing fish. Indeed due to the nearby presence of a pond the original timber structure, of late medieval times, had the north and east walls constructed on limestone footings. In contrast to the rector the village poor fared not so well. Their plight was often only alleviated by charities set up by kindly benefactors, and of these in 1573 some 40 acres had been given by Thomas Pigott, of Doddershall. His bequest included a farm at Simpson, with one acre situated in Woughton. Also some eight cottages let rent free to 'poor, industrious and deserving families.' In the early 20th century the proceeds realised £100, expended on providing coal for the parish poor. In other benefactions Sir Thomas Hanmer established a charity in 1817, bequeathing the rent due from a piece of land in Fenny Stratford. Thereby £1 was raised. Many of the ancient dwellings of the village now remain only in past writings. Of particular interest lay an 'L shaped group east of the churchyard, and indeed their sole approach appears to have been along a churchyard footpath. The original foundation was probably laid down during the 16th century. In 1841 Joseph Bodley is recorded as a beer retailer, with William Bodley in residence at the 'Plough.' In fact the Bodley family would long be stalwarts in the village, and by the close of the 19th century Frederick Bodley finds mention as a 'grocer, provision dealer, assistant overseer, farmer and agent to the Atlas Insurance Co. (fire & life).' At the sale of the Walton Hall Estate in 1902 he purchased land on which to build his family home. This would be 'The Walnuts' with construction commenced in 1903 once the previous ancient buildings had been cleared away. From the detail evident on a plan of 1781 the area had once comprised three ancient inclosures; namely Stones Orchard, a plot belonging to a Mrs. Austin, and a field possessed by John Newman. (Seemingly from Cranfield, by the Enclosure of 1770 he had received 58 acres of local land. He married Elizabeth Sear of Simpson, and is said to have built 'The Poplars' around 1792). In 1806 both the Orchard and the adjoining plot of Mrs. Austin passed to Charles Pinfold, upon his purchase of the manor house from Sir Thomas Hanmer with 200 acres of land. The two plots were thereby united, retaining diverse farm buildings and an old half timbered house. Interestingly the last tenant of this farm house is mentioned as Oliver Childs, who died at an Aylesbury hospital in 1888 on February 1st. After his death the old farmhouse then became two tenements, until demolished around 1902. Nearby, the Old Bakehouse came into existence during the 18th century, built on a site anciently known as The Holmes (a 'holm' referring to flat low lying ground near a river or stream.) The premises included stables, a paddock, various out-buildings and a bakehouse, and eventual possession passed in 1826 to Gregory Odell Clarke, of Fenny Stratford prominence. He let the property to a son, George, who being an unfortunate wastrel was destined to end his days in the workhouse. During 1873 purchase was made by Robert Stevens of Bow Brickhill, who not only continued the bakery but also divided the house into two parts. Not surprisingly the western most took the name Yew Tree Cottage from a yew tree that flourished in the front garden. Near to the Rectory a lane once led towards Rectory Farm, at the approach of which stood two cottages of brick and slate. One accommodated a smithy, and both cottages came up for auction at the Bull Inn of Fenny Stratford in 1877. The cutting of the Grand Junction canal completely re-arranged the layout of the village, which through the several springs of the area regularly flooded in winter along the main road. However said to be through the efforts of

Charles Warren, a builder of Simpson House, the road was raised 3½ feet to clear the average flood level by some six inches. As for the Simpson to Walton road, to overcome the flooding on this stretch a recommendation of the Council minutes in 1897 proposed erecting foot planks as a temporary measure. By the construction of the canal the land westwards of the main street, from Canal Cottage to the bend before the Plough Inn, which had once been part of the acreage of a large field, was sliced off by the 'Cut.' Apparently due to a default of payment by Will Kimble, of Loughton, in 1892 this strip was divided into 3 sections; namely the Mount, situated centrally and retained by Kimble, Claypit Field to the north, and Hill Crest to the south. At this southern end stood three kilns for burning lime and manufacturing bricks, for the coming of the canal had induced the creation of a small canal-side brickworks. Also a wharf, operated in 1864 by John Mead. At this time amongst the inevitable farmers his contemporary traders accounted a grocer and grazier, a beer retailer, three cattle dealers (one also a butcher), a carpenter, a blacksmith and a shoemaker. They all served a population of 562, nearly four times the mid 16th century figure. Plague had claimed many victims in 1665 and thus by 1676 the village accommodated only 120 inhabitants. Interestingly in 1901 the given population of 731 included 440 persons living on barges, whose custom no doubt

The Plough Inn today.

benefited the adjoining village pub, the Plough. This, built on a site once known as Plough Home Close, became the property of Charles Pinfold from Walton in 1806, having at that time a westerly frontage facing Boobys Lane, the main road through the village towards Newport Pagnell. Part of this old track vanished with the construction of the canal, and by 1843 the Plough, plus a few other properties, came to William Sipthorp. By the industry of his son, John, rebuilding to the present outlook was undertaken in 1877. Between the Plough Inn and Simpson House the present brick dwellings date from 1905, built by Mr. Alfred Benford. Here on April 2nd 1906 the Post Office was opened, with Mr. W. E. Smith remaining as the tenant and sub-postmaster until 1919. He then vacated the 'Post Office' and moved next door into the 'Cottage'! Now occupied by council bungalows, in 1919 the site opposite to The Walnuts, which had once been the kitchen garden for the house, was purchased by Walter Webster, a printer. Chandlers Court commemorates the famed 17th century family of bell founders, at whose foundry in Drayton Parslow a bell for the church at Simpson was cast in 1603. Simpson's parish boundaries long caused great confusion to neighbouring Fenny Stratford, and not until 1951, after four years of discussion, would the situation be resolved. During the early 19th century the parents of Simpson children could obtain an elementary education for their offspring through the services of Rebecca 'Becky' Rands. She was born the eighth of nine children to Francis Litchfield Rands, and her schoolroom was in the parlour of her small cottage at the southernmost end of Mount Pleasant. However this facility came to an end in 1876 when the school at Simpson was opened. With the extensive new developments the village of today would be an education to any past inhabitant, and one wonders what comment might be drawn from that observer in 1862, who described the contemporary scene as "one of the most wretched of many miserable villages in the county."

RELIGIOUS ORDERS AND CHURCHES

The church is dedicated to St. Thomas, the old village feast having always been held on December 21st, St. Thomas's Day. The impressive building with walls of limestone rubble can trace origins to an early structure of the 13th century. However it seems the first church soon fell into disrepair, for the present structure dates mainly from around

1330. Yet the piers supporting the tower are retained from the old smaller building, thus accounting for the apparent scaling down of the tower in relation to the rest of the plan of the church. Rebuilding of the chancel and the two transepts began around 1330, at which time the chancel was widened. Some ten years later the nave was reconstructed, and at the end of the 14th century a re-roofing at a lower level took place. The west window dates from the 15th century but the others are of a century earlier, all having since been altered. The close of the 14th century also saw a heightening of the tower, which came to house six bells. These included two from the famed Drayton Parslow foundry of the Chandlers but were re-cast around 1908. Also around 1400 the north transept stairs were built, providing access to the rood loft. Before the Reformation this crossed the chancel arch, and the doorway at the north east corner of the nave is still evident. In recent years a wooden staircase provided access to the bell ringing chamber (in the second stage of the tower) where a new ringers' floor had been inserted over the tower arches. Each of two lights, the four windows of the bell chamber are possibly of early 15th century date. However in the chancel modern windows are wholly in evidence, since the erection of the Hanmer monument in 1789 caused the square headed window of the chancel south wall to be bricked up - (the external outline is still discernible.) The transepts, one north of the tower, and one south, are an interesting feature of the church, and form its cruciform plan. Both were re-roofed in the 17th century and both incorporate a small opening, now glazed, in their end walls. Possibly these apertures allowed lepers to witness the church services without infecting the congregation. In the 1860s the north transept accommodated the parish school, and the south transept found use as a vestry. At the cost of Major Wyndham Edward Hanmer Bart, of Stockgrove, a partial restoration of the church came about in 1873, with a thorough restoration of the chancel by Mr. Agustus Brown. The ceiling and square east window were removed, and a panelled roof, 'handsomely decorated,' and a 3 light window, filled with cathedral glass, 'relieved by neat designs in coloured glass,' were substituted. Staffordshire tiles were laid in the chancel and Minton tiles in the sanctuary. The north and south transepts were restored by Miss Bidwell, sister of the rector, the Reverend G.S. Bidwell, and from funds contributed by his relatives, and those of his wife, a carved oak pulpit and reading desk were provided. As for the arch leading from the nave to the central tower this, having been in a dilapidated and dangerous state, was repaired by the parishioners 'and some other friends.' Then in 1904 at a cost of £1,300 a restoration of the nave took place, during which on removal of a false ceiling fine 17th century timbering of the hammer beam roof was revealed Also the Royal Arms painted directly onto the plaster above the chancel arch. However they pose an anomaly, for whilst the arms are of Queen Anne the upper letters G.R., dated 1742, refer to George III. Within the chancel are wall monuments to the Hanmer family, and also the most ancient tombstone in the entire county of Buckinghamshire. This commemorates William Gale, who died in 1638, and, until brought within the church to prevent further weathering, originally lay in the churchyard. Affixed to the north nave wall are two marble memorials, commemorating Charles Warren, died aged 74 on April 19th, 1872, and his wife Leonora. East of these plaques a nave window contains stained glass to the memory of George Bidwell, a past rector, and his wife Emma. This was given by their children in 1931. West of the Warren plaques is a brass plate to the memory of those men of the parish who fell in the Great war. On the opposite wall a second brass plate commemorates Jack Hawley Jones, Military Medal, who was killed in action as a stretcher bearer at Hamel in World War 1. Outside the church is a war memorial of Cornish granite, and in the 16th century south porch is an oak tablet to commemorate those who served in the two world wars. In the church are two fonts, since around 1954 an old font came to light in the Rectory garden. This was originally destined for the then newly built St. Frideswide's at Water Eaton. However today the weathered stone tub, probably of Saxon origin by size and shape, has pride of place at the western end of the church, near to the more modern but now displaced octagonal font. Interestingly the characteristic depth of these early tubs was due to the practice of the converts standing upright as the water was poured over them. In 1872 came the construction of a new rectory, to replace a half timbered predecessor of possible foundation during the 17th century. With extensive outbuildings, this accommodation seems to once have been of impressive proportions, including within the one acre site not only '6 bays of Building, tiled,' but also 'a Parlor Hall, Dairy, Kitchen and Buttery, all chambered over, and disposed into 7 several rooms.' The demise for this rectory began with the appointment in 1807 of the Rev. Thomas Walden Hanmer, 'a negligent rector, always in debt.' Indeed shortly after the Reverend's death in 1871 those engaged in demolishing the rectory were moved to remark on the 'ruinous, dirty and verminous' condition to which the building had degenerated. Through the eccentricity of his life style as much as by his fox hunting pursuits the Reverend, and often irreverent, Hanmer earned the title 'Tally Ho,' and for many years this colourful figure, replete with mahogany hued top boots, black breeches, and a low black hat with a broad and flat brim. enlivened the village scene. During much of the week, excepting Sundays, the rectory stood barred to visitors, a wise precaution in view of the many creditors seeking access to his seemingly non existent finances. By his oratory 'Tally Ho' could not only preach very good sermons but whenever necessary also convince gullible friends to not infrequently 'lend' him sums of money. However he was eventually incarcerated in a debtors' prison, but still managed to default on a payment of some £190, due to kindly friends who had supplied him with food. As for others deserving imprisonment, in October 1974 12 brass chalices and candlesticks were stolen from the church to be later, excepting one, found dumped in a ditch at Drayton Parslow. The still missing item was a 17th century chalice about 10 inches high. As for the motive, the Rev. Robin Baker said "I have no idea why anyone should want to steal something from us and then just throw it away."

ADDENDUM

1888 OCTOBER

The Post Office opened.

1893 MAY

The Local Rural Sanitary Authority began laying on the water supply to Simpson.

1898 NOVEMBER

Opinions were taken as to whether to have gas supplied to the village.

1899 JUNE

Mr. Garner reported that the Lighting Committee had definite proposals to submit regarding the lighting of Simpson. The Gas Company had asked an annual £17 10s to cover the cost of laying the mains until such time as the consumption reached 750,000 cu ft. They now offered to reduce that payment by £3 after the consumption reached 300,000 cu ft. Then by £4 10s for every 100,000 cu ft, this being after the committee proposed erecting 21 lamps to light the village and main road. The report was adopted.

1900 JANUARY

The erection of the standards and the fixing of the lamps through the village as far as the main extended was completed by the contractor, Mr. A. Taylor. However difficulty had been encountered, as the whole of the lamps wouldn't light at the same time. They would illuminate as far as Mr. Bramley's house but it was generally found that when a portion was burning his end of the village wouldn't light. On the other hand when the Fenny Stratford portion was lit the parish remained in darkness!

1902 OCTOBER

The gas main had now been extended to the school. However the last lamp was about 100 yards from the building, and with it subsequently being dark it was dangerous and inconvenient for people whenever a meeting was held there.

1903 NOVEMBER

The lighting given off by the gas lamps along Simpson road is reported to be little better than farthing candles.

1906 APRIL

The Post Office reopened on Monday April 2nd as a money order and savings bank office.

1908 JANUARY

At the sub post office a telegraph office was opened, with telegrams to be delivered from there to Walton, Caldecote, Milton Keynes, Bow Brickhill, Woughton, the Woolstones, and Simpson. The office was already a money order and savings bank office, and all sorts of licences were available. There were three daily deliveries - 6.30am, 12.30pm and 6.25pm.

1910

The Simpson Parish Provident Club is founded.[1]

1916 September

At the post office Mr. Smith had the need for a respectable youth or girl aged about 15 to assist in the shop and office. Also to take out telegrams. Live in.

1918 DECEMBER

At the post office Mr. B. Smith had for sale an inlaid, walnut, sweet toned musical box that played not only the Welsh national anthem but also 7 other tunes. £3.

1934 JUNE

Bletchley joined the first Urban District Council three years after its formation in 1895 and in the aftermath of WW1 commenced its housing programme, to include at Simpson. In the slum clearance programme of the Council in 1934 five residences in the village were scheduled for demolition, with eight houses to be built.

FREDERICK BODLEY & FAMILY

JOHN BODLEY - THE FOUNDING FATHER

Born at Bow Brickhill on May 6th 1806, in 1836 at Simpson on May 2nd John Bodley married Maria Lucas, born at Walton. As for some years past, in 1851 he was a grocer in the village, resident (ages as per the census) with his wife Maria and, all born at Simpson, their children George, 14, Ann, 12, Frederick, 9, and Eli, 1. By 1861 John was now also a farmer (grazier), Frederick a draper, Ann an assistant grocer, and Eli a scholar. John died at Simpson in 1868 on November 10th.

FREDERICK BODLEY

Baptised in 1843 on September 10th, Frederick Bodley was born at Simpson, and by 1861 was in occupation as a draper. In 1866 on October 6th at the New Wesleyan Chapel, Hockliffe Road, Leighton Buzzard, he married Mary Jane Pipkin, born at Leighton Buzzard in 1845, the only daughter of James Pipkin, a brewer of Leighton Buzzard. In 1867 a daughter, Annie Louisa, was born at Wolverton, and then in 1869 twins, John James (d1929) and Samuel Frederick.

Employed to look after the children, in July 1870 Caroline Pitkin on taking them out for recreation was set upon by the son of Noah Hill throwing stones at her. He then tried to upturn the pram, at which Frederick rushed out and boxed his ears. In consequence Noah assaulted Frederick, swearing and striking him. The offence had occurred on July 30th, and in August 1870 at the Newport Pagnell Petty Sessions Noah was charged with assault. A fine of 2s 6d and 13s costs was imposed, or 7 days in prison.

In business matters in March 1871 Frederick advertised that he was now selling 'Herington's Balsamic Cough Elixir. Prepared only by J. Herington, Pharmaceutical Chemist, Leighton Buzzard.' In April that year at Simpson his family now comprised himself and his wife and their children Annie Louisa, John James, Samuel Frederick, and now a daughter Lucy Jane, aged 5 months, born at Simpson. Also resident was the aforementioned Caroline Pitkin, age 20, born at Bletchley. Then in 1872 a son, Harry Spencer, was born and in 1874 a daughter Laura, followed in 1876 by Mary Beatrice.

Now listed as a grocer, draper and butcher, in December 1879 Frederick posted thanks to everyone who had patronised him for the last 10 years. He hoped for their continued custom, and would also be glad to assist any parish officers in the keeping of their accounts - 'Highway, Poor or any other' - being further prepared to make and collect the rates for any number of parishes. In fact apart from his daily business throughout over 50 years he would be very active in public service, and suffice to say this would include the offices of assessor and collector of taxes for 12 parishes; assistant overseer for three parishes; clerk to two parish councils; collector of water rents under Newport Pagnell RDC for two parishes; and correspondent to three Boards of Managers of County Schools. Nevertheless he still found the energy to increase his progeny, and in 1879 another son, Rupert Frank, was born. Thus in April 1881 (when he is no longer noted as a butcher) his offspring totalled Annie, John, Samuel, Lucy, Harry, Laura, Mary, and Rupert. Soon to be joined by William George, born in 1883.

By now several of the first born were of marrying age, and in 1889 on December 25th at the Baptist Chapel, Fenny Stratford, Mr. Alfred Collins of Reading married Annie Louisa, Frederick's eldest daughter. As for those siblings still at home, in 1891 these were John, single, 'assistant,' Rupert Frank, and William.

In business Frederick was still a grocer and draper but in his extensive public life in 1892 he stood for election to the County Council. However, as ungraciously recounted in a letter from 'KENTITE' to the local press this proved unsuccessful, as would another attempt.

> "Mr. Bodley, who at the invitation of the Liberal Association has contested Winslow, has deservedly been well licked. That the contest would terminate in the defeat of the aspiring grocer was all along a foreseen event, but that the County Council has been spared the affliction which the presence of this ambitious place seeker would probably have occasioned, is a matter upon which they will doubtless congratulate themselves. ... nothing now remains for Mr. Bodley but to return to the swamps of Simpson where he will be better employed dispensing soap and candles, and will be relegated to that obscurity from which he should never have emerged."

So now back in the swamps of Simpson in 1895 Mr. Bodley could offer in addition to soap and candles 'Carter's Elephant and Kangaroo Swede, and Warden Prize Mangold. Genuine in sealed packs only of Frederick Bodley & Son, Simpson.' Presumably the son was John, who from Simpson the following year advertised 'To obtain plentiful supplies of brown winter eggs, give the Orpingtons a trial. Eggs from a select pen, 2/6 dozen.' Then offered for sale in June 1896 were 'strong, sturdy plants, in quantity, cauliflower, Brussels, Cabbage, Broccoli, and winter greens, 6d hundred.'

However in 1897 John had other interests, when on January 11th at the Wesleyan Chapel he married Miss Lydia Richardson, third daughter of John Richardson of Eakley Lanes, and late of Simpson. The groom's sister Laura was one of the two bridesmaids, with the best man being John's twin brother Samuel, from Brighton. The newly weds would duly make their home at Fenny Stratford.

In 1900, in business matters came a new venture, when in September it was reported that Frederick had lately turned his attention to fruit culture. Yet not with much success, since that year he could hardly give the produce away, and having cut down between 40 and 50 gooseberry bushes had to make a bonfire of them on

November 5th. Even the plums were unwanted. More pleasingly, in 1902 on May 17th at the Baptist Chapel Regent's Park, London, the marriage took place of Mr. A.J. Welland, of Balham, and Frederick's youngest daughter, Mary.

As for Simpson, in 1903 it seems that a change of the Bodley family residence would take place. This commenced when Messrs. G.A. Wilkinson & Son, surveyors and auctioneers of 7, Poultry, London, advertised that on Thursday, May 7th 1903 at 2pm an auction would be held at the Swan Hotel, Fenny Stratford, of 'the valuable freehold property known as the Walton Hall Estate.' This was situated in the parishes of Walton and Simpson and included the Walnut Tree Farm and 'Bodley's Farm,' together with excellent farm houses and buildings. Consequent to the death a while ago of Miss Pinfold the estate had descended to Miss Seagrave, by whose instructions the sale was held. Despite being the largest room at the Swan, such was the interest that the billiard room was overflowing. The estate was firstly offered as a whole but with the only bid of £15,000 being refused lots were subsequently offered. A portion of Bodley's Farm, containing about 41 acres 3r 29p, and let at £50pa, fell to Mr. Janes of Simpson at £1,000. Another portion of the same, let at £3 10s pa, was then purchased by Mr. Pipkin of London for £350.

It seems that Frederick, who had farmed some 180 acres of the extent, which adjoined Walton Hall, also came by an interest, on which his future home, The Walnuts, was built that year to the plans of Mr. J.T. Lawrence, an architect of Leighton Buzzard. On the ground floor the extensive premises comprised a small vestibule lounge entrance hall, a dining room with French casement, opening direct onto a veranda, a drawing room and a snug morning room. Above were five principal and secondary bedrooms, a bath room etc., with the 'domestic apartments' shut off from the house and approached by a passage from the lounge hall. Also there was 'a good roof room,' formed by boarding over a large part of the second floor. It seems that at Simpson the family had previously lived at Fir Tree House, for having vacated the property in 1904 on Thursday, May 12th 'by direction of the owner' the surplus furniture was auctioned on the premises by Geo. Wigley.

17

Then in 1904 on Thursday, June 2nd at the Swan Hotel, Fenny Stratford, on behalf of Frederick Bodley 'the freehold house known as the Fir Tree,' with large pleasure and kitchen gardens 'and particularly adapted for business purposes' was auctioned. Commencing at £400 the bidding rose to £550, with the purchaser being Miss Catherine Eaton (niece of the rector), of Simpson Rectory. From an initial £200 four adjoining cottages, producing a rental of £25 11s 4d, were bought by the rector of Simpson, the Rev. William Rice, for £250. However a freehold house, grocer's shop and bakery at the corner of Aylesbury Street and Denmark Street at Fenny Stratford, let at £55pa, were bought in at £890. At this time it was announced that having passed his exam Mr. Bodley's youngest son, William, was now a member of the Pharmaceutical Society of Great Britain. He was also successful in his college exams, taking four certificates of honour and a silver medal. His apprenticeship had been served at Balham, following education at the Simpson school and Bedford Modern.

On Wednesday, August 10th an auction of 29 acres of growing crops was auctioned by direction of Frederick Bodley, 'who was now vacating the farm.' In fact he was giving up farming, and by his direction in 1904 on Monday, October 10th an auction in a field at the back of The Walnuts was held by Geo. Wigley & Sons of 3 cart horses, a cart foal, a grey nag mare and foal, Berkshire boar, 2 sows, and 18 pigs. Also 8 tons of old hay and the whole of the agricultural implements.

Elsewhere, in December 1904 it was advertised by Bodley & Co. (Proprietors, Bodley Brothers, fruit growers, seeds men, and tobacconists) of 77, Aylesbury Street, Fenny Stratford, and of Great Brickhill, that they now held a large and up to date stock of seasonable goods; 'Suitable for PRESENTS for the "festive" season.' 'Our Stock, turned over each week, ensures constant fresh supplies of choicest Fruit from the English and Foreign Markets.' Indeed, 'Our aim as heretofore, civility and personal attention, from cottage to Mansion.' Manure 'in large tins only 6d each' was also available for roses, pot plants, and all garden cops. Including pipes they could also offer tobacco products, and advertised 'Why not smoke the best cigarette in the world, DE RESKE, as supplied to the House of Commons. Only of BODLEY & Co., Fenny Stratford.' The partnership for this venture in Fenny Stratford - Messrs. Bodley and Co. nurserymen, seedsmen and florists, Aylesbury Street - was that between John James Bodley and his twin brother Samuel Frederick, who had joined John some 1 or 2 years before. However this co-operation would be tragically halved in 1905, when Samuel died in the early hours of Monday, May 15th. Aged just 36 he had been taken seriously ill early the previous week, with developing symptoms of pneumonia and peritonitis.

On the afternoon of Friday, May 19th the funeral cortege left the residence of the deceased in Aylesbury Street, and preceding the hearse a number of townsmen walked in procession to the cemetery gates. Following behind came several mourning coaches containing the family members, with other relatives and friends arriving on foot. However Samuel's brother John, of Great Brickhill, was unable to attend, from having been seriously injured in a trap accident some weeks before. In respect for the deceased the blinds of all the business premises in Aylesbury Street were drawn, and on the coffin were piled numerous wreaths. A memorial service was then held in the Wesleyan Chapel at Simpson on the Sunday evening.

In a much lighter mood, in 1905 on Wednesday, October 11th at 2pm at the parish church of Simpson the marriage took place of Miss Lucy Bodley, second daughter of Mr. and Mrs. Bodley, and Robert Charles Emerton, son of Robert Emerton of Salford. The bridesmaid was Laura's sister, Nurse Laura Bodley, with Edward Emerton, brother of the groom, as best man. A reception was held at The Walnuts, where in June 1906 Mrs. Bodley had need for 'a cook general, aged about 24. Must have good character.'

By now her third son, Rupert Frank Bodley, was living at 146, Brecknock Road, Tufnell Park, London, where in 1907 having retired to rest on Wednesday, August 28th he was found dead in bed by the maid on August 29th. At the Fenny Stratford schools he had trained as a pupil teacher under the old School Board but after serving his articles he left, and then went into mercantile work in the City, holding a post on the publishing staff of The Star newspaper. An inquest was held at the Coroner's Court, St. Pancras, on Saturday, August 31st, where Samuel J. Pipkin, uncle of the deceased, said he'd been dining with him at his home on the Wednesday evening last.

Gravestones of: Frederick Bodley (top left); John Bodley (top right); Lydia, John and James Bodley (Bottom)

On page 22: Samuel Frederick Bodley and Rupert Frank Bodley

Rupert had left his office at 4.40 to see a cricket match at Lords, and then came to his house at 7pm. After dinner they adjourned to the billiards room, and having played until 10pm Rupert then went to his home at 10.15pm. Giving evidence, Miss Dennant said she was the niece of the landlady. He had lived at the residence for 9 years and she heard him come in at 11.15. As for his health, his only ailment had apparently been a slight deafness.

In 1908 on the morning of Tuesday, June 30th Miss Laura Bodley, daughter of Mr. and Mrs. Bodley of The Walnuts, married Philip Richard Stevens, the son of the Rev. Philip Stevens, the Wesleyan Minister of Edmonton. In occupation as a nurse, Laura was held in high regard for her skills and cheerful disposition, and at the Wesleyan Chapel at Simpson an arch of flowers adorned the approach. Other floral arrangements had been placed on the walls by the villagers, with carpets laid from the road to the porch. Somewhat stormy, with some heavy showers, the weather proved hardly ideal but nevertheless the chapel was filled with a large gathering. In fact this was the first wedding to be held at the chapel, and in commemoration on behalf of the Trustees a copy of the Word of God and Wesleyan Hymn Book, bound together, was presented to the couple inscribed; "Presented by the trustees of the Wesleyan Methodist Chapel, Simpson, to Mr. and Mrs. Philip Richard Stevens, on the occasion of their marriage, being the first marriage in the above place of worship." The wedding breakfast was held in a marquee on the lawn at the south side of The Walnuts, and after a honeymoon at Cromer the newly weds would make their home at Bushey.

Then in 1908 on October 21st at St. Martin's Church, Fenny Stratford, the marriage took place of Mr. and Mrs. Bodley's third son, Harry Spencer Bodley, to Annie Pulham, eldest daughter of the late Mr. William Pulham of Fenny Stratford. Their offspring having now flown the nest, in 1911 at The Walnuts just Frederick, 'assistant overseer and tax collector,' and his wife were resident with 2 servants.

Then in 1915 shortly after the death of his elder brother, George, Frederick was bereaved by the death of his wife at The Walnuts on April 13th.

As for Frederick, in 1917 having suffered a serious illness the previous winter, which had begun with an attack of flu, leading to

IN
LOVING MEMORY OF
SAMUEL FREDERICK BODLEY,
WHO DIED MAY 15, 1905,
AGED 36 YEARS.
ALSO OF
RUPERT FRANK BODLEY,
WHO DIED AUGUST 29, 1907,
AGED 28 YEARS.
"Until the day break and the shadows flee away."

subsequent complications, he had resumed his duties during the spring and summer but died in 1917 on Sunday, October 28th. Probate (£884 4s 8d) was granted to Samuel James Pipkin, 'gent,' and also John James Bodley, 'farmer' who for a number of years had been his father's right hand man in practically all his public work. This he would now continue.

On Thursday, November 1st at The Walnuts in accordance with his father's wishes a short service was conducted, before which the pupils of the school were permitted to take a last look at the oak coffin and flowers. Afterwards they lined the walk and roadway to the hearse, with the cortege proceeding to Fenny Stratford where all the blinds were drawn and business suspended. Here the cortege was joined by amongst others the Inspector of Police, members of Fenny Stratford UDC, the managers of the Simpson school and Bow Brickhill school, Overseers of the Poor of Simpson, Woughton and Bow Brickhill, the manager of Barclays Bank, Dr. E. Nicholson, the Rev. W. Rice, tradesmen of the town, and many of those attending the market. A staunch Wesleyan Methodist, having held every office open to a layman, at the time of his death Frederick had been the Circuit Chapel Secretary, and it was by members of the Wesleyan Chapel that his coffin was borne to the grave. As instructed by his executors, on Friday, December 14th 1917 the whole of the furniture of The Walnuts was auctioned by Geo. Wigley and Sons, to include a governess car with rubber tyres, pony harness, and 58 head of poultry. Then at the Park Hotel, Bletchley, on the afternoon of Friday, April 26th 1918 they auctioned The Walnuts. This had the incentive of main drainage, public water supply, and town gas, whilst as for the grounds these were laid with lawns and flower beds. Also included was an orchard, and in the kitchen garden a small greenhouse. Additionally there was stabling for 4 horses, a thatched barn, piggeries, cow sheds etc, and at the side of the premises a grass paddock, with another piece of grazing land of about 4a 0r 1p. The whole was freehold and tithe free, as was the inclusion of two freehold and tithe free enclosures of feeding land. These amounted to just over 60 acres, and having a frontage of over ¼ mile to the Fenny Stratford road, and a frontage of nearly 1,000 ft to the Simpson and Walton road, were let to Hugh Sipthorp. The property was first offered at £4,500 and on rising to £6,200 was purchased by the Rev. Wlliam Rice, rector of Simpson. However after a short illness he died at the Rectory at Simpson in 1919 on February 5th, and by order of his executors The Walnuts was again put up for auction on Thursday, April 10th. [2]

THOMAS KENCH & ROBERT KENCH PERRY

Thomas Kench, baptised at the church of St. Mary, Harrow on the Hill, in 1809 on July 23rd, was the son of Thomas and Mary Kench, of Harrow. In 1837 on May 30th he married by license, since she was a minor, Anne Maria Evance, and with Thomas as a builder in 1841 they were living at Harrow on the Hill. Then in 1861 with Thomas as 'a landed proprietor' they were resident at Lymington. However in 1862 he is recorded as being of 221, Strand, Harrow on the Hill, in ownership of freehold houses and land. Again in ownership of land and freehold houses in 1863 and 1864 he and his wife were at Yew Tree Villa, Tilehurst, near Reading. In 1871 with Thomas now as a 'landholder, formerly a builder,' they were living at Park Villa, Stanwell, but in 1875 he purchased a property in Simpson from Octavius Burrell for £1,500. This he named Simpson (Sympson) House and in March 1880 advertised the need by April 5th for a man to attend a garden and horse, 'and to make himself generally useful' - 'To a suitable person liberal wages would be paid.'

However in 1884 Thomas put the house up for sale, instructing Geo. Wigley to auction the property on Thursday, June 12th at the

Swan Hotel, Fenny Stratford. Yet despite having nearly 3 acres of grounds, flower gardens, unique summerhouses, an ornamental fish pond, fountains, statuary, a conservatory, kitchen gardens, 'well stocked with fruit trees,' stabling and coach houses, a grass paddock at the rear, and a cottage for the groom or gardener, with the bidding beginning at £1,500 it failed to sell. In the wake of this there was still no success when Mr. Wigley invited private offers, and so, with no prospect of a new owner, instead of their intention to leave the country Thomas and his wife remained at Simpson. In August 1888 another attempt proved unsuccessful, and the following year Thomas and his wife both died at the house on May 18th. They had no children and in 1889 on June 29th as the administrator's solicitor C. Wyatt Francis of 61, Carey Street, Chancery Lane, London, posted;

'Notice is hereby given that all creditors and other persons having any debts, claims or demands upon or against the estate of Thomas Kench, formerly of Harrow on the Hill, in the county of Middlesex, but late of Sympson, near Fenny Stratford, in the county of Buckingham, formerly a builder, but lately out of business, (who died on the 9th day of May, 1889, and of whose personal estate, letters of administration, with a will annexed, were on the 26th day of June, 1889, granted to Robert Kench Perry, his lawful great nephew, and one of his next of kin, by the Principal Registry of the Probate Division of Her Majesty's High Court of Justice, are hereby required to send particulars in writing of their debts, claims and demands to me, the undersigned, the solicitor for the said administrator on or before the 17th day of August, 1889.'

Thomas was buried at St. Mary's churchyard, Harrow on the Hill, and, having the previous year been living at 4, Princess Terrace, Church Road, Acton, Robert Kench Perry and his wife and children took up residence at Simpson House. The couple had married at the parish church of Acton in 1880 on October 13th. Aged 20, at that time Robert, of Grove Place, Acton, was employed as a coachman, being the son of 'a school board visitor.' Also of Grove Place his bride was 19 year old Emily Clara Shelley, the daughter of a road foreman. In 1881 they were living in Horn Lane, Acton, with Robert now working as gardener. On moving to Simpson he soon became involved in the local scene, and in 1890 on the evening of Friday,

January 17th was chairman at a meeting of the Wolverton Liberal Association. This was held at the Science & Art Institute, being his first appearance at a Liberal meeting. Then on Easter Monday 1890 he captained a cricket team of Simpson Club in a match against the Fenny Stratford Town band. Despite the cold and stormy weather many spectators were in evidence, to witness him being run out for 1.

With the weather again inclement, not least from frequent storms, that year on a Wednesday and Thursday in July a Fancy Bazaar was held in the Rectory Grounds. This was in aid of the church restoration, and in a large marquee included a Fine Art Exhibition under the care of Mrs. Robert Kench Perry and Miss Rowland. As for Robert he had lent numerous articles, amongst which were some interesting models of torpedo boats etc., the work of the late Mr. Kench of Simpson House.

In other presentations, on Wednesday, August 20th 1890 at the meeting of the Newport Pagnell Board of Guardians he offered to present the inmates with 30 or so books from his library. Also old papers such as the Daily Graphic etc., which he purchased from the Reading Room in the village every quarter. Suffering severe head injuries, which entailed him being placed under medical care, on Thursday, November 27th 1890 he met with a serious trap accident between Newport Pagnell and Simpson.

It seems he duly recovered and in April 1891 with the attendance of 3 servants was still resident at Simpson House with his wife and, ages as per the census, children - Ada, 8, born at Shepherds Bush; Ernest, 6, born at Acton, and, also born at Acton, Robert, 5, and Frank, 2. However that year he decided to leave Simpson, and on October 27th having been put up for auction at The Mart, Tokenhouse Yard, London, Simpson House was sold by private treaty. The family would now be resident in London, where of 178, Seven Sisters, Road, Holloway, he was in occupation as a fruiterer.

As such he tragically died in 1892 on September 3rd, and at the inquest on Thursday, September 8th the details of the distressing circumstance were given. Frederick Nasielski, who was also a fruiterer and a friend of deceased, said that he had met him on the previous Thursday afternoon at a pub at Manor Park. Afterwards with both having their light spring carts outside they set off for home together, and from stopping at various pubs on the way Robert was somewhat worse for wear on arrival. He gave his horse and trap to his man to put away, and getting astride a newly bought black mare said he would accompany Nasielski to Winchmore Hill, where the latter had to go. On the way Robert told him to drive on in his cart and he would see how soon the mare could overtake him. However when near a blacksmith's shop at Palmer's Green the farrier called out "Your friend's over," whereupon Nasielski looked back to see Robert lying on the ground with the mare beside him. At the inquest Dr. G. Wight, who attended the deceased, said that death had occurred on the Saturday from epileptic convulsions due to concussion. This had been doubtless caused by the fall, and a verdict of accidental death was recorded. Robert was buried at Camden, with probate granted to his widow, and Arthur Jones (£551 17s 6d.)

LETTER FROM INDIA

THE MURDER OF THOMAS WEBB

The letter is addressed to her father in law, William Webb, of Simpson, from Annie Webb. She is the widow of his son Quarter Master Sergeant Thomas Webb, and she recounts the incident in which he was murdered by Sepoys in the general slaughter at Gwalior on the night of June 14th 1857. The letter arrived after William Webb's death at Simpson on October 24th 1857.[3]

"Fort of Agra, Sept. 1857.

MY EVER DEAREST FATHER, - I know how dreadful the shock will be to you to hear of our sweet Thomas being killed by these brutal Sepoys: he put too much confidence in them. Thomas was really a good-minded man, and he thought everyone the same. However, I could not persuade him they would kill him if ever they mutinied. I will give you an account of the dreadful night of the 14th of June, when my dear husband was killed. Father, don't think I forsook him in that dreadful hour. No; I was by his side all the time. I thought to receive the first ball they shot at him, but they pulled me away from before him, and then fired. The ball went through his left arm, and he told me not to shriek in that way, as he was only wounded; so I went into the other room where, I think, some sixty or seventy Sepoys were. I told them if they wanted to shed blood to take my life, but to spare my husband. They told me they had orders to take the life of every European - man, woman, and child. They would not kill me as I never interfered with any of them since I came to the regiment, nor did dear Thomas; but if they did not kill him others would come and torture him to death, so they thought it best to shoot him at once. In fact these they had any dislike for they cut up in pieces when they killed them. They would not allow me to go near Thomas. They said they should not be buried, as they threw all of them into a ditch, and dragged me away. There were nineteen killed that night - officers, sergeants and women. Dearest Father, they would not allow me to take one stitch of clothing to put on me. I had to walk six days and nights without a shoe on my foot or a cover on my head, and the burning sun was so fearfully hot, that it scorched me all over; all I had to eat was one piece (sic) not one halfpennyworth. In fact when I came into this station, no one ever thought I could possibly recover. I was not the only one; we were sixteen in number - ladies and sergeants' wives. I am not able to stand, much less walk; it is quite wonderful to see how I have kept my senses at all, after the fearful sight I witnessed at Gwalior on the 14th of June. Now, dearest Father, let me beg of you to put on Christian fortitude and arm yourself against giving way to fretting, as you only are now left to me to call back the fond recollection of our dear son and fond husband. I am coming home when it is safe to travel down the country, and I will take every care of you in your old age. Your affectionate daughter.

"ANNIE WEBB."

HYACINTHS, HYMN BOOKS, & HONEY BEES

CHRISTOPHER BOURNE & ALBERT WARREN

Simpson has accommodated two acclaimed specialists. Christopher Bourne was a renowned horticultural expert and bulb grower. He then took Holy Orders and became a vicar. Albert Warren, a railway worker, was nationally renowned as an apiarist, winning numerous prizes for his honey at prestigious shows.

ALBERT WARREN

Born at Simpson in 1888 on November 15th, Albert Edward Warren was baptised at the parish church in 1889 on March 1st. He was one of the children of Francis John Warren, a painter, and his wife Susan (nee Rands), who worked from home as a dressmaker on her own account. In 1911 at Willen he married 24 year old Edith Lathall of the village, whose father, William, was a hop grower. A daughter, Gertrude, was born in 1913 (d1990) and at that time Albert was a platelayer on the railway. However his hobby was bee keeping, and between the wars he won many prestigious prizes for honey. In August 1919 at the Cannock Show he took the 1st and the 3rd prize; the following year in May two first prizes for honey at the Oxfordshire Agricultural Show, and in July at the Royal Show the 2nd and 3rd prizes. In 1924 at the Sutton Coldfield (Birmingham) Show, held on Wednesday, September 3rd, he was awarded 2nd prize in the shop window display, this being for an exhibit of 200lbs of honey. He also won 2nd prize for comb honey, and was reserve in 3 other classes. The show was open to all England, and all the leading apiarists of the country were exhibiting. In 1929 in May at the Oxfordshire Show he took 1st prize, and then at the Prescott and District Agricultural Show two 1st prizes and the bronze medal. Also that year in July at the Watford Home Counties Horticultural Show he was awarded three 1st prizes, three 2nd prizes, and two 3rd prizes. In 1930 on January 25th a son, Dennis, was born, who in 1939 was living at Simpson with his parents at the aptly named The Apiary. (Gertude had married in 1910.) Of The Apiary, Albert died on April 14th 1960 at Renny Lodge Hospital, Newport Pagnell, with administration granted to his widow. She died in 1962 on June 14th, and both are commemorated on the same gravestone.

CHRISTOPHER BOURNE

The son of the Rev. Stephen Eugene Bourne and his wife Charlotte Edith (nee Andrews), Christopher Bourne was born in 1884 on March 7th, baptised on March 31st at the church of St. Andrew's, Lincoln. With his father being warden of St. Annes's, Bede Houses, Lincoln, the family were resident at St. Anne's Lodge.[4] From that year his father next became vicar of New Basford, Notts., until 1888, in which year he became vicar of Dunston, Lincoln. In 1891 attended by a cook, a nurse & a housemaid, he was resident at the Vicarage with his wife and children Christopher, Agatha, age, 1, born at New Basford, Notts, and Cyprian, age 5, also born at New

Basford. By 1907 Christopher was engaged in the large estate office 'of a nobleman in Yorkshire,' and on January 30th at the church of St. Thomas, Cliffe, Lewes, he married 19 year old Alice (sometimes Alys) Harrison. Born in 1887 on March 3rd she was the daughter of Robert Harrison, a farmer of Radstock House, Lewes, with the witnesses to the marriage being Cecily Penn Munby and John Cecil Munby. (Cecily was Christopher's half sister by an earlier marriage of his father.)

That year on May 10th Christopher's father, vicar of Dunston, died aged 61, with the chief mourners at the funeral on May 14th being his widow Charlotte, and children Cyprian, Agatha, and Christopher. In 1908 on June 16th a daughter, Dorothy Irene Monica Bourne, was born to Christopher and Alice on June 16th at Pocklington. She was baptised at Londesborough, and on July 10th 1909 came the birth of a second daughter, Joan Augusta Mary Bourne. At that time the family were resident at Market Weighton but in the same year Christopher moved to Olde Wharf House, Simpson, becoming renowned as a bulb grower and horticulturalist.

In 1910 on April 6th he was instituted to the St. Martin's Lodge of Freemasons at Fenny Stratford, whilst in business life on the lawns of his residence he hosted a meeting in August 1910 of the Bletchley Workingmen's Association, of which he was vice president. As a daffodil and bulb specialist he was a Fellow of the Royal Horticultural Society, and at their Forced Spring Bulb Show in March 1911 secured the Silver Flora Medal for the finest exhibit of 70 varieties of daffodils and narcissi. The competition was open to all, and would be his first occasion of exhibiting as a trader. In other activities, that month in the polling for council representation for the Fenny Stratford and Simpson wards of the Fenny Stratford UDC he was elected for the Simpson ward. Then in July 1911 he was awarded second prize in the open Sweet Pea class at the show at Leighton Buzzard. With his growing renown in such realms, in 1912 dated August 17th he corresponded from Olde Wharf House - 'Telephone No. 2 Fenny Stratford' - with the horticulturalist E.A. Bowles, of Myddelton House Waltham Cross. This typewritten letter is now held in the archives of the Royal Horticultural Society, and in the contents he apologised for not sending a copy of his catalogue for

1912; "We have been making out a new address book this year and it is always difficult to make sure that no name has been omitted that ought to have been included." He says he will forward one 'by this post,' and adds "I am rather pleased with the illustration of Nar: SILVER SPANGLE." Also that year a son, Edward, was born on September 16th. In April 1913 at the Breconshire daffodil show Christopher was awarded the Gold Medal in trade exhibits.

However his career at Simpson was nearly curtailed on Wednesday, August 6th, when while driving his car to Bletchley, on proceeding around the corner near the Old Post Office he collided with a Rolls Royce belonging to Mr. F. Konig of Tyringham Hall. Coming from the opposite direction this was being driven by Mr. Konig's chauffeur, and although Mr. Bourne swerved on to the grass his vehicle was hit broadside, forcing him into the rails guarding the brook. Despite severe damage to his car he only suffered a few bruises, and in court the case was dismissed on payment of costs. In April 1914 he took first prize at the Royal Horticultural Society's annual daffodil show, this being for an open collection of trumpet and Barri daffodils. Also he was awarded a 1st prize for a batch of seedlings, 'not yet in commerce,' and one Sunday that month he opened the grounds of Olde Wharfe House for the public to inspect his prize winning daffodils. As for anyone aspiring to such expertise, in September 1914 he published 'Some Beautiful Bulbs and How to Grow Them,' a catalogue of daffodils, hyacinths, tulips, iris, gladioli etc, 'which have gained many awards at the leading shows. Post free from Christopher Bourne the Bulb Gardens Bletchley.'

With the outbreak of WW1, at a Council meeting on October 13th he proposed, seconded by Colonel Peter Broome Giles, that a Committee should be formed to consider how best to help Belgium refugees. As for the Bucks Volunteer Defence Corps, on Friday, January 29th 1915 they attended a meeting at Aylesbury, where Mr. Bourne and Mr. W. Watson, of Bletchley, were appointed as Company Commandants. The Corps had been formed following the Lord Lieutenant of Bucks decision to raise a County Regiment of three battalions for Home Defence, each a thousand strong, In horticultural matters, on Mr. Bourne's instructions in the empty premises in Aylesbury Street, Bletchley, 'lately occupied by the

International Stores,' on Wednesday, October 13th 1915 a sale of English grown bulbs was auctioned at 3pm by Foll and Bawden. These were surplus stocks of daffodils, narcissi, tulips etc., and the 20,000 bulbs had all been grown in his bulb gardens at Bletchley and Simpson. In 1916 he became vice chairman of Bletchley Urban District Council, moving to Bletchley in 1917.

There at the Bucks Military Service Tribunal at the Police Court on Monday, July 23rd 1917, he applied for military exemption. Categorised as Grade 2 he had been called 'on review,' with the National Service Representative, Captain Porter, saying that consequent to a re-grading by the Medical Board he had been compelled to pursue this course of action. With the case having been heard on previous occasions, a grant of conditional exemption had been made in February 1917. This was subject to his working on the land for a number of days a week. However this had now been challenged, and the appellant asked to be left until the end of the present bulb season. In conclusion exemption was granted until November 1st. As the holder of a lay reader's licence, in 1917 on the evening of Thursday, October 4th he conducted the Harvest thanksgiving service at St. Martin's Mission Room in Bletchley Road, Bletchley.[5] However the spectre of military service remained, and in December at the Buckinghamshire Appeals Tribunal he was stated as being of Bletchley and married with three children. In testimony he said he'd invested £12,000 in bulbs, and in seeking exemption told the Tribunal that he didn't rely on his business as a grower of bulbs, although some were worth £20 each. He shortly expected to be ordained for Holy Orders, and in his support the Bishop of Buckingham had written to say that he was doing very useful work as a lay reader in the scattered parish of Fenny Stratford. Nevertheless it was pointed out there was nothing to prevent him from taking Holy Orders after the war, and exemption was refused.

Following the Armistice, under the auspices of the League of Nations Union a public meeting was held in the Picture Palace at Bletchley. Having organised the gathering Mr. Bourne attended as joint honorary secretary with Oliver Wells, and during the event the Reverend Firminger said "their hope was that such a League of Nations would bring about better times, and a better life for one and all." In 1919, as being of Cuddesdon Theological College on Trinity Sunday, June 15th Christopher was ordained as deacon by the Bishop of Oxford. He was duly licensed to the Assistant Curacy of Fenny Stratford, and on June 22nd a daughter, Ruth, was born. Then in the absence of the Rev. Firminger it was now as the Rev. Christopher Bourne that on Saturday, July 19th 1919 he gave a short address at the formal peace celebrations for Bletchley and Fenny Stratford, followed by prayer and a hymn. During the recent railway strike both he and the Rev. Firminger had supported the local railwaymen, who in appreciation in December 1920 presented each with an inscribed fountain pen.

On the afternoon of Sunday, November 7th 1920 at St. Martin's Church, Fenny Stratford, there was a large gathering for the formal dedication of the memorial 'tablet' which, commemorating those parishioners who had given their lives on active service, took the form of three copper panels on a dark wood base'. The Vicar, the Reverend Firminger, officiated together with the Assistant Curate, the Reverend Bourne, who read the lesson. In 1921 on July 11th a daughter, Margaret Alys Bourne was born at Bletchley. However the family would soon be leaving the town for he had now been appointed to a curacy at St. Bartholomew's, Reading. For the past two years he had been assistant curate in Fenny Stratford, and having been in charge of St. Martin's Mission Room, in Bletchley Road, it was here that he preached his farewell sermons in 1921 on Sunday, October 2nd. For his past devotion the members of the congregation presented him with a clock and vases.

In April 1929 from being the curate he was then offered the living of St. Bartholomew's, duly instituted and inducted on Tuesday, July 2nd. On family matters, in 1930 at Reading a son, Michael, was born. Then in 1934 on April 13th Dorothy married the Rev. James Walker at her father's church, where the groom, the son of Mr. and Mrs. Walker of Hawridge Rectory, Berkhamsted, was assistant priest. (Dorothy died aged 95 at Stockport in 2004 on January 14th.) Also in 1934 on May 3rd at the speech competition of Kendrick Girls' School, Reading, her sister Ruth gave as her chosen subject 'England is justified in the purchase of the Codex Sinaiticus.' Ruth's unmarried sister Joan also attended Kendrick Girls' School, and in October

1937 was amongst the successful candidates at the Hammersmith municipal elections. A graduate of Reading University she had long been interested in politics and was an ardent member of the Labour Party. In 1938 on Wednesday, April 20th at St. Luke's, Slyne-with-Hest, the wedding took place of her brother Edward Christopher Eugene Bourne and Miss Mary Monica Scott, daughter of Canon E. Scott and his wife of Hest Bank Lodge, Lancaster. The groom's sister Ruth was one of bridesmaids with his brother Master Michael Bourne as page. The couple had met while students at Reading University, and the groom was to be ordained deacon on Trinity Sunday.[6]

During their residency at Crofton, near Preston, a daughter was born in March 1939, in which year Edward was ordained as priest on Trinity Sunday. In 1939 they were resident at Yarrow Cottage, Chorley Road, Chorley, Lancs. As for the Rev. Christopher Bourne (who had now joined the ARP) he was resident at 174, London Road, Reading, with his wife and daughters Ruth, who was now a student at Reading University, and Margaret. Both were in the VAD Red Cross Berks., and Margaret would pursue a career as a midwife. (She died at Bournemouth in 2002.) Meanwhile Joan was living at Hammersmith, and having been resident there for several years was employed as secretary to the Chief Woman Officer of the Labour Party. (She died aged 90.)

After the war in December 1945 the engagement was announced of Ruth and the Rev. Lawrence Hibbs. Educated at Reading school he had formerly been a choirboy and server at St. Bartholomew's Church, where on Tuesday, May 7th 1946 the couple were married. They would make their home at Holy Trinity Rectory, Jersey. Alice (Alys), the wife of the Rev. Christopher Bourne, died at Bournemouth in 1959, and the Rev. Bourne died in 1970 on November 19th, when resident at 24, Fitzharris Avenue, Bournemouth. As per a notice placed in the Bournemouth Echo; 'BOURNE, Canon Christopher. At Bournemouth on November 19th, aged 86, devoted priest, father, and grandfather. Vicar of St. Bartholomew's, Reading, 1929-1956. Requiem St. Alban's Bournemouth, 11.30am Wednesday, November 25th. Cut flowers only to the church on Tuesday or donations for C.of E. Children's Society, c/o The Vicar. Memorial service at St.

Bartholomew's, Reading, at a later date.'

WESLEYAN CHAPEL

Of other non-conformist elements, a mention is made of a house in the possession of George Ethridge at Epiphany 1701/2, which was licensed as a meeting place for Quakers.

A Wesleyan Chapel was built in the village in 1842, and then in 1870 a new chapel on a different site was constructed to accommodate 100. In October 1879 the first of a series of social teas at the houses of friends involved with the chapel was hosted by Frederick Bodley. 24 persons attended, and music, reading, and singing was afterwards indulged. In fact the Wesleyans had thoroughly renovated their chapel with a new floor laid, the pews widened and updated, the ceiling cleaned, and the walls painted. New 'patent ventilators' had been installed, and sermons would be preached towards raising the funds.

Funds would also be needed in 1896, when during a service on the evening of Sunday, February 23rd a lamp fell without warning, smashing the lamp's chimney to pieces and stunning the congregation into silence. The lamp was one of two, each of 100 candle power, of the central draught type, and had been suspended from the ceiling in front of the rostrum, directly above seats usually allotted to the children. Indeed it narrowly missed several small girls and having rolled under one of the seats attempts to retrieve it were made by the chapel keeper, who had a shawl around her. With the imminent danger of this and her other clothing catching alight a member of the congregation rushed forward, and carrying the lamp outside extinguished the flame. Then in December in the early hours of the 17th came the potential for further damage when the village was shaken by two earthquake tremors. Perhaps not surprisingly a thorough renovation of the chapel took place soon after, and with Mr. Wright having been awarded the tender the reopening took place in 1897 on Whit Sunday, June 6th. With Miss M. Stevens at the harmonium a sermon was preached in the afternoon by Mr. J. Read, who again preached in the evening with Frederick Bodley at the harmonium. Leaving a deficit of £4 a collection was taken, and for adorning the chapel Mr. Geo. Hazelwood, of Simpson, presented the trustees with a velvet pile Bible cushion and tassels.

In 1908 on the morning of Tuesday, June 30th Miss Laura Bodley, daughter of Mr. and Mrs. Bodley, of The Walnuts, married Philip Richard Stevens, the son of the Rev. Philip Stevens, the Wesleyan Minister of Edmonton. In occupation as a nurse, Laura was held in high regard for her skills and cheerful disposition, and at the Wesleyan Chapel at Simpson an arch of flowers adorned the approach. Other floral arrangements had been placed on the walls by the villagers, with carpets laid from the road to the porch. Somewhat stormy, with occasional heavy showers, the weather proved hardly ideal but there was nevertheless a large attendance. In fact having been licensed for such on June 3rd 1908 this was the first wedding to be held at the chapel, and in commemoration on behalf of the Trustees a copy of the Word of God and Wesleyan Hymn Book, bound together, was presented to the couple inscribed; 'Presented by the trustees of the Wesleyan Methodist Chapel, Simpson, to Mr. and Mrs. Philip Richard Stevens, on the occasion of their marriage, being the first marriage in the above place of worship.'

In 1935 with the Rev. Francis Hudson, the Superintendent minister, presiding, on Wednesday, July 24th the stone laying took place for a new Methodist church and school, each able to accommodate some 100 persons. A partition between the two buildings enabled the whole to be used for special occasions, and included was a vestry and a kitchen. The General Chapel Committee had made a grant of £95, and with £20 having been donated by Mr. and Mrs. Stevens, for the rostrum and Communion, Mr. Stevens announced that £238 13s 2d had already been made by appeal. £500 had been raised in total. Six stones were laid on behalf of the Trusteees; Mr. G. Bowler on behalf of the Sunday School; Miss M. Stevens on behalf of the Trustees; Mrs. A. Matthews on behalf of the Sewing Meeting; Mr. W.G.P. Bodley in memory of his parents; Mr. A.J. Stevens in memory of his parents; and Mr. A.J. Sharp JP on behalf of the Circuit and in memory of John Rose (the Rose Legacy). Of the many bricks one was laid by Master Billy Bowler, and in the foundations were deposited a parchment and other papers containing various records. After the ceremony tea was served in the village recreation hut, which was filled for the evening meeting. It was expected to open the chapel in November, whilst as for the debt, with the total expense having been £1,530 this was finally paid off in July 1937. In 1983 the chapel was sold and today the parish church of Simpson is part of the Woughton Team Ministry, Local Ecumenical Project, this being an arrangement whereby several churches in the area co-operate, with one building generally used for all services.[7]

A REFUSNIK RECTOR

THE REVEREND WILLIAM RICE

William Rice was born at Llanelly, Carmarthen, in 1845 and when 11 weeks old was baptised in the parish of Llangennech on June 27th. With the family abode as Glyngwernen (sometimes written as Clyngwernen) he was the son of Cornelius Rice, a farmer, and his wife Ann Eaton, who had married in 1835. In 1851 the family was resident at Llanelly comprised of (ages as per the census) Cornelius, aged 50, farming 100 acres, Ann, 49, and, all born at Llanelly, their children Catherine 10, Elizabeth 8, and William. Cornelius died in 1859 and now as a widow in 1861 Ann was farming the 100 acres, living with William and her unmarried daughters Elizabeth and also Mary Ann, born in 1838 and baptised on June 17th. By 1871 Ann was an 'annuitant,' as was Elizabeth, and in addition to William also resident with them was a nephew, 12 year old William Eaton. Educated at St. David's College, Lampeter, (now the University of Wales) William Rice was now a student of theology, and gaining a BA in 1875 he was ordained that year as deacon, proceeding to priest's orders in the diocese of Worcester in 1876.

Following positions as curate of St. Paul's, Birmingham, 1875-77; Ashover, near Matlock, 1877-79; Melbourne, Derbyshire 1879-88; and Hodnet, Shropshire 1889-90, in April 1891 he was living as head of the household at Yoxall, Staffordshire, where he was the curate. Also resident was his nephew William Seys Eaton, age 31 and single. A graduate student of theology he was born in 1860 on November 23rd at Swansea, the son of his namesake father, a draper, and his wife Angelina.

By the patronage of Sir William Hanmer, in 1891 William Rice became rector of Simpson, where at Christmas Eve in 1892 not only did he distribute money and tea to many of the aged and poor of the village, but also entertained the bell ringers to tea at the rectory. In 1872 a visitor to the village had noted that the church was in a very dilapidated condition, and indeed with his predecessor having been ill for the past four years, on arrival the Rev. Rice found the parish in a less than desirable state.

Sadly despite the initial harmony such would also become his relationship with many of the parishioners. Hardly surprising when he caused an early splash by stipulating that church attendance was a condition for those wanting to fish! This came about when on June 9th 1895 some youngsters asked Mr. J. Hoskins if they could fish in a pond in a meadow that he rented. He raised no objection but when the rector came along he said "I cannot allow you to fish here unless you attend church, and I can give you a ticket to fish in the canal if you attend church." In fact it seemed that bait was sorely in need for church attendance, since the previous Sunday evening the 'faithful' had numbered 4 old women, 4 or 5 children, and the sexton. Yet not too far away an open air Wesleyan service on the lawn at the back of Mr. Bodley's house attracted a presence of over 50.

As for Mr. Hoskins, he would again make the rector's acquaintance later that month, arising from an animosity on June 22nd. With many people attending from Simpson the case was heard at Fenny Stratford Petty Sessions on Thursday, June 27th, when the rector was summoned for assault and battery on Albert Truby Ennals. Additionally there was a cross summons by the rector against Ennals for assault at the same time and place. The defence for Ennals stated that having always been a cripple he lived with his father at Simpson, and had gone to Rectory Farm to take tea with the tenant, John Hoskins. Later the rector came to Rectory Farm, and taking exception to a copy of some printed verses pinned to a door began to rub them out. In clarifying this circumstance the defence for the rector said he was the tenant of some land beyond Rectory Farm. There he kept some horses in the fields and being usually accompanied by his niece, Miss Catherine Eaton, he often went to look at them in the evenings. On the way he had to pass Rectory Farm, which was approached by a public way, and situated about five yards from the footpath were the two farm doors. On one of these a large hand drawn in chalk pointed to the verses on a printed paper. On seeing these the rector then knocked on the door, and tried to destroy the paper while he waited. Mr. Hoskins came out to see what it was all about, whereupon the rector asked him who had put the paper on the door. Mr. Hoskins claimed he didn't know, to which the rector retorted that he must be what his brother said of him, "suffering from mental depression." Then after a few more remarks "Well, you must be a lunatic not to know who put this up." At this Hoskins took a step back, and having signalled for Ennals they both rushed towards the rector, who fended them off with his walking stick. In court Ennals showed two prominent bruises but Miss Eaton said the rector had acted only in self defence. After consulting briefly in private the Bench dismissed both the summons and cross summons, with each party ordered to pay their own costs.

A right old ding dong, and on the subject of bells in September that year the four in the church tower were taken down and transported to Loughborough, to be tuned by Messrs. J. Taylor & Co. and to have their clappers refitted. At the same time a new bell would be cast, with the whole ring of five to be re-hung on a steel frame in place of the centuries old oak beams, one of which had the date 1623 inscribed. The bell founder's estimate came to £123 14s, with £10 to be paid for the work of the masons and carpenters. In 1896 on Monday, February 3rd the bells were duly returned from Loughborough, to include the one recast at the expense of the rector's niece, Miss Eaton. This bore her name whilst as for the rector's name, this again cropped up when he was fined £3 that year for assaulting a boy named Bodley.

In fact the members of the Fenny Stratford UDC had probably also raised his temper that year, for at their meeting in October their response to his threatening letter about inadequate measures for flood prevention was to laugh heartily, before moving onto the next business. Other encounters with the authorities would include fines for driving without lights and for allowing heifers to stray on the road. These were part of a herd of Jersey cattle which he personally superintended. Also a bull, but in 1898 when he went to its quarters on the evening of Saturday, January 8th he discovered too late that it had got loose. On hearing her uncle's cries his niece rushed in from the yard, and picking up a pitchfork managed to fight off the animal. Medical aid was summoned but his severe mauling ensured that although favourable progression was made the rector had to be confined to his bedroom for awhile.

On other farmyard matters, in February 1900 on inspecting the rector' premises the Surveyor of Fenny Stratford UDC found that animals were being kept in a portion of the cottage tenanted by 'his man' Yates. This he judged injurious to health, and when informed the rector agreed that this should be abated. However he called the Surveyor's attention to the state of the flooded yard, and asked him to bring this matter to the Council's attention. Then on February 26th in a letter to the council he wrote:

"My farmyard is flooded again today, and adds further to the damage which you saw last week. A gentleman remarked here today to me, that all my 'cake' in the manure was, by the colour of the water, being washed away to the river. I have had 8 tons of cake lately, so you may fairly estimate the loss in that respect, besides other damage. I had to turn about 20 cattle out of the yards and sheds to the land, where they were exposed to the inclemency of the weather after being shut up, and to remove the calves from the flooded sheds. The loss and inconvenience of having to be knee deep in water is really awful. I trust you will, as you promised, bring this matter before the Urban Council, and that they will consent to your plan of stopping

Rectory Farm

the flood by means of two valves. The County Council have all the material ready to turn the storm water into the brook, so that you will only have to deal with the sewerage, and prevent that finding an outlet onto my yard.."

However the council thought the best thing he could do was to move his premises further away from the river!

In 1901 the rector was living at the Rectory with his unmarried niece, Catherine Eaton, age 36, in occupation as his housekeeper, and one servant. His income was £106 per year and on the subject of finance in 1904 he stood for election as Guardian of the Poor for Simpson. Not that he seemed much valued by the electorate, for the announcement on Monday, March 28th of his 20 votes against the 104 of Mr. A.J. Stevens 'was received with expressions of surprise, but with an approving cheer.' Election to Fenny Stratford UDC fared no better, with those for William Heady being 67, and those for the Rev. Rice 9; 'The figures demonstrating Mr. Rice's defeat at Simpson were received with exclamations of surprise and with some laughter.'

Nevertheless that year he would help to raise funds for a church restoration, with a meeting held of the relevant committee on Monday, February 8th. This was chaired by the rector, with the other members to include W.J. Levi, and the Reverends F.F. Field, of Woughton, and H. Smith, of Woolstone. About £600 had been raised, and after some consultation it was decided to apply to the Diocesan Building Society for the renewal of a grant sanctioned some 10 years ago. Subscriptions could be paid to the churchwardens Messrs. G. Evans-Jackson and Mr. J. Austin.

Indeed progress would be made and with the restoration work carried out by Messrs. Yirrell & Son, of Leighton Buzzard and Bletchley, and with Mr. Scott, son of Sir Gilbert Scott, as architect, on Tuesday, November 1st 1904 the church was re-opened by the Bishop of Oxford and re-dedicated to St. Thomas. The service was full choral with members of the Fenny Stratford and Bletchley choirs conducted by Major Levi. Also the new portion of the churchyard, a lately enclosed part of the Rectory garden, was consecrated.

However the rector had less cause to celebrate that month when at Newport Pagnell County Court a claim was entered against him by Alice Joan Fawcett, of Woburn Sands. This was for breaking and entering her house on September 8th but he counterclaimed for £9 17s 6d, comprised of £3 for one quarter's rent, 2s 6d for water rate, £1 15s for seeds and cultivation of garden, and £5 damages for breach of contract as organist. Alice stated that on September 8th she opened her door to the rector, who in angry tones said her chickens were scratching up the potatoes in the garden. Unless she put a stop to it he wouldn't take the garden produce. When she replied that she couldn't prevent them he said, "You will have to, or I will set my dog on them." Fearing his temper, and being alone in the house, she shut and bolted the door, which with a blow of his fist the rector burst open. She then fled into the dining room and when he followed she slammed the door and shouted for him to go away, or she would call the police. He then tried to burst the door open and when unable to do so went to the dining room window, shaking his fist and threatening to set his dog on the chickens. When questioned in court he denied having an uncontrollable temper but admitted having previously been summoned and fined for assault. He had also been sued for trespass and ordered to pay £10 in damages. However he refuted that a lad he engaged from Northampton workhouse had felt the need to escape from the Rectory at night. Also that he had received a lawyer's letter with regard to thrashing a boy. In conclusion the judge found the case of breaking and entering proved. Also that Alice Fawcett was justified in refusing to act as organist. However she would have to pay one quarter's rent and the water rate, although for the unlawful entry she was awarded £5 damages and costs. For the rector, regarding the rent and water rate he was awarded £3 2s 6d plus costs.

In a more benevolent mood, at Christmas 1907 he gave joints of beef to nine of his tenants and also gifts of plum puddings, oranges, apples, tea etc. supplied from the rectory. Others in the village were also remembered, with gifts of tea, fruit, plum puddings etc.

However for one of his tenants such goodwill evaporated in 1911 in a case that was heard in April at Newport Pagnell. Not appearing in person the rector applied for a judgment of notice to quit against Arthur Barringer, a labourer of Simpson. The latter admitted owing £2 and said "the parson" had stopped him a week's salary to cover it. He had to go home to his wife and children with no money, and when he complained the rector allegedly said "If you say any more I shall have an action for violence against you," adding "If you do not get off my premises I shall punch your head." The case was adjourned pending the rector's attendance, with it being the opinion of the judge that the man's wages should be paid. As for the rector, having been unable to let his glebe of 225 acres he farmed the land himself, and indeed in 1911 at the Rectory a farm assistant was also accommodated.

Then in 1912 there would be another resident, for on April 9th at St. George's, Hanover Square, he married Lady Sydney Montagu (in the marriage register Montague is struck out and Montagu inserted!) Ogilvie-Grant. She was the daughter of the late 10th Earl of Seafield and of the Dowager Countess of Seafield and, born in 1882 on July 23rd, at the time of her marriage was resident at 5, Blenheim Street, New Bond Street, London. Many Society people were present at the ceremony, after which the couple left for their honeymoon.

As for Simpson the population was now around 134 and after the outbreak of WW1 due to the conflict 13 of the 40 cottages were unlet. With regard to the rector matters were hardly peaceful on the home front, for in 1915 when drunk a parishioner named Cook struck him across the head with a stick. William spoke to his niece about this assault and the next day Mrs. Cook abused him, and also hit him with a stick. She later charged him with assault, whereupon he issued a cross summons against the Cooks. They then called a witness named Fitzpatrick, and having found in their favour the Bench fined the rector £2. In other matters the rector had been seen driving his sheep through the village on Sunday evenings, and eventually a few of the parishioners sent a memorial to the Bishop of Buckingham. In this they stated that prior to the rector's institution in 1891 the church had been well conducted but for some years now this had not been the case. Accordingly in January 1917 a commission sat at the Parish Room, Bletchley, comprised of the Bishop of Buckingham and six others, to include the Rev. Eaton. He was the nephew of the rector and had been appointed to the living of the nearby village of Walton in 1902. (He remained as the incumbent until 1927). In consequence the commission reported that including the choir the Sunday morning congregations had dwindled to an average of 15 to

Lady Sydney Montague Ogilvie-Grant and the Rev. William Rice, rector of Symp-son (Bucks), leaving St. George's, Hanover-square, after their wedding yester-day. The bride is a daughter of the late Earl of Seafield and of the Dowager Countess of Seafield.—("Daily Mirror" photograph.)

20; that under the 'persistent pressure' of certain parishioners early Communion was held at irregular intervals; that no candidate had been presented for Confirmation for many years; and that there was no systematic visitation of the sick, although the rector had never refused when sent for. In conclusion the Commission found that the Church had lost its former hold, and that the rector no longer retained any influence over his parishioners. This they attributed to two causes;

a) 'As a keen agriculturalist the rector had subordinated his duties as a parish priest to his interests as a landowner and a farmer. He had been seen to walk with his sheep through the village on Sunday evening on their way to the station to go to London, whither he followed after service to market them on Monday morning. He had as many as 500 sheep and 33 beasts. Due to a preoccupation with these secular matters his ministrations in the church had suffered. Witnesses said prayers were gabbled through so hastily and indistinct that it was difficult or impossible for the congregation to join in the worship. Some sermons were good but others at times were incoherent, with no connection with the text and rarely containing

43

any reference to Church doctrine.'

b) 'He was always in dispute with someone or other about petty matters, such as land boundaries, or rights of way. In these he had sometimes confronted persons with very intemperate language and alarming gestures. He had also been in frequent trouble with the local authorities and police on minor charges, resulting in his being brought five times before the magistrates and fined. Also personal attacks had been made from the pulpit.'

After their sitting the members had tea together at Bletchley Station, where the Bishop took a vote of those present on the point 'that the minimum of services had been performed.' To this no one dissented. However regarding 'that the services had been inadequately performed' four members voted with the Bishop, the Rev. Eaton voting against. Thus a recommendation would be sent to the Bishop of Oxford that the rector should be inhibited from performing clerical duties at Simpson, with a curate to take his place. Such an order was duly made by the Bishop of Oxford but in the wake of this the rector launched an appeal, which in 1917 on Tuesday, June 12th was heard before a judge and the Archbishop of Canterbury at the Royal Courts of Justice in London. Indeed this was the first case to be heard under the Benefices Act of 1898. Also the first time that the Archbishop of Canterbury had sat in the Court alongside a High Court Judge in the trying of an ecclesiastical action. The defence stated that partially caused by the war there had been a reduction in the congregation, but the great body of the parishioners supported the rector and regarded him with affection. He had never neglected the church services but since the death of his agent, and unable to find a replacement, he had driven his sheep to Bletchley on Sunday evenings to catch the 9 o'clock train to London. There he would market them early on Monday and then return to Simpson to arrive back at the Rectory before noon, and sometimes before breakfast. He had never neglected visiting the sick and had even left his meals when called upon to do so. As for being absent from the parish, the only occasions had been 15 years ago, when he was absent for two Sundays, and also five years ago when he was away for three Sundays, during which time he was married. Excepting some newcomers his relations with the parishioners had been friendly, and until the appointment of the Commission there had never been any complaints that he mumbled the prayers too rapidly. Nor had there been any suggestion that his sermons were detached from the church doctrine. His services included early celebrations on Christmas Day, Easter Day, Whit Sunday, and Harvest thanksgiving day. Also mid day celebrations once a month, and in addition at the request of Mr. Bourne and Miss Webb he had held early celebrations every Sunday for two years. However these he ceased in September 1910 due 'to certain rumours about motor driving scandals.' At elections for the School Board he had twice been returned at the head of the poll, and since arriving at Simpson he always strived to faithfully carry out his duties. On acrimonious matters Mr. Brooke and Mr. Bourne, the landlord and tenant of a farm adjoining his glebe, had 'abused' him one day for one of his carts having cut their hedge. He denied calling Mr. Brooke "a thief, liar, and loose character." Also that he called the churchwarden a liar, and amongst other denials refuted having shouted or sworn at his labourers. At the adjourned hearing on Wednesday several of the 20 or so witnesses called by the rector vouched for him having satisfactorily performed his duties. His niece, Miss Catherine Eaton, who had served as his church warden, said whenever she brought messages from those who were sick he always went to visit them immediately. As for the evidence for the Bishop, during the proceedings Christopher Bourne, of Bletchley, in stating that he held a lay reader's licence, and was a candidate for Holy Orders, said that until last March he had lived at Simpson from 1909; "When I first went to the Church, the whole appearance of the place struck me at once as extraordinarily slovenly. I regret to say that if I had not known the prayers I should have had extreme difficulty in following them. They were rapidly and extremely carelessly read, and quite indistinct. The conduct of the early service grieved me very much, and did not come up to the ordinary standard of reverence." On one occasion he asked the rector not to trespass on his land, at which the rector allegedly flew into "an absolutely disgusting exhibition of temper, quite incoherent and literally frothing at the mouth." Then several months later when driving his wife and her companion to Bletchley the rector abused him for running into some young calves he was herding along the village street. Flourishing a stick the rector then made for him, at which people came out and laughed at the spectacle, "which was, unfortunately, not uncommon." Indeed it was his opinion that the parish was in a state of spiritual destitution. One elderly man, a Naval pensioner, resident in the village since 1905, said he'd kept a diary of the rector's 'sayings and doings.' One entry regarded a morning service in March 1905, when "The Rector made some horrid statements. He called Jackson by name, and said he was a liar. ... Many people left the Church during the Rector's abuse." Saying that her brother had been killed in action, Alice Mary Howard of The Cabin, Simpson, said she was behind in the rent owed to the rector, who notwithstanding her circumstance three times called her a hussy. She had heard him use bad language to his sheep, whilst Mrs. Bowler said that in calling her a liar he shook a stick at her. On the final day of the hearing the defence admitted the rector's 'defects of an over virile temperament, and was afflicted with a violent, choleric temper, but had done nothing unworthy of a man of honour, and no persecution or tyranny had been alleged against him.' They asserted that the hostile witnesses 'were actuated by petty grievances and ill will.' Nevertheless judgement for the Bishop was entered with costs, and as one who had witnessed the proceedings would later recall; "It was a painful affair, but the Rev. William Rice seemed quite impervious to criticism." Indeed he seemed quite unfazed by events, and as a national newspaper would comment; "Sympson being a small place, Mr. Rice naturally knows everybody within it. As he walks along the road, exchanging the time of day, no stranger would think that he no longer exercises the cure of souls of the village. He has the look of an open air man, with a sunburnt, clean shaven face, and plentiful grey hair."

He also owned half the village, and showed scant empathy for any tenants who fell into rent arrears. Not least Alice Howard, whom he sued at Newport Pagnell court on Friday, August 24th for possession of a cottage and premises. Also for rent arrears of £9 4s. With judgment found in his favour the rent arrears were to be paid at 5s a month, with possession of the premises to be complied with in 28 days. Arthur Clarke fared no better, for at the court on October 26th in a claim by the rector for recovery of possession of a cottage and premises, let at a rental of 3s 8d per week, an order was made for possession in 6 weeks, with the rent arrears of £2 4s to be paid at 2s 6d per month. It seems the rector's niece was also not gifted with Christian fortitude, for at the same court she made a claim against Albert Eldridge, a lance corporal in the Army, for possession of a cottage in the village known as 'The Old Post Office.' She also asked for an order in respect of £2 5s rent arrears. However, with the rector's name frequently mentioned in the case, it seems the judge had the measure of him, saying "We know the reverend gentleman; he has a hasty temper." The judge then asked the defendant, "When in peace and quietness, can you turn out?" The soldier replied "As soon as I possibly can, and when it is convenient." To this the judge replied "Say no more about it. Give up possession in six weeks, pay the rent, but I will make no order as to costs."

As for his own accommodation, despite the ruling of the appeal court there was no power to remove the rector from the Rectory! Nevertheless as an inhibited incumbent he had to pay the stipend of the curate in charge. Appointed by the Bishop of Oxford this was a Mr. Legge, who acknowledged on July 3rd, as the day of the Bishop's speech, a cheque for his first quarter's salary of £20 17s 4d. This was the estimated value of the living minus an amount for repairs to the rectory 'and the Queen Anne's Bounty mortgage.' Thus not only did the Reverend Rice continue to occupy the Rectory but he also continued to farm the glebe. Additionally he asserted his rights as rector, and summoning and presiding at the annual Easter Vestry in 1918 appointed his wife, who for awhile had been in London, as Rector's Warden, and secured the election of his niece, Miss Eaton, as Parishioners' Warden. As for his church attendance, not having attended at Simpson since March 1917 he now patronised the church at Walton where his nephew, the Rev. William Seys Eaton, was incumbent. Nevertheless he still maintained property interests in the village, and in April 1918 purchased at auction at Bletchley 'The Walnuts' with the attached 860 acres of land for £5,200.

After a short illness he died at the Rectory at Simpson in 1919 on February 5th and with effects of £12,835 19s 9d probate was granted to the Rev. William Seys Eaton and Catherine Eaton. Then at the Rectory at noon on Tuesday, March 18th 1919 an auction by order of his executors was conducted by Geo. Wigley and Sons of the household furniture, to include 400 volumes of books. The following day the live and dead farming stock at the Rectory Farm were sold, and in completion on April 10th the sale took place of grazing grounds, accommodation grass land, and some 16 or 17 cottages at Simpson. As for his widow, she died at a nursing home in Hove, Sussex, in 1944 on July 23rd.

COBBLERS TO SHOEMAKING

Many of working age in the village were content to follow the usual occupations of farming or pursuing a trade. However some had higher ambitions, to include William Warner who in 1915 was elected Mayor of Wednesbury. His father had been a boot maker in Simpson and many of the older residents still recalled him as a boy. One was Frederick Bodley of The Walnuts, who wrote;

"Mr. William Warner was some 40 years ago residing in the village. His father was the village bootmaker, and was Superintendent of the Wesleyan Sunday School. The son did not do much in the bootmaking line, he aspired to something higher. I well remember going in one Monday morning with some boots to be repaired, and Mr. Warner said; 'What do you think, Mr. Bodley, our Will says he does not mean to remain here at this job; he has made up his mind to strike out for himself and see what he can do.' He joined the Prudential Assurance Company as one of their collectors, and by strict attention to business he rose step by step until finally he became District Superintendent for the district where he now resides, and for which he is now the mayor. Some years ago he retired from the

Garden Party at the Old Rectory 1912

Prudential Company into private life. For many years he has been a most acceptable preacher, and has held all the offices open to laymen in the Wesleyan Connexion."

A HAT TRICK OF BOWLERS

WILLIAM BOWLER 1868-1956

William Bowler was born in 1868 on January 27th at Aspley Guise. Then in 1888 on October 16th at Walton he married Annie Pollard, who in 1867 had been born at Simpson on September 27th. The wedding was conducted by the Rev. Field, of Woughton, and at the time of his marriage Mr. Bowler was in the employ of 'Squire Burton' at Walton Hall. In 1891 William and his wife were living at Walton, where in 1893 on May 27th a son, George William Bowler, was born. With William in occupation as an agricultural labourer in 1901 the family were living at Simpson where, resident with his wife, son, and his wife's mother, in 1911 he was now in a 'gentleman's service' as a general labourer. It seems the 'gentleman' was Frederick Bodley of The Walnuts, Simpson, and after many years in this employ William became a smallholder, besides driving for a year the mail horses and van from Bletchley to Newport Pagnell. By 1939 he had retired, and in 1948 he and his wife celebrated their Golden Wedding. Still quite active he helped his son out on his holding, and even maintained a large allotment garden with a small orchard. During their last years he and his wife lived with their son and daughter in law at Simpson at Bridge House. William died in 1956, predeceased by his wife in 1951.

GEORGE WILLIAM BOWLER 1893-1970

Born at Walton in 1893 on May 27th, and christened on June 25th, George was the son of William and Annie Bowler. From Walton he moved to Simpson in 1898, and on leaving the village school at the age of 12 he worked with his father on their smallholding, later also having a small milk business. At the outbreak of WW1 he joined the Royal Artillery, serving in France, Belgium and Italy. Having left Woburn to live with his parents, during this time his wife to be, Rose Matthews, carried on his milk round. She had been born at Woburn in 1895 on August 30th to Harry Matthews, a carpenter, and his wife Jane. On George's return they married at Simpson in 1919 at the Wesleyan Chapel, of which for many years he would be a trustee and chapel steward. In 1920 the couple purchased Bridge House, adjoining Bowlers Bridge at Simpson, with George in occupation as a dairyman and smallholder. Then in 1927 a son, William Harry Bowler, was born. At their Golden Wedding in 1969 George and Rose celebrated with family and friends at Bridge House and, to include Mrs. G. Woodward, who had been their bridesmaid, many of the guests who had attended the wedding were present. Of Bridge House, George died in 1970 on July 27th, and having been resident at 426, Simpson village, to where she and her son had moved in

Bowler's Bridge

September 1971, Rose died in 1975 on February 19th

WILLIAM HARRY BOWLER 1927-2019

William was born on September 12th 1927 at Simpson, where he would live all his life. He began his education at the local school in April 1932, and in 1939 secured a special place at Wolverton Secondary School. During WW2 until 1944 he served as a messenger at the Civil Defence HQ based at Simpson Rectory, and then began work at Bletchley as a railway cashier. In this employment he then remained until taking early retirement in 1984. As with his father and grandfather he took active participation in the village Methodist chapel, teaching at the Sunday School and playing the piano for services. Shortly after the death of his father, in 1970, he was approached by Milton Keynes Development Corporation about their need to acquire Bridge House and the land to the north. This was to construct one of the early grid roads, H9 Groveway, and in consequence in September 1971 William and his mother moved to 426, Simpson village. Aged 91 William died in 2019 on August 10th at Milton Keynes University Hospital.

A BLEAK WYNTER'S TALE

In 1942 on the morning of Sunday, March 22nd fifty five year old Paul Wynter, brother of the rector of Simpson, the Rev. Reginald Wynter, committed suicide by throwing himself in front of an express train at Bletchley Station. From suffering the after effects of a nervous breakdown he had been staying at Simpson Rectory since January 18th. At the inquest held at Bletchley Station a verdict was recorded of suicide while the balance of his mind was disturbed. The Rev. Wynter became rector of Simpson in 1936, and at the outbreak of WW2 was resident at the Rectory with his wife and daughter. In the wartime measures he was an ARP Warden and his wife a First Aid worker. Also accommodated, no doubt as a safer refuge, were Mary Geraldine MacRae, born in 1869 on May 14th, a short hand typist 'stock exchange,' and David Macrae, born in 1932 on August 10th. Due to ill health at the age of 67 the Reverend left Simpson with his wife in 1944, with an auction held that year of household furniture etc. on Wednesday, November 22nd. Also included was an oil painting by Mrs. Wynter entitled 'Bolton Woods.' He would now take up a position at Brighton to help the churches and undertake parochial mission work. Of 78, Rowan Avenue, Hove, Sussex, he died in 1956 on February 17th, with probate granted to his widow.

GONE TO THE DOGS
GROVEWAY STADIUM - THE ORIGINS

In June 1946 the idea of a greyhound racing track was originated by Robert Beckett of The Poplars Farm, Simpson. He duly gave notice of his intention to apply for the issue of a licence to operate a track on his land in Grove Road, with the application to be heard by the County Council on October 16th. However prior to that in July objections to the scheme were put forward at Bletchley, with the Urban Council opposing the application on the grounds of the public expenditure involved in the maintenance of the road, and the provision of a footpath. This was decided at a meeting of the Council on July 9th, when Mr. F.A. Bates said he thought the Council should also take the lead in opposing the scheme on moral grounds. Indeed the chairman, Mr. S. Maycock, said the Council had received a copy of a resolution forwarded to Bucks County Council by the Bletchley United Christian Council. Several members in thinking that the Council should seek the views of residents suggested that a town meeting should be called, with it decided to discuss the question at the next meeting. Meanwhile the recommendation to object to the proposal on financial grounds was approved without dissent. Then in September that year at the quarterly meeting of the Wolverton and Bletchley Methodist Circuit, held at New Bradwell, Mr. G.F. Adkins was appointed to represent the Circuit in objecting to the proposed dog track. Nevertheless the scheme went ahead, and its history of hosting greyhound races, speedway, and stock car racing is variously told on the Internet, to include 'Greyhound Racing Times,' and 'Speedway Magazine on line.' Suffice to say that the stadium was bulldozed in 2006, and the site now lies under the developments of modern housing.

SCHOOLS

In 1841 is mentioned that 20 year old Robert Bodley was a schoolmaster at Simpson. Then in November 1860 a cottage in the village was hired for use as a Sunday School and evening school by the Rev. F. Wilson. Before the introduction of a formal State education many villages had 'dame schools,' usually run in their own homes by an elderly woman, who, with their parents paying a few pence per week, would provide an elementary education for local children. One such school was that of Becky Rands at Simpson.

BECKY RANDS

The eighth of the nine children of Francis Litchfield Rands, a farm labourer, born at Bradwell Abbey in 1756, and his wife Ann, Rebecca Rands was baptised at Simpson in 1799 on May 12th. By 1851 she was living with an elder sister, Elizabeth, head of the household, with both in occupation as lace makers. Then by 1861 she had set up a dame school in the little parlour of the southernmost of the three cottages at Mount Pleasant. With a small cane she was allegedly a strict disciplinarian, and for this education parents of the village children paid a few pence per week in fees. However in 1876 when the Simpson and Woughton Board School opened she then had to find an alternative income, and thereon eked out a meagre living by lace making, needlework and odd jobs. She became impoverished, and in 1890 at the meeting on August 27th of the Newport Pagnell Board of Guardians her relief grant was renewed. This was on the recommendation of James Horton, the relieving officer, and provided an increase of 1s per week for additional nursing. However she died in December that year and was buried in an unmarked grave in Simpson churchyard.

THE WOUGHTON AND SIMPSON BOARD SCHOOL

A TIMELINE OF TEACHING: THE FIRST 50 YEARS

Allegedly the origins of the school were commenced in the 1850s by the Church of England, accommodated at that time in the old Sunday School building near Church House, Woughton. Then under the Elementary Education Act of 1870, in 1874 on May 21st a proposal was made to unite the school districts of the parishes of Woughton on the Green and Simpson. Thereby this entailed not only the need for a school for 85 children, midway between the two villages, but also the election of a School Board. Thus in January

1875 the members elected without opposition were the Rev. George Shelford Bidwell, rector of Simpson, the Rev. Maurice Farrell, rector of Woughton, William Levi, of Woughton House, and Messrs. John Sipthorp and Robert Stevens, both of Simpson.[8] In consequence the members of the 'United School District of Woughton on the Green and Simpson' held their first meeting that year on Thursday, February 4th. The venue was a room near the rectory at Simpson and with all members present William Levi was unanimously elected as chairman. The Rev. Maurice Farrell was appointed as vice chairman with Mr. Frederick Bodley, of Simpson, as the unanimous choice as clerk to the Board. In September 1875 tenders were invited for the construction of the school building and the master's house, to be located halfway between Simpson and Woughton. Prepared by A.E. Browne Esq, of Clifton Chambers, Lincoln's Inn Fields, the plans and specifications could be inspected between 10am and 5pm at the clerk's residence on and after September 6th. Tenders, 'sealed and endorsed,' were to be delivered to Mr. F. Bodley on or before 10am on September 27th, with the stipulation that the Board would not be committed to the lowest. Mr. Bodley was also the recipient of applications for a certificated master for the school, 'Wanted on or about October 1st 1876.' The appointed person would have charge of the pupils from Simpson and also Woughton, for the school would now accommodate any children from the latter village who previously attended the old Sunday School building (now demolished). Herbert William Bates was duly appointed from the applicants, writing as the first entry in the school log book;

"November 13th 1876 Monday.

Opened the school today when 32 children presented themselves for admission. No apparatus arrived yet, the only school furniture being desks for the boys. Examined the children and found the majority had no idea of tables or arithmetic; very few could write anything; the only knowledge they possessed being a slight one of reading. The greater part of the week was spent in teaching them their figures; learning them to write the letters of the alphabet; also the multiplication table by two. These exercises were done on their own slates with a piece of whiting for chalk and the dark wall for a blackboard."

Additionally he notes the arrival of the school books - "two dozen and one Bibles and a set of wall maps." That year Esther Hodge is mentioned as the mistress although it's uncertain if she was the one referred to in this entry;

"The first pupil teacher - "Dec. 20th 1876. "Miss A' came this morning on trial for the office of pupil teacher. She is, however, very backwards in her attainments and as yet rather quiet." In fact her lessons would prove rather poor, with parents complaining of her "beating and frightening the children." Not surprisingly by August she had received her notice, and another pupil teacher had been taken on. Thus in further entries;

"1876 July 27th. More teaching being required in this school, Kate Greenacre came on trial today and promises to make a good teacher." (However her performance would gradually decline although she nevertheless stayed on for 4 years.)

In 1877 on the evening of Monday, January 15th an entertainment was given in the new Board School room by Messrs. W. & J. Piggott of Leighton Buzzard. This comprised 'dissolving views illustrating a tour through districts of Central and Southern Europe.' Also the adventures of John Gilpin, 'which greatly amused the children.' The superiority of the limelight over the old fashioned oil lanterns was evidenced by the remarkable brilliancy of the views.' Also shown were some enlarged photo transparencies of the neighbourhood, and, being the first occasion for such use, the room was filled.

As for school work, the numerous entries in the log book would include;

1877 Jan. 25th. "The second standard wrote dictation on paper for the first time."

1877 Feb. 8th. "A ladies committee was appointed to assist in the Sewing." (This was mainly comprised of the Managers' wives, lead by Mrs. Bates, and as recalled in later life by a former pupil; "In the afternoon the head teacher's wife used to come in and take us for needlework and she was a nice old lady. She used to wear a big silver thimble and if we didn't behave she used to bang on our heads with her thimble.")

1877 July 5th. "The first surprise visit I have yet had in any school."

1877 Sept. In the Inspector's report of the school on June 18th is stated; "Mixed School: This school, recently opened, promises well under Mr. Bates. Some weaknesses was shown in the arithmetic of the First Standard, but the results of the examination generally show careful teaching and time well spent."

1878 Feb. 12th. "Several loads of fine gravel for the playgrounds and some ornamental tiles for the garden arrived today."

1878 Aug. The report on the Woughton and Simpson Board School states "The school is in a thriving condition. The order is good, and the elementary work is neatly and accurately done. The sewing is good."

1878 December 16th. "William Hawley was drowned this evening while sliding on the canal just after afternoon school. No one was present at the time and the body was recovered about two hours after. Attention was called to the place by finding a favourite stick upon the ice."

1879 Aug. 9th. " Only a very small school this morning, there having been a great flood yesterday causing many of the houses to be flooded thereby preventing the scholars from leaving their homes."

Then in December on Monday 8th came another sliding tragedy on the frozen canal. After leaving the Simpson school, in the company of two other boys the son of Charles Hurley of Walton

Village School: Pupils and teachers.

went to the canal and began sliding towards Simpson. Then opposite the farm buildings of Mr. Sipthorpe the ice gave way, submerging the three boys. Two were rescued but Hurley was already dead when recovered. On the Wednesday an inquest was held at the Plough, at which a verdict of accidental death was recorded. On happier matters throughout 1879 and 1880 satisfactory reports by the Inspector were given. However during April 1881 the school was closed due to an epidemic of measles resulting in 7 or 8 deaths in the village. School attendance was understandably poor and a consequent lapse in the pupils' behaviour was perhaps evidenced by Mr. Kenny-Herbert, the Inspector, in writing his report for the year;

> "I am sorry to report a great falling off both in order and attainments. No amount of warning or talking seems to have the least impression on the children; they whisper, laugh and play without any hesitation. I hope I shall never have to send up another schedule like this one from this school. The infants are moderately fairly forward. The sewing specimens are not good and the knitting consisted of one pair of cuffs and a stocking and a half. Great improvement will be expected as a condition of an unreduced grant next year."

For those seeking an alternative education, it was advertised in June 1881 that Dunmore House School at Simpson, 'for Boarders and day pupils,' was transferring to Fenny Stratford. Assisted by his wife the principal was Mr. Alfred Holloway, whose establishment could offer 'Thorough instruction in 20 subjects, with Languages and Accomplishments.' 'Notice of removal. Mr. and Mrs. Holloway, of Dunmore House School, Simpson, desire to intimate to the inhabitants of Fenny Stratford and neighbourhood that they have decided to remove into the town of Fenny Stratford as being a more central position, and trust to receive the support of parents who may wish for their children a sound and liberal education.' The next term would commence on July 4th 1881. (The first pupil of their school had been Miss Rachael Belinda Austin, the only daughter of Mr. Austin, the blacksmith, and his wife of Simpson. After an illness which had confined her for the past 6 years she died in August 1895 aged 27, being buried in Simpson churchyard. Of the many wreaths was one from Mr. and Mrs. A. Holloway with the words "In loving and affectionate memory of our first pupil, Mr. and Mrs. A. Holloway.") The Board was also in need of premises in Fenny Stratford, and it was reported in 1882 at their meeting on Friday, February 3rd that since the previous meeting a letter had been received from the Education Department. This requested a plan to be forwarded of the existing British School, Fenny Stratford, with a surveyor's certificate as to its saleable value. Also the plans, specifications, and an estimate for the additions it was proposed to make. Mr. Gotto, an architect of Leighton Buzzard, had been asked to furnish these, to be sent together with his certificate. Regarding the value he stated a figure of £435, the Board having purchased the premises for £400. As for the position of mistress at Fenny Stratford many applications were received, with Miss Adelaide Eliza Wilding, of Hereford, eventually chosen. Her salary would be £75 to include sweeping the school, which would be opened as soon as possible after completing the alterations. Then on the morning of Monday, June 19th 1882 the Board opened their school at Fenny Stratford - with the result that not a single scholar attended;

> "The ratepayers of Simpson have been put to great expense in providing this accommodation, which appears to be almost unnecessary. It is another proof of the necessity of throwing that portion of the town which is now in Simpson parish into Fenny Stratford parish. A vast amount of expense and inconvenience would then be avoided."

Meanwhile at Simpson in 1882 Kate Greenacre's term of apprenticeship expired, and she applied to the School Board for a testimonial. This was reported at their meeting on Monday, July 3rd, and the chairman was asked to draw this up, to be signed by all the members. However when she left on July 8th it would be with the Inspector's note that 'Kate Greenacre is to be informed that she is not qualified.' As for Mr. Bates, in his general opinion he wrote in the log; "The school has appeared in a much better light this year." Somewhat ironic, for in November 1882 he notes a meeting of the Board at which "I was informed that the Board intended to dismiss me." Supposedly they intended to employ a mistress, and he would be given three months notice from the next meeting. However there was unanimous agreement to award him the highest testimonials. These no doubt helped him to secure another post in February 1883 which, as he proudly noted in the school log, was from 51 applicants. As for his time at Simpson, his last entry in the log book is on March

2nd 1883, in which he writes "absent most of the day sending my goods by railway." That evening he was afforded an appreciation, with a presentation made to himself and his wife for their 6½ years at the school. The meeting comprised some of the subscribers, and Mr. Cowlishaw, head master of the Fenny Stratford school, in addressing Mr. Bates included; "I have great pleasure in presenting to you on behalf of the subscribers this handsome and valuable timepiece, sincerely hoping that when you are located in your new home on the banks of the Humber you will often turn your thoughts to those you left behind on the banks of the Ousel. In departing from them you carry away with you the good wishes of all present. We all unite in wishing you a safe and prosperous journey, and may your efforts in your new sphere meet with the same appreciation as they have done at Simpson." He then presented a locket to Mrs. Bates,[9] and in a suitable, albeit pointed reply, Mr. Bates responded;

> "I thank you all for your kind feelings towards us and most especially for the handsome presents you have made us. We both appreciate and value them very much. Our time spent here has been six years of happiness, and our leaving is not our seeking. We are obliged to submit to the dictates of the Board whether good or bad. I have always endeavoured to do my duty faithfully and conscientiously, and it gives me very great pleasure to find those services appreciated and recognised. We shall always value these presents, and when we look upon them our memories will return to Simpson and the great kindness we have always met with from its people. I thank you most sincerely on my own and Mrs. Bates' behalf, and also Mr. Cowlishaw for presiding and for his kind utterances; also Messrs. Plumb and Edwards for their labours in raising the funds and to the subscribers generally for their kind assistance."

In 1883 at the meeting of the School Board on Friday, March 23rd the clerk was directed to have the school and house cleaned, and the house repaired for the new occupant who, with the Board having seemingly been somewhat economical with the truth, was not a mistress but instead was Mr. Richard A. Rawling of Roborough National School, South Devon. However of the five applicants invited for interview only two turned up, and thus from this limited choice Mr. Rawling was unanimously appointed at a salary of £80, to include sweeping and cleaning the school. In other appointments in

1883 on Monday, July 16th Miss Emily Jane Wall was unanimously appointed as mistress at £50pa. Born at Aspley Guise she was the daughter of Mrs. Jane Wall, the mistress of the Woburn Sands school in connection with the Aspley Guise school, and she had already been a pupil teacher at the school. (In 1871 Jane was schoolmistress at Aspley Guise, with her husband John as master at the National School. Then in 1901 Emily and her now widowed mother were schoolmistresses at West Farleigh). During the winter a night school had been held at Simpson, and in April 1884 an evening tea was given in recognition of the satisfactory examination of the scholars on March 31st. In April 1886, due to the fracture damage to the stonework and brickwork caused by frost the clerk was instructed to have the front wall of the school repaired. As for opinions of the school, some of these also appeared a little fractured, for in July 1886 William Smith, of Little Woolstone, in writing to the Agricultural Gazette remarked; "Look to Simpson, two miles from here. At twelve o'clock daily, you may see a string of pinch-faced, starved, ragged looking children coming from the Board School, real paupers as they are, for a child that has its head crammed by a "standard" from the poor rate is as much a pauper as one thus having its belly crammed with bread." At the meeting of the School Board on Friday, July 6th 1888 the Inspector's Report was considered;

"Mixed School

The school has passed another very successful examination, and has secured a high percentage of passes. What is wanted to make the work completely satisfactory is a little more attention to style and uniformity as regards the handwriting, and to neatness and carefulness over forming figures and setting down and arranging sums. The order is good and the sewing fair."

Infant Class

"The infants read well and write very fairly, but the formation of figures and knowledge of numbers are not so good as they should be. The general condition can be rated at very fair."

(Additionally he reports that the ventilation of the infants' class room is not satisfactory. Also 'E. Burtcher is contained under Article 84.')

In 1889 at a meeting on Friday, March 1st a long discussion took place regarding the charge applied for the use of the school for other purposes. Considerable damage to desks, etc. had been caused, and with it carried unanimously Mr. Levi proposed, seconded by Mr. Sipthorpe; "That in future the charge for the Simpson School for those who are non resident and the proceeds not for a local object shall be 10s per night; for those residing in the district and for all local purposes it shall remain as before, viz., 6s, per night." Yet there were no grumbles regarding the teaching ability of the schoolmistress, 26 year old Miss Emily Jane Wall, who was now residing in Simpson with the Clarke family. Nevertheless that year a report stated "There is a great lack of intelligence in regard to expression and the meaning of words." In September 1891 at a special meeting of the School Board the replies received at the last meeting were considered regarding a master to replace Mr. Burtcher, whose term would expire on November 14th. Of the five requested to appear again only two turned up, with letters from the others stating their inability to attend. Therefore the testimonials of the two hopefuls, Mr. Davis, of Andover, and Mr. Edward Bevan, of Stafford, were read by the clerk, and with both called before the Board they were questioned by the chairman. The nature of their duties was explained but both objected to the requirement of having to sweep the school and light the fires etc. without extra payment. Nevertheless to include this requirement Mr. Bevan would accept the position at £85pa. That year an Inspector's report had stated; "The infants class will be reported as inefficient unless the children are taught with intelligence and their school life brightened and made interesting to them." With the point so starkly made, no doubt in consequence in August 1892 an advert was placed for the need, by September 12th, of a young lady aged over 18 to take charge of the class at 5s a week. In 1893 on Tuesday, January 3rd the children attending the Woughton and Simpson Board School performed a Cantata entitled 'Santa Claus.' Piano accompaniment was by Mr. W.J. Levi, and the event reflected great credit on Mr. and Mrs. Bevan, the new master and mistress. The proceeds provided a much welcomed tea for the children. Also during the month six cookery lessons in connection with the County Council Technical Education Scheme were undertaken in the schoolroom by Miss Clara Fallows. Instruction in the afternoon was given to 12 girls, who made various dishes under the direction of Miss Fallow, and

'The evening demonstrations were much appreciated.' As for other instruction, in April for women only a course of lectures on Health in the Home was given by Miss Bella Deyns. An attentive presence of 20 ladies greatly appreciated the first lecture, and her offer to visit their homes for the purpose of advising on sanitary matters was accepted by four of those attending. For displaying on the walls of the school, on Thursday, July 27th 1893 the school chairman, Mr. J. Sipthorpe, presented portraits of the Duke and Duchess of York, with Mr. Levi undertaking to have frames carved by the boys' school.

In the routine oversight of the school, the Inspector reported;

"Infant class - The infants, for whom Mr. Bevan is responsible in addition to the upper school, are doing as well as circumstances permit. Mrs. Bevan takes the class in some Kindergarten exercises and needlework, but she does not interfere beyond this. It is an arrangement which would try most masters severely, and one which I cannot regard as satisfactory. Mr. Bevan will receive his certificate in due course."

With regard to these findings, after protracted discussion Mr. Levi proposed placing an advert for a female teacher over the age of 18 to take over the infants' class. Thus in October 1893 at the monthly meeting of the School Board a letter was read from Miss Ellen W. Langley. In this she accepted the appointment as pupil teacher under the Board, with her duties to commence from September 11th. Then in December having been master for two years Mr. Bevan applied for an increase in salary. One member thought the fact that he had a house and inclusive coal worth some £15 to £20 a year should be taken into account, but another member said that might be, but they should consider that the house was in a lonely position, and therefore who would be likely to give that sum for it. As for Mr. Levi he concurred with an increase, albeit suggesting that the master should be told it was consequent on the merits of their next report. This was agreed. In March 1894 the master's report showed that for February the school had been opened 40 times, with 93 pupils on the books. As for other matters, the clerk in handing in Miss Langley's doctor's certificate reported that she had been away for a week through illness. Subsequently Mr. Bevan, the master, had sent up and asked what he should do, to which the clerk had replied that he should cope as best he could. If there was a girl in the school capable of such work then allow her to do it, and additionally Mrs. Bevan had assisted with the teaching. At the meeting of the School Board in April 1894 Mr. Bevan reported that the number on the books was 89. The average attendance was 73, and in other news the path from Simpson to the school was to be put into good order. Regarding Technical Education, in 1894 on the evening of Friday, May 4th a public meeting was held in the village schoolroom. In the absence of the Rev. J.B. Higham, who failed to attend, the rector stepped in, and having explained the meaning and objects a local committee was afterwards appointed comprised of Messrs. Levi, Bramley, Bevan, Field, Garner, G. Biggs, Mrs. Field, Mrs. Levi, Miss Higgins and Miss Clinch. The initial four were then elected as delegates to serve on the District Committee. In other activities the Ambulance Classes which began at the Board School on October 23rd 1894 were now flourishing, with Dr. Buxton instructing a full class of 30 men from Woughton and Simpson. On similar matters the usual carpentry classes were being held in the schoolroom, laundry classes would commence shortly, and 'It is hoped that parents especially will urge their young people to attend the classes regularly.' In January 1895 the parish council had concerns that some 40 children who went to the school from Simpson had to tramp all the way along a muddy road. It was therefore proposed that the clerk should write to the County Surveyor and ask if a path could be made. Then in December 1895 the Board had further concerns, when in furtherance of her illness a letter was read from Miss Langley resigning her post as the teacher of the infants at the end of the month. In consequence the clerk was instructed to advertise for an assistant capable female teacher by January 6th 1896. Applicants, to take charge of the infants, 'average 25,' would need to be aged over 18, and in 1896 it was reported on January 7th at the meeting of the Board that Miss Rebecca B. Barrows, who every weekend lived with her mother at Fenny Stratford, had replied from Ridgmont, accepting the position at £25pa. However she asked for her salary to be reconsidered, which, if she met the Board's requirements, would be discussed at the next meeting. In fact she wasn't alone in thinking the remuneration insufficient, for in a letter that month to the local press 'Indignant' wrote;

"I noticed that the Rev. W. Rice proposed, and Mr. Levi seconded, that a teacher should offered the "liberal" salary of £25 a year. Would either the Rev. Rice or Mr. Levi like a daughter of theirs to teach in a school for a year for £25? A teacher would have to pay at least 10s a week for board and lodgings, for, say 45 weeks in the year, which amounts to £22 10s, leaving her £2 10s, or nearly 1s per week, for pocket money, clothing, etc. She might earn much more than that as a servant in the meanest place in the country. A girl of 14 earns more in her first place, and yet a teacher is supposed to be apprenticed for four years, during which time her parents have to keep her, as she barely earns sufficient in books, clothing, and pocket money, and then, after studying for that time, and passing four examinations, she is offered £25 a year. I noticed that the Chairman wants no more "blocks of wood." Can he expect to get more for £2 10s a year? Why, he would have to pay that per year for a wooden image. I would like to point out that if the Board really want the school to improve (which appears to me very doubtful) they must appoint a competent person as teacher, and pay the salary required, namely, from £45 to £50 a year. If they get a teacher for £25, she is only a teacher by name, as no one really competent to teach would think of accepting an appointment unless a salary, on which she could "live," was offered." The writer concludes that the Board "will have to open their shallow hearts very wide, or the school will remain closed."

Nevertheless Miss Barrows accepted the appointment, and it was reported at the meeting of the School Board in 1896 on Monday, March 2nd, that having visited the school on Thursday the chairman and Mr. Field found the master, Mr. Bevan, sufficiently pleased to recommend her permanent employment. On other issues they noticed the stove filled the room with smoke, and that the gate between the boys and girls playground was in a rotten condition. Since then Mr. Bevan had mentioned the need for some paper hanging and white washing at his house. As for Miss Barrows, her appointment in view of Mr. Bevan's assessment was confirmed subject to 3 months either side. This was on the proposition of the Rev. F. Field, seconded by Mr. Garner. Also there was unanimous agreement to present Mrs. Bevan with the sum of £2, in recognition of her services as teacher during the period from Miss Langley leaving the school until the appointment of Miss Barrows. Money was also available for the maintenance of the school, for in July 1896 tenders 'to be received not later than Saturday, July 18th, were invited for 'painting etc.' of the school and house, to be sent to Frederick Bodley, clerk to the Board. In fact having been elected by the ratepayers in January 1896 the Board now consisted of Albert Bramley, Frederick Francis Field, Joseph Garner, and William John Levi. Also John Sipthorpe, and regarding the Inspector's report at their meeting in 1896 on Monday, July 20th it was stated;

> "Mixed school. Mr. Bevan is maintaining the efficiency of this school with some success. Map drawing is not sufficiently taught. This be should attended to.
>
> Infants' class. The infants will, I think, do well under Miss Barrows, in course of time. Their general condition is now very fair. Miss Barrows is continued under Article 68 of the Code."

Then in other good news it was reported in September that the school had been thoroughly renovated. In 1896 at the meeting of the Board on Monday, December 21st the clerk, Mr. F. Bodley, asked for an increase in salary. Having been clerk and attendance officer for nearly 20 years his work had now increased from the district being more scattered. With a £5 increase his request was unanimously agreed, thereby providing £20 for both positions. Welcome news, but not so welcome in 1897 was Mr. Bevan being caught by a surprise visit of the Inspector. This was on the first day of term and at a time when he hadn't marked one of the registers. With an explanation demanded he explained "I was endeavouring to make a good start and get into the general routine as quickly as possible ... the marking of the registers entirely slipped my memory until the change of lessons took place when the matter suddenly occurred to my mind and I immediately commenced to mark them. While I was doing so H.M. Sub-Inspector came into the school." Not that it seemed a major misdemeanour, for it was written in the Inspector's report in July 1897; "Mr Bevan is working as well as he can with his school, and meets with such success as a single handed teacher can expect. He ought certainly to be given the help of a monitor. ... The infants' division is doing very fairly. ... Here, too, a monitor is much wanted to attend to the babies' class. Drawing at Simpson is 'excellent.'"

Indeed all seemed very convivial, as also had been the annual tea given on Tuesday, June 8th to the children attending the Simpson

School and also the Branch School in Fenny Stratford High Street. The pupils from Fenny Stratford were conveyed in vans and horses supplied by J. Baisley Esq., JP, and Mr. F. Bodley, and as they passed through Simpson they loudly cheered. At the school they were met by the Board members, the clerk, the Simpson teachers (Mr. and Mrs. Bevan and Miss Barrows,) and the Branch teachers, (Misses Sangster, K. Clarke and L. Clarke) and despite the indifferent weather after tea games were played in an adjoining field. This was followed at 6pm by cake, tea, sweets etc. in the school, and in conclusion a vote of thanks was proposed by the chairman, W.J. Levi, to the teachers, friends and especially the master. In 1898 the Inspector's report was read at the meeting of the School Board on Monday, July 4th; "The school is doing well on the whole. An effort is being made to improve the children's intelligence with some success. The teaching of geography must never be of a mechanical kind. Infants' Class. Miss Barrows is doing well with the infants' class."

Not for long though, for in 1900 at the meeting of the School Board on Monday, January 8th the clerk read the following letter from the 'Assistant Head Mistress, Miss Barrows.'

"2, Western Villas,

Western Road,

Fenny Stratford.

To the Members of the School Board.

Mr. Chairman and Gentlemen.

I beg to resign my position as Assistant Head Mistress to the Infants at your School; my duties to cease three months hence.

I take this opportunity to thank the Board for the kindness shewn me during the four years I have been in your service, and shall esteem it a favour if you will kindly grant me a testimonial as to the manner in which I have carried out my duties during that period.

I remain,

Mr. Chairman and Gentlemen,

Most obediently yours,

ROSE BEATRICE BARROWS."

As per instruction the clerk would reply that the Board very much regretted her departure, as they thought she had been consistently satisfactory. Thus in February 1900 an advert was posted for a replacement. Then in May another such advert would have to be placed, for at the meeting of the School Board on Monday, April 30th the resignation was accepted with regret of Mr. Bevan, who had accepted an appointment in London. In a letter he wrote;

"Simpson Board School.

April 3rd, 1900.

To the Members of the Woughton and Simpson School Board.

Gentlemen, - I have just recently received an offer of a good appointment in London, and I believe it will be to my interest to accept it.

To enable me to do so, I must ask you if you will kindly allow me to vacate my present position by June 8th. Also, should you favourably consider my request, I shall be glad if you will grant me a testimonial at the earliest possible date, as I have to submit the same to my future Managers. My reason for wishing to take up this appointment is purely personal, and not in any way connected with the slightest dissatisfaction at my position here, as I have always received the greatest kindness and courtesy from the Board.

Trusting this may meet with your favourable consideration.

I am, yours obediently,

E. BEVAN."

The chairman said they would be very sorry to lose Mr. Bevan and that he had given the Board every satisfaction. It was agreed for June 8th, and to advertise for a replacement. Consequently a special meeting was called in May to consider the applications received for the post of headmaster and headmistress. This carried a combined salary of £120pa, with house, fuel, and garden, and after consideration the clerk was directed to communicate with John Bool of Nash, near Buckingham, and Mr. T. Best, of 38, Havelock Street, Sheffield. Both were asked to meet the Board members on May 5th at 7pm, with Mr. Bool proving the successful candidate. Applications for the position left vacant by the resignation of Miss Barrows had also been received, including one on behalf of Kate M. Spiers, sent by Susan Besson of the schoolhouse at Little Woolstone. At a special meeting of the School Board she was duly engaged as assistant teacher with a month's notice either side. However it seems there had been a misunderstanding at the interview, for at the meeting of the Board on Monday, October 15th the clerk reported that she had sent the following letter;

"Woughton Schools, Sept. 27th.

Dear Sir. If I had known the teacher was required in the upper department I should not have accepted the appointment. I have always been used to an infants class, and I therefore wish to resign and give the Board a month's notice.

Yours faithfully,

K.M. Spiers."

In view of this there was unanimous resolve to appoint Miss Hosey as the assistant teacher at £37pa, with the promise of an increase to £40 after the Inspector's visit. As for Mr. Bool, he had now settled into his role as headmaster, but on October 19th he had to send the children home as only 19 turned up. Mr. Sipthorpe said the absentees had taken 'French Leave' to see a circus! Mr. Bool had further cause for complaint in December, when he deemed that paraffin to light the school fires was inefficient. In response the Board decreed that fire lights should be used in future. In 1901 at the meeting of the School Board on Monday, November 4th, held at the clerk's residence, Mr. Bramley reported that the chairman, clerk and himself had interviewed Mr. G. Wigley, auctioneer, with reference to the sale of the Branch School at Fenny Stratford. A solicitor for Mr. Wigley would be needed, and in consequence Mr. Bull of Newport Pagnell had been appointed. The clerk had handed over the letter to him from the Education Dept. sanctioning the sale, with the building to be sold by auction. With regard to any of the stock being of use to the Simpson school the committee had inspected that available, to include some of the maps. From being out of date and now replaced by a new series the many books would be distributed among the children of Woughton and Simpson. In other business the tenders for providing and fixing three No. 4 Tortoise slow combustion stoves were opened, with that of Mr. A.H. Lee of Fenny Stratford accepted at £4 18s 6d. On the instructions of the Woughton and Simpson Branch School Board, in 1901 on Thursday, November 21st

Mr. Geo. Wigley conducted an auction at 4pm at the Swan Hotel, Fenny Stratford, of the freehold property known as the Woughton and Simpson Branch Board school, Fenny Stratford. This comprised the spacious brick and tile building previously used as schoolrooms, having a long frontage to the High Street adjoining the Mount Pleasant path to Church Street. Then with regard to the school at Simpson, 13 applications were received in January 1902 for the post of master and mistress. At a special meeting each of the candidates was interviewed, with Mr. E.D. Roberts of 42, St. John's Road, Polsloe Park, Exeter, appointed at £120pa. This would include fuel, with £5 for sweeping the school. The post was subject to 3 months notice either side and would commence at the end of March. Of 12 years experience Mr. Roberts was 27, and his wife was also a certificated teacher. At the meeting of the School Board on Monday, February 3rd 1902 the clerk was directed to write to the Loan Commissioners stating that the Branch School had now been closed and sold by auction. This was on the instructions of the Board of Education, and with their stipulated reserve price of £230 having been reached the Loan Commissioners were asked to take over the money, which was now in the bank. Those children who had attended the Branch

Simpson Village School

School now attended the Fenny Stratford Board Schools, and at the meeting of the Simpson & Woughton School Board on the evening of Monday, June 23rd 1902, held at the school at Simpson, the Rev. Rice said that in view of this perhaps the salary of the clerk should be reconsidered. In fact he had submitted this intention at the previous meeting, and in moving that their clerk, Frederick Bodley, should be reappointed said he would leave the question of salary to Mr. Bodley's consideration, as to whether he would accept a reduction. However Mr. Bodley said the same issue had been brought up by the Reverend three years ago, and he held the office in accordance with the terms of his agreement. As long as he did the work of the Board properly and to the satisfaction of the Board of Education there was no law as to his reappointment. At this a heated argument broke out between the rector and the clerk, such that a messenger at the rector's request was sent to the clerk's house for the Education Acts. When these arrived the rector then quoted a section of the 1870 Act, after which further discussion 'of a very personal nature' was indulged. Nevertheless the motion of the rector was seconded by Mr. A.J. Stevens and carried. However there would soon be no scope for further altercations, since by the Education Act of 1902 came the abolition of School Boards, with at a local level a re-organisation to place elementary schools in the hands of local education authorities (L.E.A.s) under the control, as regarded the Woughton and Simpson school, of the County Council. An Education Committee was appointed, approved by the Board of Education, and in 1903 at its monthly meeting at County Hall, Aylesbury, on the morning of Thursday, July 16th, the Elementary Education Sub Committee resolved that three representatives of Fenny Stratford Urban District Council should meet three representatives of Woughton Parish Council, with these six then appointing the two managers of the Woughton and Simpson school. In 1902 a new window had been ordered to brighten the infants room, and in March 1903 once the builders had finished the infants moved back in, to find the room "quite bright and cheerful." However with the introduction of the 1902 Education Act not so bright did Mr. Roberts now deem his future prospects at the school, and in a letter of resignation from himself and his wife, read at perhaps the last meeting of the Board in 1903 on Monday, July 27th, he explained his concern, namely that the decreasing number of scholars under the working of the new system would affect his future salary and promotion. Thus with testimonials to be given his termination of employment would be on November 1st 1903. A new master was appointed to take over from that date but through failing health Mr. Roberts left a week early on doctor's orders. Two lady teachers from Bletchley then filled the break until the arrival of John Cullom and his wife. As for further developments in the new educational administration, in 1904 at the Aylesbury meeting on Thursday, March 24th, the Bucks Educational Committee recommended that regarding the management of the Fenny Stratford and Woughton and Simpson schools the following arrangements should be adopted ;

a) That the two schools be grouped under one body of Managers (Education Act 1902 s. 12).

b) That the number of Managers be nine.

c) That of the three Managers to be appointed by the Minor Local Authority, two be appointed by the Fenny Stratford Urban District Council and one by the Woughton Parish Council.

On the national scene, in that 'long hot Edwardian summer' the sun was still shining on the British Empire, and in the school log book in 1908 is contained the customary 'Empire day was celebrated this morning by singing the song 'The Flag of Britain' around the flagstaff and saluting the flag.' The flagstaff, the gift of the Rev. Field, was erected by Col. Levi, and after the celebration Mrs. Levi, of Woughton House, presented the school prizes for regular attendance and good conduct. Mr. Bramley addressed the children on the 'Empire,' and the following year in continuing the tradition the "School closed this afternoon for Empire Day. The ordinary work was suspended this morning and explanation of the Union Jack and singing of patriotic songs taken instead." No doubt in the contemporary circumstances the occasion was a boost to morale, and indeed in the Inspector's report it was stated that "the children are lively and intelligent. The curriculum is being strengthened by the introduction of cardboard modelling." In 1910 Empire Day had an additional bonus, for as the log records; "Ordinary work was suspended and lessons given on the Empire." As a further cause for celebration at the close Col. Levi presented each child with a bun and an orange. Then in August 1914 the storm clouds gathered and the First World War commenced.[10]

That year also saw the departure of the headmaster, for on December 22nd he wrote, "I, John Cullom, terminated my engagement as headmaster of this school." This was due to having secured 'a more important appointment' under the Beds. Education Committee at Luton, and that day he and his wife were presented by the scholars with a massive pair of silver candlesticks. Also a cathedral gong hall clock in oak, with the presentation made by Mr. F. Bodley on behalf of the managers. Mr. Cullom's successor would be Edmund Badger, who in October 1917 in aid of the British Red Cross Society (Bletchley Division) arranged the programme for a 'Concert-Entertainment.' Organised by Mrs. J. Kilpatrick this was given in the school on a Friday evening, with the bill provided by the senior scholars and staff assisted by Frank Morrison of London. Of the many contributions Mr. Badger sang quaint West Country ditties, and together with Miss Alice Mould rendered several musical duologues in character costume. Mrs. Badger provided the accompaniment and with almost every family from Simpson, Woughton and Walton in attendance £7 7s was raised. (Miss Alice Mould was the infants' teacher who lived in the schoolhouse at Little Woolstone and rode a bicycle to school every day.) Mr. Badger seems to have encouraged school concerts but in 1921 on January 18th he wrote in the school log book; "I have been rather 'below par' in health for several weeks." In fact he was certified as suffering from septic anaemia, and was ordered to rest for three weeks. He duly returned to work on June 1st but in 1922 on March 10th the doctor certified him unfit for school duties, and again ordered three weeks rest. Then on April 18th 1922 came the poignant entry "Mr. Edmund Badger, head teacher of this school, died on this date." Subject to the approval of the County Council and the Board of Education, in January 1925 it was proposed to pay £50 for land at the rear of the school as a playing field and school garden. Also in recreational matters, in 1926 at the breaking up for the Christmas holiday an entertainment was provided for the children. Mr. B. Kilvington assisted by Miss Gladys Young and Miss Alice Mould (assistant teachers) arranged a substantial tea and the part of Father Christmas was played by Captain Hudson, who, together with his wife had presented a large Christmas tree. In December 1927 Clifford Bayley Mould became the headmaster, and in 1929 was resident at the school house with his siblings Ellen, Alice, and Harold. As told in the book in this series 'The Woolstones & Willen' he would leave for a school at Wadhurst. Thus in 1931 on March 2nd George Lionel Owen Williamson became the new headmaster. However when the school broke up for the Christmas holidays in 1933 there would be the departure of a longstanding member of staff, Miss Alice Mould, who in leaving gifts was presented by Mrs. B. Hudson, of Woughton House, with a leather attaché case. This was on behalf of the teachers and children, and there was also a present from the parishioners of Woughton and Simpson of a gold wristelet watch. Miss Mould had been a teacher at Simpson since 1909 but was now going to join her brother Clifford at his school at Wadhurst.

A TIMETABLE OF TEACHERS

HENRY WILLIAM BATES   1876-1883

The son of John Edmond Bates, a furrier, Henry William Bates was born at Portsea in 1846, baptised on December 27th. In 1851 he was living at 12, College Lane, Portsea, with his mother Elizabeth, age 37, head of the household, a 'furriers wife,' together with his siblings. Living in Commercial Road, in the parish of St. Paul, Newport, Monmouthshire, in 1867 on July 9th at St. Paul's Church he married 19 year old Jane Johnson, also of Commercial Road. She was the daughter of William Johnson, a sadler, and Henry was now employed as a schoolmaster. This was probably at 144, Commercial Road, on the corner with Capel Street, where in 1877 the headmistress would be a Miss Hill. Meanwhile, elsewhere at Barkisland, West Yorkshire, the Barkisland Endowed School opened in March 1868, and perhaps as the first in the role by 1871 Henry had become the headmaster, living at the schoolhouse with Jane, employed as a schoolmistress, and (ages as per the census) son Henry age 2, born at Newport, Monmouthshire, and daughter Elsie age 1, born at Caerleon, Monmouthshire. Also William Johnson age 26, single, brother in law, a seaman, born in London, and Elizabeth Johnson, single, sister in law, age 20, born in London. Then in 1871 on October 21st a daughter, Eva Alice, was born. When an advert appeared in the relevant journal Henry applied for the position of headmaster - 'Wanted on or about October 1st 1876' - for the new school at Simpson, built to accommodate the pupils from Simpson and also those from Woughton. He was duly chosen and in 1881 was settled at the schoolhouse with his wife Jane, as schoolmistress, and (again ages as per the census) son Henry; daughter Elsie; daughter Eva Alice; son William, age 7 born at Barkisland; daughter Winnefred age 6, (actually born in 1874 on November 26th at Barkisland); and infant son Eneas, born at Simpson. As for his time at Simpson, his last entry in the school log book on March 2nd 1883 states "absent most of the day sending my goods by railway." In 1891 he was now at New Holland in the parish of Barrow on Humber, resident in Magna Lane at Southwell Terrace as schoolmaster with his wife Jane, daughter Winnefred, who was now a pupil teacher, son William, son Eneas, and daughter Annie Gwendoline. In 1901 he remained as the schoolteacher, resident with his wife and two lodgers, one of whom, Edith Barnett, single, age 29, was a certificated school mistress, born at Hull. Sadly Jane died in 1903, buried in Barrow upon Humber cemetery, and in 1911 Henry, of Southwell Villa, New Holland, was the head teacher of the Elementary School, resident with his unmarried 29 year old daughter Annie Gwendoline. In 1914 he then moved to Bridlington, Yorkshire, where, when resident with his daughter Annie at 9, Carlton Street, he died aged 97 in 1944 on Saturday, November 18th. Until prevented by old age he sung in the choir of Christ Church, and in former years had been a lay reader. The funeral was held at Christ Church, with the vicar saying in the service; "We are thankful for the example he set in his home among those he loved and in life's work among young and old." Cremation was at Hull with interment at Barrow on Humber cemetery, being commemorated on the same gravestone as his wife. Administration was granted to his son Eneas Percy Bottomley Bates, 'retired college principal,' with effects of £1,782 3s 2d.[11]

WILLIAM BURTCHER 1884-1891

William Burtcher was born in 1858 at West Rainton, County Durham, the son of George Grey Burtcher, a boiler smith, born at South Shields, and his wife Isabella, born at West Rainton. In 1883 on January 3rd at West Rainton he married Eleanor Atkinson, and in October 1884 secured the position of headmaster at Simpson at £85pa with house and fuel. However he and his wife suffered a loss in September 1888, when whilst they were away on holiday their house was broken into. As well as clothes, a watch and a revolver, all the valuables were stolen, and what was left was deliberately smashed. Even the fruit in the garden was stolen. Nevertheless despite the trauma in 1889 at the meeting of the School Board on Friday, August 2nd it was stated in the Inspector's report for the Mixed School;

"Mr. Burtcher has again succeeded in producing a very satisfactory percentage of passes, and I am pleased to see improvement in the style of the work. I think I may now say that the school deserves the excellent merit grant."

Then at the first meeting of the newly elected School Board in 1890 on Thursday, January 30th he asked for an increase in salary, it being stated that he'd greatly improved the efficiency of the school, earning them excellent grants, and that Mrs. Burtcher had been highly complimented by the Inspector on her efficiency as sewing mistress. The increase was duly approved. However, trouble was pending, to become manifest at a special meeting of the School Board in 1891 on Thursday, August 6th. Here the clerk read the notice convening the meeting, namely to pass a minute to serve the master with three months notice to leave their employ. Col. Levi said he understood this had been decided at the previous meeting, with Mr. Stevens saying the master had made a serious omission in regard to the matter of "cutting out," as regarded the sewing classes. When this was discovered he allegedly tried to evade the responsibility and 'screen' Mrs. Burtcher. This apparently arose from a time when she had been unwell and an assistant was taken on. As per Mr. Stevens, "It was all very well for Mr. Burtcher to contend that he was not responsible for the needlework and cutting out but they had paid Mrs. Burtcher to do the work, and they were under the impression she was doing it." According to Mr. Burtcher his wife had resigned in 1888, but that was incorrect since at the close of the last Board, in January 1890, they had both applied for, and received, a testimonial. Yet this was his first omission and he had been an excellent master. Nevertheless Captain Levi thought there was deceit involved, since the master had claimed a salary increase which the Board had been lead to believe was partly for work being undertaken by Mrs. Burtcher; "And now he came and said she resigned in 1888. ... The Board had appointed an assistant to Mrs. Burtcher and he now states that she had been doing the work that should have been done by Mrs. Burtcher; and further that she is incompetent." Thus the Board had 'got into a mess' with the Education Department; "Surely if a member of their staff was incompetent it was his duty to at once give information to the Board." He was a very good master but he had deceived the Board and he thought he should go. The chairman said he was the best master they'd ever had, "and had got the children on first rate." Their grants had been larger and he should not like to get rid of a good master and get a bad one. Despite this, after much discussion it was unanimously agreed to impose three months notice, with his term to expire on November 14th 1891.

JOHN BOOL 1900-1901

Born at Rawmarsh, Yorkshire, the son of Benjamin Bool, a mason, and his wife Martha (nee Dickinson), John Bool was baptised at the church of St. Mary the Virgin in 1861 on February 3rd. His father died in 1870 on March 22nd and in 1881 resident on The Green, Rawmarsh, Martha, in occupation as a milk seller, was the head of the household. Of her several children John was now a pupil teacher. In 1886 on April 28th he married Elizabeth Eardley, born at Tunstall, Staffs., at the Wesleyan Chapel, Broad Street, Nottingham. At Nottingham in 1887 a son, Frank Eardley Bool, was born, and then in 1889 a son Perceval Stanley. In, or by, 1891 John had become schoolmaster at Gawcott, Bucks, resident with his family and also a boarder, Alice Parrott, age 22, born at Adderbury, Oxon. In 1894 a son, Reginald, was born. Then in 1898 on June 23rd a daughter, Fanny Kathleen Bool, was born. In May 1900 John was successful in applying for the position of headmaster at Simpson 'successive from Church Street, Gawcott.' However he would resign in late 1901 and Mr. E.D. Roberts would be his replacement, to commence duties in March 1902.

JOHN CULLOM 1903-1914

John Cullom was born at Tadley, Hants., in 1869 on September

8th, the son of George Cullom, a farmer, and his wife Maria, born at Cheltenham. In 1881 he was living at Tadley with his parents and several siblings. Then in 1895 on December 14th at Cranfield he married Elizabeth Catherine Harpur, born at Cranfield in 1868. In 1896 they were resident in Ellington Street, London, with John employed as a schoolmaster, the school probably being at 45, Ellington Street, Arundel Square. (It was established in 1856, with a girls' school connected with it in 1879.) That year a son, Stanley Arthur, was born, baptised in 1897 on March 7th at the church of St. Clement, Barnsbury, Islington, London. Later in the year John was appointed as headmaster at the board school at Elsing, Norfolk, writing in the school log book on November 8th, "I, John Cullom, C.M., with my wife, Elizabeth Catherine Cullom, C.M., took charge of Elsing Board School this day … Find children in all subjects very backward." Not for long though, for in the Inspector's report for the year ending 1899 February 28th was written "The school has made gratifying progress during the year, under the present teacher, and is now in a creditable state. Staff J. Cullom, E.C. Cullom." In 1901 they were living at the schoolhouse, Elsing, and in April 1902 a daughter, Mildred Eleanor, was born. In 1902 came another pleasing report by the Inspector; "The discipline is firm and kindly, and the children are attentive and interested in their work. The Master works with energy and intelligence, and the state of the school is very satisfactory."

Perhaps too much energy, for due to his illness in March 1903 the school was closed by the Board for a week;

"March 6th 1903 School closed one week as the doctor would not allow me to return."

"March 16th 1903 School closed for another week as I could not return to duties."

Then on March 23rd he wrote in the log book, "I, John Cullom, returned to my duties this morning." However with his address being 'Heath Road successive Church Street,' on September 29th 1903 he wrote; "At a Board Meeting held in the Schoolroom this evening, I, John Cullom, tendered my resignation as Head Master of the Elsing Board School, also Mrs. Cullom as Sewing Mistress." Consequently on October 30th 1903 "I, John Cullom, resigned charge of his school today." He then became headmaster at Simpson, although early in 1904 his address is still given as Church Street. Resident at the schoolhouse in 1911 the family comprised himself and his wife and their daughter Mildred, although his son, Stanley, was noted as being away. That year on October 22nd a son Philip George was born. (As Sergeant Philip George of the RAF (VR.) 5 Photographic Reconnaissance Unit, he died in 1945 on June 16th, leaving a widow, Vera May Cullom, of Orpington. He is buried in the war cemetery, Salerno, Campania, Italy.) In 1914 on December 22nd John wrote in the school log book, "I, John Cullom, terminated my engagement as headmaster of this school." In 1921 he and his family were resident at Midhurst, Sussex, and having retired by 1931 he and his wife were living in Arthur Street, Ampthill. Of that address, Mrs. Cullom died in 1931 on January 29th. In 1939 as a widower John was living at 143, High Street, Cranfield, recorded as an 'Elementary schoolmaster retired' and air raid warden. Also resident was a housekeeper, Eleanor Cullom, born in 1874 on September 25th. Of Orchard House, North Crawley, John died in 1951 on December 9th and was buried in the churchyard of Cranfield parish church. Probate was granted to Stanley Arthur Cullom, school porter, and Mildred Eleanor Cullom, spinster. (Stanley died in 1966 at Horsham, Sussex. Mildred married Archibald Harper in 1952. She died in 1979.)

EDMUND BADGER 1914-1922

Edmund Badger was born at Derby in 1860 on April 13th, baptised on July 1st. In 1861 he was resident at Conisbrough, Yorkshire, with his father Benjamin, age 27, a joiner, born at Conisbrough, his mother Elizabeth (nee Laughton), age 27, born at Conisbrough, sister Mary, age 5, born at Doncaster, and brother Thomas, age 2, born at Conisbrough. At the age of 7 Edmund became a chorister in the parish church of Conisbrough, where many years before his grandfather had been the conductor and leader of the choir and orchestra. In 1871 Edmund was living with his grandparents, Thomas and Ann, in Doncaster Road, Conisbrough, but presumably in a family move he left Conisbrough in 1878, and in 1881 was living as an 'unemployed schoolteacher' at High Melton, in Doncaster Road with his mother, his, father, who was now a builder employing 3 men and a boy, and siblings Mary, Thomas, and now William, age 14. Then at least from 1885 to 1888 he was employed as a teacher at Rabone

Lane School, Smethwick, Birmingham. In other pursuits he was an enthusiastic cricketer, and the previous year in a thespian foray had made his first stage appearance with J.W. Turner's Opera Co., when he essayed the part of Thaddeus in the Bohemian Girl. Seeming this to be an aspiring vocation, in 1888 as announced in the contemporary local press he was to leave Birmingham in April to study in London, 'preliminary to a plunge into the musical profession next season.' In fact he would spend 3 or 4 years in London and Italy for further study (Edwin Holland and Genlio Moretti). In 1889 the first part of a book collection of West Country songs was published by the Rev. Sabine Baring-Gould MA, and the Rev. H. Fleetwood MA, and their endeavour would become popularly known by the shortened title of 'Songs of the West.' [12] The Rev. Baring-Gould was squire and parson of the village of Lew Trenchard, in West Devon, and featuring songs from the book a touring company was established, with Mary Frances Anne Bussell involved from the beginning as pianist in the Baring-Gould's shows. She had been born at Great Marlow, where her father, the Rev. Frederick Bussell MA, was vicar, but now she was resident with her widowed mother at Lew Trenchard. Born at Great Marlow in 1862, her brother, the Rev. Frederick William Bussell BD, of Brasenose College, Oxford, also had involvement with the Songs of the West, and it was possibly at Oxford that he made the acquaintance of Edmund (who used 'Frank Pemberton' as his entertainments name) who became enthused with the subject and content. In 1892 Frederick purchased Exbourne Manor for £4,000, and in the wake of this his mother and sister moved from Lew Trenchard to live at the Manor House. Then in 1893 Edmund became proprietor and director of S. Baring-Gould's 'Songs of the West' organisation, and at Exbourne performed with Mary in local village musical activities. Indeed romance was kindled and in 1894 they were married in a choral service at the parish church on Monday, April 2nd. Exbourne had been decorated by the villagers for the day, and at the church a Union Jack fluttered on the tower, with an arch of evergreens over the church gate. Mary was given away by her brother, Frederick, with Mr. J.A. Laughton as best man. After the ceremony Mrs. Bussell held an 'at home' at the Manor House, and at 5.15 the couple left for Somerset from Okehampton, with the honeymoon to be spent in Weston Super Mare. The couple would then make their home in Exbourne. As for renown in his former Birmingham, the local press reported that year, 1894, "The Songs of the West costume recitals organised by Edmund Badger formerly of this town have proved so successful that the Crystal Palace management have engaged him to give three more on Saturdays June 16th, 23rd, and 30th. Since 1893 he has continuously toured his own concert and operatic companies through Britain, Ireland, and America."[13] When Frederick sold his interests in Exbourne (for £6,200), Edmund and his wife and mother in law moved to London and in 1901 were living at 211, Cornwall Road, Kensington. From there Edmund operated as a wine & spirit merchant, and apparently at some time as a boot dealer. However by 1908 Frederick and Mary had moved to 37, Hagley Road, Edgbaston, where 'Edmund Badger (tenor) late professional pupil in Milan, and in London of Dr. W.H. Cummings and Edwin Holland is now resident in Birmingham and gives lessons in voice culture and singing.' In addition Mary gave tuition in piano and music lessons. Then the next year came this recognition in his home county;

'Edmund Badger as Frank Pemberton is one of the best tenors of the present day. After a long and honoured connection as manager with George Edwards and Mr. Mouilot's Toreador Co. he is now sole proprietor of the Frank Pemberton English Opera Co. and the Lunoun Glee Singers. For some time he was principal tenor for Moody Manners Opera Co.'

In 1913 the production The Arcadians was being variously performed under the direction of 'Frank Pemberton,' but in 1914 on June 3rd he commenced as a temporary teacher at Dunstable Ashton Elementary Boys' School. That year he left on July 31st and in November was at Steppingley Church Lower School. Following the departure of John Cullom on December 22nd 1914, he then became headmaster at Simpson, writing in the school log that he assumed duties after the Christmas holidays in 1915 on January 11th. Nevertheless he continued with his musical interests and at Simpson advertised 'Mr. Edmund Badger (tenor) late professional pupil in Milan, and in London of Dr. W.H. Cummings and Edwin Holland gives lessons in voice culture and singing.' Indeed during

October he and his wife contributed to the performances in the two concerts given in the YMCA tent at the Royal Engineers depot at Staple Hall, Fenny Stratford. He also participated in several school concerts, to appropriately include singing 'West Country ditties.' Working his way up through the ranks, during WW1 Edmund served as a Special Constable, in which capacity during one night time patrol he traced a stray collie dog to the residence of the village rector. In consequence the Rev. Rice was fined 5s 6d, plus 5s as Mr. Badger's expenses. Allegedly Mr. Badger had a fierce temper which was perhaps not surprising from having to teach nearly 40 children of 6 different 'standards' with no help. As he wrote in the school log book; "I have now been 4 years entirely alone in the main room." "There are a few backward children who require a good deal of individual attention … without any assistant I find it quite impossible to give time to such cases." Perhaps in consequence on January 18th 1921 he wrote; "I have been rather 'below par' in health for several weeks." In fact he was certified as suffering from septic anaemia, being ordered to rest for three weeks. He returned to work on June 1st but in 1922 on March 10th the doctor certified him unfit for school duties, and again ordered three weeks rest. Then on April 18th 1922 came the

Staple Hall Depot August 30th. 1915.

poignant entry "Mr. Edmund Badger, head teacher of this school, died on this date." He left effects of £649 12s 11d to his widow Mary Frances Anne Badger who when of All Saints Vicarage, Clapton, died in 1938 on November 16th at Hackney Hospital, London.

BENJAMIN PEARS KILVINGTON   1923-1927

Benjamin Pears Kilvington was born in Hull in 1882 on November 29th and in 1891 was living at Sculcoates, Kingston Upon Hull, with his parents Benjamin, a joiner age 33, born at Easington, Yorks., Annie age 34, born at Scarborough, and his siblings. Then in 1901 with his mother as head of the household he was resident at Sculcoates employed as an Elementary School Board teacher, as was his 20 year old sister Maria. From 1902 until 1904 he was Assistant Master at Day Street School, Hull. Built in 1868 this had originally been titled the Day Street British School, and with a capacity of 765 pupils the average attendance in 1904-6 was 600.[14] However from 1904 Benjamin was now a supply teacher under Bucks Education Committee at Bletchley, in Bletchley Road. Then in 1907 on Monday, December 2nd at the monthly meeting of the Fenny Stratford School Managers the correspondent read a letter from the Secretary of the Education Committee at Aylesbury. Therein he suggested that from being a supply teacher Mr. Kilvington should be appointed to the permanent position of assistant teacher in the Boys' Dept. at Bletchley. At present he was uncertificated but that day had gone to Bedford to take the necessary exam. Having a good record he had been a supply teacher in the county for 3½ years, and, with the headmaster, Mr. Shardlow, being very pleased with his performance, it was resolved that he should be appointed at £85pa. Thus at the monthly meeting of the Fenny Stratford school managers on the evening of Monday, January 6th 1908 a letter from the secretary of education committee at Aylesbury was read confirming his appointment as an assistant teacher in the Boys School of the Bletchley Road Council School, Bletchley. He had now obtained his certificate and in 1910 at Fenny Stratford was admitted on April 4th to the National School Admission Register. In 1911 he was boarding at 6s a week at 35, Victoria Road, Fenny Stratford, where the head of the household was Richard Daniel, a commercial traveller, resident with his wife Emma and their unmarried daughters, all born at Fenny Stratford,

Winifred Maud, born in 1892 on July 9th, Florence age 17, a pupil teacher at the council school, and Dorothy age 16. In May 1911 the Bletchley Station Choir devoted their talents to a benevolent concert for a railway guard killed working at Bletchley station. Tellingly a duet was given in the performance by Winifred and Benjamin, for on Thursday, August 8th 1912 they were married in Bletchley at the Albert Street Primitive Methodist Church. The couple were well known locally and many friends were present. Mr. W. Kilvington, brother of the groom, was best man, and a reception was held at the Wilberforce Hotel. After a honeymoon at Filey the couple then made their home at 5, Oliver Road, Bletchley. In 1913 a son, Kenneth D. Kilvington, was born (he died at Northampton in 1921) and in 1915 on January 2nd another son, Edward Guy Kilvington. With the country now at war, in August 1916 Benjamin was examined for army service. However from being medically unfit he was rejected on the 29th of the month and from September 5th was placed as an ordinary seaman in the RNVR, serving on several vessels. After the war in 1923 he was general secretary of Bletchley Sports Club and that year was appointed as headmaster of the Woughton & Simpson Council School, with Miss Gladys Young and Miss Alice Mould as assistant teachers. He soon proved a popular choice, and during 1925 by his organisation of whist drives and entertainments he raised sufficient money to install a wireless in the school. This was used for the first time one Friday in December, when the pupils listened in to the funeral service of the Queen Mother. The children took a great interest in the broadcast and also the wonders of radio. Sadly between Benjamin and his wife there now seemed little interest in their marriage, and in 1926 a judgment was made for maintenance. Then in 1927 on Monday, June 20th at the County Court, Aylesbury, in the case of Winifred Maud Kilvington, Bletchley, v Benjamin Kilvington, schoolmaster, Woughton & Simpson School, a claim was lodged for arrears under a maintenance order for £32 16s 4d. An order was made for payment in 14 days. Yet the same year at the County Court on Monday, August 15th a judgement was made in respect of a sum of £46. Appearing for Winifred, Mr. W. Law of Buckingham said the matter had been before the court on previous occasions. The defendant was a schoolmaster, and had executed a maintenance deed granting alimony at £12 a month. However he was greatly in arrears and his client and child needed the money to live. With this being the third time that he'd had to deal with the matter, the judge asked if Kilvington was present, to which Mr. Law said there was no reason why he shouldn't be, as the schools were closed for the holidays. Mrs. Kilvington of 5, Oliver Road, Bletchley, said her husband was a school master employed by Bucks County Council, but since August 1st he had not been attached to any school. He'd been paid between £6 10s and £7 a week until he relinquished his position as headmaster of the Simpson and Woughton School. She didn't know if he left or whether he had to leave. He was now living at the Shoulder of Mutton, Bletchley, and although having the use of a bicycle, with the school being 4 miles away he was seen on a motorbike the previous week. Saying it was a question of how much to set, the judge made an order for payment of the full amount in 14 days, or else a committal for 28 days. In 1928 Benjamin became Assistant Master at the Thomas Gray Council School, Slough.[15] Nevertheless the acrimony continued, and in 1932 in July at Bletchley County Court - 'in the case of Winifred Maud Kilvington of 5, Oliver Road, Bletchley, v Benjamin Peers Kilvington, schoolmaster, Thomas Gray Council School, Slough' - Mr. Law said the claim was for £81 17s 6d in respect of a judgment made in December last. The defendant had paid nothing, but had sent a letter saying he would pay £27 on the 29th of this month. Saying he was a most difficult man who never kept his word, Mr. Law said an order for £15 a month was made in that court. There was no doubt he could pay as his salary was £265 10s 6d a year. The judge made an order for £10 a month or else prison. In 1939 Benjamin was still living at Upton Park, Slough, whilst in Bletchley the aggrieved Winifred was living at 5, Oliver Road, Bletchley, with her son Edward, a wholesale confectioner.[16] Benjamin died in 1949 at Windsor and it seems Winifred died in January 1950.

SCHOOL MEMORIES

With acknowledgement to the booklet 'Village Memories,' by Ouida Rice.

John Rose "I was born in 1893 and I started school when I was three. We had to walk down to the school. … If you could pass the labour examination you could leave school at twelve. I passed this with four others - George Bowler, Fred Purcell, Fanny Goodman and Ethel Warr - we all left school."

Mrs. Sinfield recalled that children came all the way from isolated farms at Coffee Hall and Bleak Hall. "They used to leave their donkey where the allotments are, that used to be called 'The Patch.' We used to ride the donkey at dinner time and get late for school, because we didn't have dinners at school."

Mrs. E. Lovell "We had two masters while I was at school, Mr. Cullom, and Mr. Badger. They used the cane quite a lot, and the big boys were put across the desk and thrashed. If they had time they put a book or thick paper down their trousers. Mrs. Badger often gave us a crack on the head with a thimble, or a sharp crack across our knuckles with a ruler, if we talked in our sewing class."

Mrs. Powell was a pupil at the school from the age of 3 until she went to the grammar school. She later returned to teach at the school for 15 years.

"I started school when I was 3½ and we sat on long desks without backs and we had to sit up straight. We had to sit still an awful lot. There were about 50 or 60 children and they were any age from 3 up to 14. We only had two teachers, the infant teacher up to the age of seven and the Head Teacher had to take all the rest."

"In the afternoon the head teacher's wife used to come in and take us for needlework and she was a nice old lady. She used to wear a big silver thimble and if we didn't behave she used to bang on our heads with her thimble."

"There was only one tap in the whole school. The girls were fortunate because they had the Simpson end lobby and they had the cold tap. In the summer when it was very hot we used to take a bucket of water out so that the boys could have a drink."

"Of course we had no electricity, so we had hanging oil lamps and on very rare occasions the oil lamps were lowered and lit and we thought it was lovely, nearly a party for us."

"We used to go to school bowling our hoops, then in the top season we all used to have whips and tops; every game had its season."

"Our art lessons weren't all that thrilling, we had to draw ink pots made of stone and of course the red ink was sacred to the head teacher to mark his register. One day the head teacher said we had to draw this wretched ink pot. And it was a very cold afternoon and we had the stoves going well and he set the ink pot on top of the stove so that we could all see it. Suddenly there was a glorious noise and whoosh, pop, up went the cork to the ceiling and a glorious fountain of red ink and it made our afternoon."

"We had great fun when we went swimming. We used to go down Bury Lane across the fields at the bottom to what was known as the ford across the river Ouzel. In those days the girls had frocks that either buttoned or hooked from the neck right down to the waist at the back, and then you had a petticoat with a string around the neck to tie up at the back. As we walked along in a line the girl in front found her buttons being undone by the following girl, right along the line."

(Two entries from the school log book relate to the swimming:

1920 June 9th "A proper bathing place has been arranged in the river Ouzel at the bottom of Bury Lane. The boys, accompanied by the master, bathed there this morning and found the steps etc. very convenient."

1920 June 24th "4 girls, accompanied by Miss Mould, bathed this afternoon. The portable canvas tent is now completed and in use.")

MEMORIES OF WARTIME

SIMPSON'S WAR MEMORIALS

On the green near to the parish church, on the afternoon of Sunday, February 4th 1923 a grey granite pillar some 8 feet high, purchased by public subscription, and bearing the poignant inscription 'Lest we forget 1914-1918,' was unveiled as the village war memorial by the Bishop of Buckingham. A guard of honour from the Woburn Depot stood with arms reversed, and also in the ceremony the Bishop unveiled a mural tablet which, placed on the north interior wall of St. Thomas' Church, commemorated those who had made the ultimate sacrifice;

C. Baker; G.F. Bridge MM; A.E.B. Coles; W.E.G. Eaton; C.R. Hill; A.J. Huggins; J.H. Janes MM; F. Nicholls; A. Rose DCM; F.T. Rossiter; W.H. Webster DSO.

The War Memorial.

All those men from the village who had served in the war were also remembered, their names listed on a large board in the church porch. Some 450 people attended the service and also present were ex Servicemen, Boy Scouts, and Girl Guides. Many of the local clergy took part in the ceremony with the Lesson - taken from Wisdom iii., 1-9 - read by Mr. A.J. Stevens JP, a local Wesleyan. In giving an address the Bishop firstly unveiled the tablet and then the monument, and at the close of the service buglers from the Wolverton Territorials sounded the Last Post from the heights of the church tower. A few moments of silence then ensued, after which the buglers sounded Reveille. As did many parishioners, floral tributes were placed at the base of the monument by relatives of the fallen, and with the Bishop offering prayer two hymns were sung. After the Benediction the Bletchley Station Band played the Dead March. Then at the close the National Anthem, in the singing of which the congregation joined in.

AN AERIAL ENCOUNTER

In late April 1917 three aeroplanes suddenly landed in a field at Simpson, but the next day took off at noon, performed aerial manoeuvres over Bletchley, and departed, with no one any the wiser as to where they came from, why they were there, or where they were going!

A SONG FOR PEACE

In 1919 the Reverend Julius T. Lawson of Simpson composed the music of a new song, 'Peace.' With the words by John Harris, this was published by West's, of Moor Street, London, W1, with the local publishing agents being Purrett's, Victoria Road, Bletchley.

DOMESTIC STRIFE

In July 1917 a Simpson man asked the Bletchley magistrates to give his wife time to pay a fine, so that she could pay it herself and 'know something had happened'!

A SOCIAL AMENITY

In February 1920 the hut at Staple Hall Depot, Fenny Stratford, which served as the ante room to the officers' mess, was purchased through the energies of the rector of Simpson, the Reverend J. Thomas Lawson, and his friends, for relocation as a social centre on a central field site called Abbey Yard. At the sale of the Simpson properties of the Reverend William Rice, the site had not reached the reserve price, and being withdrawn was then considered by Bletchley Urban District Council as possibly suitable for housing. However, instead it passed into the ownership of Mr. W. Webster, of The Walnuts, Simpson, and it was he who not only gave the site, but also provided a substantial sum towards taking down and re-erecting the hut. Thus on the afternoon of Wednesday, September 8th 1920, with a guard of honour of the 1st Wavendon Troop, drawn up under Scoutmaster R. Franklin, the opening ceremony was performed in

World War 1

Private Christopher Herbert BAKER
1st Battalion, Oxfordshire & Buckinghamshire Light Infantry
Died: 20 April 1915 at Ploegsteert
Buried at Ploegsteert Military Cemetery, Hainaut, Belgium

Private George Frederick BRIDGE **M.M.**
1st Battalion, Northamptonshire Regiment
Died: 2 August 1919 at Fenny Stratford
Buried at Bletchley Cemetery

Private Archie Edgar Benjamin COLES
1/1st Buckinghamshire Battalion, Oxfordshire & Buckinghamshire Light Infantry
Died: 28 March 1916 at Hébuterne, Somme
Buried at Hébuterne Military Cemetery

Guardsman William Ewart Gladstone EATON
2nd Battalion, Grenadier Guards
Died: 1 September 1914 at Villers Cottérêts
Named on La Ferte-sous-Jouarre Memorial, Seine-et-Marne

Private Cyril Ralph HILL
42nd Battalion Canadian Infantry, (Quebec Regiment)
Died: 9 October 1916 at Courcelette, Somme
Buried at Warloy-Baillon Communal Cemetery Extension, Somme

Sergeant Alfred John HUGGINS
5th Battalion, Oxfordshire & Buckinghamshire Light Infantry
Died: 19 August 1917 at Passchendaele
Buried at Brandhoek New Military Cemetery No.3, Ieper, Belgium

Private Jack Hawley JANES **M.M.**
5th Battalion, Oxfordshire and Buckinghamshire Light Infantry
Died: 5 April 1918 at Le Hamel, Somme
Named on the Pozieres Memorial, Somme

Private Frederick George NICHOLS
1st Battalion, Bedfordshire Regiment
Died: 13 March 1915 at Neuve Chapelle
Buried at Ramparts Cemetery, Lille Gate, Belgium

Corporal of Horse Arthur ROSE **D.C.M.**
1st Life Guards
Died: Zillebeke, Ieper
Buried at Kemmel French Cemetery

Lance Corporal Frank Theodore Reginald ROSSITER
Grenadier Guards
Died: 1 December 1917 at Cambrai
Named on the Cambrai Memorial, Louveral

2nd Lieutenant Walter Henry WEBSTER **D.S.O.**
4th Battalion, Royal Fusiliers, The London Regiment
Died: 10 February 1917 at La Basse Road
Buried at Rue-Petillon Military Cemetery, Fleurbaix

War Memorial detail, top.

Register of lives sacrificed in the church, above.

Plaque to the memory of Jack Hawley, right.

89

Simpson men who served in the Great War.

Simpson Social Club. The 'x' marks The Poplars Farmhouse.

the presence of a large assembly by Colonel Broome Giles, who duly signed the visitors book. The grounds and fete were then declared open by Mrs. Harley, of Walton Hall, and, with music by the Fenny Stratford Town Prize Band, the events included a sale of work, a rummage stall, swings, hoop la, coconut shies, and Aunty Sally, etc. Refreshments and teas were provided at modest prices, and in the hut at 7pm a grand concert was staged, followed from 9 to 12 by a grand masked dance, with fancy dress optional. Admission to the ground had been 3d, to the enclosure for the opening ceremony 1s 3d, to the concert 1s 3d and 8d, and to the dance 1s. Some £40 was taken during the day, from which it was hoped to put £25 to the credit of the hut fund, leaving a debt of about £250.

THE SHAPE OF THINGS TO COME

With the beginnings of the New City, the future of the village as envisaged in 1971

'Special attention is to be given to the integration of the new development with the old and it is hoped to make significant improvements to the village scene. The Corporation is to have a look at ways of preserving familiar and structurally sound buildings such as the church and forge, of reinstating the village green, and opening up a length of Simpson Brook to make a further attractive feature for the village. Off street parking will be discussed with Bletchley Urban Council and encouragement will be given for the improvement of Simpson by putting as many overhead cables as possible underground, and removing broken down fencing and dilapidated outbuildings. This Spring will see a start made on H9, a city road that will form the future northern boundary of the village and give an improved link between the A5 at Bletchley and the A50 near the M1 junction at Broughton. The A5 relief road which runs south of Simpson is due to be completed in December 1975. The present through road taking traffic from Newport Pagnell to Bletchley will be cut by the H9 near Bowler's Bridge. To give a convenient alternative route round the eastern edge of the village a new link road between the C11 (Walton) road and H9 will be built. It is also proposed to build a short temporary road between Bowler's Bridge and the H9 across the north west corner of the village during the construction of the grid and new bridge roads to give Simpson respite from contractors' traffic. Some 54 houses in middle and upper price ranges are planned on six acre and two acre sites in the village. There will probably also be a one acre extension to Simpson House flats to give extra accommodation for new employees arriving at Milton Keynes. Simpson House may possibly be renovated for development corporation offices. The village school outside the village on the Newport road will remain open until the new combined school on Grove Way replaces it by the end of 1972. The new road system will enable children to walk in safety across

This plan was developed by the Milton Keynes Development Corporation for Simpson in 1971.

WOUGHTON

An old photograph of Woughton on the Green

The old rectory at Woughton on the Green

THE EARLY HISTORY OF WOUGHTON[A]

'Woughton, though now a village of little, or no, importance, has a distinguished history. The Manor was surveyed in Domesday Book as partly the land of the Earl of Morton. The first of these Manors came, on the rebellion of William, son of Robert Earl of Morton, against Henry I, to Stephen de Blois, afterwards King of England, with the earldom, and was later bestowed by Henry II on his son John, subsequently also King of England, whom he made Earl of Moreton or Mortaigne. In the reign of Henry III both these Manors belonged to the Verleys, the patronage of the Church being also vested in the same family in 1223. By heirs female of the Verleys this Manor seems to have come to the Muxons, Bottetourts, and Greys, and so to have been at length acquired by the Vavasours, who conveyed the demesne to the Mordaunts, to whom this Manor belonged in 1608, when Henry Lord Mordaunt died possessed. His successor, John Mordaunt, Earl of Peterborough, gave his interest to his kinsman, Lewis Mordaunt, who, in 1642, conveyed to Roger Nicoll two parts of the advowson and Manor, and in this family they continued until 1717, when Nicoll sold them to Mr. Edward Troutbeck, though a third part remained to the Longuevilles, which had come to that family from the Greys, and in 1732 a third part; namely one turn in three of the advowson belonged to them, the other two turns belonging to Edward Troutbeck, who lived at Westbury. His son, or grandson, Thomas Troutbeck, Rector of Woughton, was possessed of this Manor and advowson in 1760, and on a dispute about his title to the lordship he had a trial at law, and at Buckingham Assizes, 1759, it was adjudged to be his right. The present Lord of the Manor and Patron of the living is Col. Bowles, but he is not resident at Woughton. The principal house in the parish now is Woughton House, built by the father of the late Lt. Col. W.J. Levi, and sold after the latter's death to Capt. B. Hudson, the present owner, and occupier. Woughton, like many of her neighbours, had, in the 17th century, a coining apparatus, and a coiner, both, however, of an illegal character. The tradesman in this village who ventured to issue his own money was a grocer named William Coale, and his coinage,

---

A From an article in the *North Bucks Times* 1925 Aug. 18th.

as far as is known, consisted only of brass farthings, issued between the years 1651 and 1671. This token is particularly interesting as it was unknown to Boyne, the great authority on the tokens of the 17th century. This Woughton token is as follows, on the Obverse and Reverse:- Ob. A star at the top, with round the coin "William Coale," and in the centre the Grocer's Arms. Rev. The same star; round the coin; "Of (a small star) Woofton-W.E.C." The initials being in the centre, and from the inclusion of the "E" denoting that William Coale was a married man. His death appears to have taken place in 1699, for in the Church Register is the following entry. "1699. Wm. Coal buried ye 30 of April."

The village is built in the form of a rectangle and has a very neat appearance, being about a quarter of a mile long and half that distance broad. The Church stands about a middle of the east end of the square or green, whence the name Woughton-on-the Green. The main road from Newport Pagnell to Fenny Stratford crosses near the west side of the Churchyard, and the western end of the green is bounded by the Grand Junction Canal. The whole parish was enclosed by Act of Parliament, 1769. The population, as given in a return made to the Bishop of Lincoln in 1712, was 50 families and 243 inhabitants. By the Census of 1841 this number had increased to 354, but during the ensuing hundred years the population has declined, for the Census of 1911 gave it as being 209, and the last figures available, those of 1921, show a further decrease to 182'.

The Church, which is dedicated to the Assumption of the Blessed Virgin Mary, is an ancient fabric having a chancel, nave, south aisle, and porch, and an embattled tower. The general style is decorated Gothic. The porch is good with a two light window on each side and a handsome cross on the top. The tower is in perpendicular style. The aisle and nave are divided by four pointed arches supported by clustered columns, and the chancel arch is a fine pointed one. The font is plain, but the pulpit is of handsomely carved oak and depicts Christ as the Good Shepherd. The beautiful rood screen, surmounted with a large cross and Christ crucified, is also carved oak, as well as the choir stalls, and the open benches in the nave. The roofs are open timber, stained to represent oak. In the south wall of the chancel is a piscine niche with a finely carved head. The nave is lighted by two windows with good mullions, one with a transom and three large lights below, and six small ones above. The other window is of three lights with tracery in the head. The chancel is lighted by three windows, one in the east end, of three compartments with tracery in the head. The other two, one on the south and the other on the north side of the chancel are also good. The priest's door is in the south wall, and also the sedilia. On the north wall of the chancel is a brass: "In memory of Margaret, wife of Maurice Farrell, rector of Woughton, who died 8 October 1881," and a mural tablet to the memory of David James, Esqr., and family. Under an anchoret, or arch, in the north wall of the chancel, is a recumbent figure of a man in freestone, and a dog couchant at his feet. The head rests on a pillow, and the hands are clasped in the attitude of devotion. This is probably the builder of the Church in the reign of Edward I. There is no inscription on this monument. In the south aisle the steps to the rood loft are visible. The entrance has a fine canopied head supported by corbels of singular design. Here too is another piscine, with the head filled with tracery, the shaft in the centre having been destroyed. The west window is seen through the tower arch. The porch retains the stone sediles and there is a trefoil headed niche in the centre. There are four bells in the tower, these being inscribed: 1. Chandler made me 1653; 2. Richard Chandler made me 1717 (this bell is cracked); 3. Chandler made me 1701; 4. Park and Chapman, of London fecit, Thomas Lucas, Churchwarden 1771, Barnard Chervall, Gentleman. In 1887 Gillett and Johnstone recast the first and second bells, and erroneously attributed the second bell to Richard Chandler, whereas it was originally cast by Anthony Chandler.

The (old) rectory house is a good substantial building of red brick in the domestic Gothic style, situated in well laid out grounds, about a quarter of a mile from the Church. The site appears to have been surrounded by a moat. From the fact that the rectors were for some time also Lords of the Manor, it is probable that this is the site of the ancient Manor House. In 1868, Rev. Maurice Farrell built the new rectory, borrowing for the purpose the sum of £890 from Queen Anne's Bounty, under the Gilbert Act. There have been several extensions for the repayment of capital and interest, the last having, apparently, been in 1887, by which the instalment due in 1888 was

£15 2s 1d. By this time the whole debt has probably been liquidated.[17]

WOUGHTON HOUSE

'Small private mansion, now (1986) a hotel and restaurant. C. 1840 extended to the rear, and remodelled in 1876 by W.J. Levi. Red and yellow banded brick, since whitewashed. Two storeys, five bays with central projecting flat roofed porch with a round door opening. The windows have segmental heads and built in blind boxes. The front wall is raised as a parapet to conceal the shallow pitched slate roof, and has ball finials. The added block to the rear is in a similar style. Until recently it had a lean-to conservatory on the south side with a vine of local repute. The building occupies the site of one of the two manor houses of Woughton, probably the one owned by the Longuevilles at least up to the Civil War.'[18]

THE OCCUPANTS

THE LEVI FAMILY

WILLIAM LEVI   1779-1823

William Levi was born in 1779 at Moulsoe and in 1807 on July 8th at Bramham, Yorks., married Dorothy Oldfield (1777-1856.) She was the daughter of the late Joshua Oldfield of York. A son, William Levi, was born in 1810 at Moulsoe and a daughter, Frances, at Moulsoe in 1813, baptised on March 14th.[19] William senior died at Moulsoe in 1823 on April 14th and in his will left all his messuages and tenements etc to his brothers in law, Joshua Oldfield of York, gent, and William Tyler Smith of Northampton, gent, as his executors. These they were then to sell and pay the proceeds to his wife Dorothea, and then after her death to his children William and Frances. However it seems she intermeddled in the affairs of the executors. She died in 1856 on December 18th, after which administration was granted to her son William in 1861 on February 8th. In Moulsoe church in the nave is a memorial to William Levi and of his wife Dorothy.

WILLIAM LEVI   1810-1889

William Levi, the namesake son of his father, was born in 1810 at Moulsoe. In 1837 he was a land occupier at Newport Pagnell 'on the Green,' and then in 1841 at Newport Pagnell as a farmer, resident with his mother Dorothy, of independent means, and Frances (Fanny), his sister, also of independent means. In other activities he joined the Royal Bucks Yeomanry but it was as a farmer of 200 acres, employing 10 men, that he came with his mother and sister to Woughton House in 1846, attended by a domestic staff of a cook, a housemaid, and a dairy girl. In 1862 on October 1st at York he married Sarah Jane Mills who, born at York, was the daughter of Robert Mills. In 1863 on March 18th he was appointed Major from Captain on the promotion of the Duke of Buckingham and the following year a son, William John Levi, was born. William was now also a JP and at the formation of the Woughton and Simpson School Board in 1875 he was appointed chairman. In 1877 he resigned from military on March 3rd, being allowed to retain his rank and wear the uniform of the regiment. Less distinguished however would prove to be his butler, who in 1880 was charged with theft from another part of the country.

More of a loss was that of Edwin Payne, who having for many years been coachman to Major Levi died that year. Following his father's tradition his son William John Levi was a captain in the Royal Bucks Hussars, and having attended a course of yeomanry instruction at Aldershot was returning on Saturday, September 7th 1889 to spend Sunday at Woughton House. Having arranged to meet him in the afternoon at Bletchley station, his father set off from Woughton House in a horse and trap but on having turned from Aylesbury Street, Fenny Stratford, into Denmark Street the horse took fright and careered along a fence. The Major desperately tried to haul the horse back but was thrown out of the trap and smashing against the wall of a house his skull was fractured. Two doctors were called but he died within 40 minutes. The inquest was held at the Foundry Arms on the Monday morning, at which Joseph Eaton said he was a groom in the Major's employ. The horse was about

14 years old and had been in the Woughton House stables for 10 years. On the Saturday he harnessed the horse to a dog cart at about 3.15 and the Major then started off for Bletchley. Alfred Gurney, a telegraph clerk, said that about 3.50 he was going past some new buildings in Victoria Road when, on hearing a commotion, he saw an out of control trap coming from Denmark Street run into a kerb. It pitched onto a wall and railings in front of Alfred Taylor's house and the Major on being thrown out was flung against the wall, and fell between the overturning trap and the railings. Alfred ran to give assistance and with others lifted up the Major and conveyed him to the house of Alfred Taylor. Medical attention was swiftly summoned and Dr. McGachen found him lying unconscious in the back bedroom. Dr. Simms had already arrived and they both carried out an examination. However the Major expired soon after. The funeral was held on the afternoon of Thursday, September 12th with, to include the housekeeper, Mrs. Goodman, the procession leaving Woughton House at 1pm. The service was conducted by the rector the Rev. Field, who had just returned from a holiday in Paris. Of polished oak with solid brass mountings the coffin bore the inscription on a plate at the foot; 'W. Levi, J.P. FOR BUCKS, BORN JANUARY, 1810, DIED SEPTEMBER 7th, 1889.' The coffin was then lowered into a brick grave lined with moss collected from Bow Brickhill woods by the Misses Higgins, Graves, Lines and Knight. Having been presented by his widow and son, in 1892 on the afternoon of Thursday, February 25th a beautiful organ in his memory was opened in the church by the Lord Bishop of Reading at a special evensong. In the presence of a large congregation, followed by Dr. Mann of King's College, Cambridge, presided at the organ, and with the procession of clergy having entered the church at 3pm in silence, the Bishop stopped before the organ and pronounced the sentences of dedication. At 7pm the Bishop gave a short address which was followed Dr. Mann performing a recital on the organ. The offertories throughout the day were for the nave restoration fund, raising £1. Costing about £1,250 the organ, the whole action of which was 'tubular pneumatic,' was manufactured by Messrs. Norman Bros. and Beard of Norwich, and within the church a brass plaque was placed inscribed; "To the Glory of God, and in memory of W. Levi, who died September 7th 1889,

aged 79. This organ and chamber are erected by his wife and son S.J. and W.J. Levi, February 25th, 1892." Major Levi's widow died at Woughton House in 1920 on November 10th, leaving £5,942 18s 1d to her son William John Levi.

Woughton House in the 1920s.

WILLIAM JOHN LEVI   1864-1921

William John Levi was born at Woughton in 1864, baptised on July 11th. In 1881 the family were resident at Woughton House with his father (a JP for Bucks.), his mother Sarah Jane, and a cook, a housekeeper, and a footman. Having been celebrated the previous day with a dinner, given to his friends and relatives, in 1885 on Thursday, June 11th William's coming of age was the scene of village rejoicings. The day was marked by a holiday, during which the church bells rang out all day, and sports and games etc. were indulged. As the work of the parishioners, over the entrance to the grounds adjoining Woughton House a triumphal arch of evergreens and flowers had been erected, surmounted by 'Many Happy Returns of the Day,' composed of blue and red letters. Above in gold letters on a white ground were the initials W.J.L. on a black shield encircled with flags. A similar motto was displayed on the reverse. Music was provided by the Fenny Stratford band, and with catering by Mr. Sheppard, of

Friday August 12th 1904. W J Levi at Quainton

Woughton House. The writing on the reverse states it's August 1902. Left to right William John Levi, Mrs. Levi with Scrap, Hon. Mrs. W. Lyttelton, LM Levi.

Fenny Stratford, a substantial tea was provided. Shortly before 8pm the company transferred to the Board school room, where Major Levi had engaged a conjuror from London. Of the many gifts was included a marble time piece from the villagers, a photo album from the choir, and a walnut wood stationery cabinet from the servants of Woughton House. In public life William aspired for election to the County Council and in November 1888 in seeking candidature wrote from Woughton House;

> "At the request of a number of influential Gentlemen in this Division … I am fully alive to the great responsibilities of the position I am seeking by your favour. … In offering myself for your suffrages, therefore, I shall be in no respect the candidate of a political party, and if you do me the honour to elect me the interests of all alike will be of equal interest to me."

Following the tragic death in 1889 of William's father, Major Levi, in 1891 at Woughton House the family comprised Sarah Jane, living on her own means, and unmarried son William, now a Captain in the Royal Bucks Hussars and also a JP for Bucks. A housemaid, a kitchen maid, and a footman were employed as the domestic staff. Then that year on Wednesday, June 10th William married Lillian Maude Yorke. Born at Kensington on December 2nd 1862 she was the only daughter of the late Joseph A. Yorke, born in

W.J. Levi - the writing on the reverse states it's Gayhurst, August 1903, W.J. Levi & W. Hulford going to Buckingham, Goodmans motor.

1831, Stipendiary Magistrate of South Shields, and his wife Marian. (Joseph was the son of the Rev. Hon. Grantham Munton Yorke, who amongst other distinctions was Dean of Worcester from 1874 until his death in 1881.) The day proved warm and bright for the wedding at All Saint's Church at Milton Keynes, and in various parts of the village triumphal arches spanned the road. Another one, *Health and Happiness*, adorned the entrance to the Rectory grounds, and flags and streamers were in abundance. Under the command of Sgt. Major Barber the 'A' Troop of the Royal Bucks Hussars, of which the groom was a captain, were drawn up along the route from the rectory to the church. Here a large attendance had gathered both inside and out, and shortly before 2.30 the A Troop entered the church and lined the nave. Dr. Mann, organist of King's College Cambridge, presided at the organ, and just before 2.30pm the groom arrived with his best man, Mr. Gerard Fiennes. The bride was escorted by her uncle, the Hon. & Rev. Wingfield T.W. Fiennes, who gave her away. With the united choirs of Woughton and Milton Keynes in attendance the first part of the service was read at the chancel arch by the Rev. Lewis Lloyd, cousin of the groom. The latter part was then read by the rector of Woughton, the Reverend Field. After the ceremony the wedding party were entertained at the Rectory on the lawn, where the happy couple, bridesmaids et al, were photographed. Addressing the contingent of the Royal Bucks Hussars, in thanking them for having come such a long distance William said he was greatly honoured, especially since during the very short time that he had been Captain of the Troop they held him in such esteem. Throughout the afternoon the band of the Royal Bucks Hussars played selections in the rectory garden, and during several intervals the church bells rang out. A 'feu de joie' was also fired by the Hussars. Then shortly before 6pm the couple left the rectory for Woburn Sands, en route for Cambridge. Being numerous and expensive the presents included one from the foreman and workmen employed in the restoration of Woughton church. Indeed in April 1893 William gave £100 towards defraying the debt on the work, and as the organist and choirmaster he had entertained the choir with tea and games at the church on the evening of Friday, January 13th.

Then by railway on Tuesday, September 4th 1894 he took the

female and junior members to Euston for a steam boat trip from London Bridge to Hampton Court, where time was spent at the Palace. As for his wife, now as a Woughton resident in November 1894 she gave a considerable sum towards the balance of the cost of re-glazing the nave windows. In fact she seemingly had practical skills of her own.[20] In February 1896 William was amongst those elected to serve on the Woughton and Simpson School Board, and also on the parish council. In married life in 1901 William (who was now a Major) and Lillian were living at Woughton House with Sarah, attended by a domestic staff of a maid, a cook, a housemaid, a kitchen maid, and a footman. William had now been initiated into the Freemasons - St. Peter & St. Paul Lodge - (he would become Worshipful Master of both the Newport Pagnell and the Fenny Stratford Lodges) and had also been promoted to Lt. Col. in the Royal Bucks Hussars.

In 1911 he was still resident at Woughton House, as at the beginning of WW1, when in September 1914 he was appointed honorary treasurer at a County Meeting for a relief fund. This would be the Bucks County Relief Fund, and then on the evening of Monday, October 18th 1915 he presided at a public meeting to discuss organising a local committee to work in conjunction with the Central Association for the supply of fruit, vegetables etc. to the Navy. He was also military representative of the Newport Pagnell Tribunal but that year he suffered a severe nervous breakdown, and in July 1916 was ordered to take a complete rest from public work. Indeed among his responsibilities he was Chairman of the Bench, Deputy Lt. for the County, a County Councillor, President of the Fenny Stratford Choral Association, a member of the Education Committee, and as a skilful musician he usually played the organ at Woughton church.

In the wake of this in 1918 in June at the meeting of the War Pensions Committee it was reported that Mrs. Levi had sent a letter. In this she stated that due to the serious illness of Col. Levi she thought that from not being able to attend the meetings she must resign. However the committee decided to write urging that although not attending the meetings she should stay as a representative for Woughton, for any cases that arose. Col. Levi had now decided to

Grave of Sarah Jane Levi

Grave of William John Levi

give up farming, and on his instructions Wigley Sons & Gambell auctioned at the Swan Hotel, Newport Pagnell, on Wednesday, March 19th 127 acres of grass and arable land, together with a small house and an excellent range of buildings. Vacant possession could be had at Michaelmas 1919. Having never fully recovered from his breakdown, at a time when he was Past Provincial Senior Grand Warden and Senior Grand Deacon (England) of the Freemasons he died at Woughton House in 1921 on November 5th. Interment was in the churchyard of St. Mary's at Woughton. With effects of £61,887 7s 2d probate was granted to his widow. She left Woughton House in 1924 and the following year was resident at Havant, Emsworth Road. By 1930 she had moved to Bouverie Road West, Folkestone, and at the outbreak of WW2 was resident, 'of private means', in Earls Avenue, Folkestone. She died in 1947 on October 20th at Earls Court Hotel, Tunbridge Wells.

Captain Barton Hudson

Born on October 11th 1895 at 16, Harley Street, London, Barton Hudson was a son of an eminent surgeon Charles Elliott Leopold Barton Hudson FRCS (usually known as Leopold) and his wife Ethel Vaughan Hudson (nee Morgan.) She was the daughter of Septimus Vaughan Morgan, one of six brothers whose firm would become Morgan Brothers (Publishing) Ltd.[21] The couple had married in 1895 on January 9th but in 1897 Charles died, and in 1901 with the attentions of domestic staff his widow, 'living on her own means,' was resident at Gledhow Gardens, Kensington, with her sons Barton and Austin, who had been born in 1897 on February 6th.[22] Both Barton and Austin were educated at Eton, being there together in 1911 when their mother was resident at 46, Hans Mansions, London SW. (In 1917 on January 27th at the church of Holy Trinity, Brompton, she would marry Lt. Col. Edward Hall Stevenson RFA, a bachelor, aged 44). As Surgeon Lieutenant Charles Elliott Leopold Barton Hudson, Middlesex Yeomanry, (Duke of Cambridgeshire's Hussars), the boys' father had been placed on the Army Medical Reserve of Officers in 1892 on December 7th. As for Barton, he entered military service at the beginning of WW1 in the Territorial Force Yeomanry. Promoted to Second Lieutenant in 1915 he served at Gallipoli with the County of London Yeomanry but in 1916, with the same rank in the Middlesex Yeomanry, on November 23rd he applied for the Freedom of the City of London, this 'by redemption, in the Company of Ironmongers, of London.'

His address was now that of his mother at 46, Hans Mansions, whilst in his military career he was promoted to Lieutenant and then Captain, being noted as such in 1919 on September 10th when, at Holy Trinity Church, Brompton, he married Hope Vere Inglis Chalmers. (There seems a degree of confusion as to which was actually her first name, but at the ceremony she signed as Hope Vere Inglis Chalmers.) Born in 1899 on May 15th she was the daughter of Robert Chalmers, 'gentleman,' and in October 1917 had married Ralph Windsor Parker, who, as a Captain in the Grenadier Guards, had been killed in action in 1918 on March 28th. At the time of her second marriage Hope was resident at Cookham, Berks. Meanwhile Barton was resident at Bookham Cottage, Great Bookham, Surrey, and it was there that the couple were living in 1921 when their first son, Philip Alexander Hudson, was born on April 28th. A daughter, Faith, was born the following year, but it was at Kensington in 1924 on December 21st that a son, Martin Morgan Hudson (d. 2005) was born.

In fact with his now increased family Captain Hudson had bought, or was in the process of buying, Woughton House as the family residence. Local staff were recruited, of which Miss Amor, whose father had been the last village policeman in Woughton, living in North Cottage on the Green, recalled; "I worked for Captain Hudson after I left school, I was the nursery maid. We had a whole wing for the nursery; there was a day nursery and two night nurseries. I stayed there until the boys went to boarding school and the girl had a governess. Many's the time I've taken them all out on ponies and with two dogs. The baby was in a basket on the saddle of the pony. There was a servants' parlour; there were a lot of staff, but we ate upstairs in the nursery wing. We wore a uniform, grey dresses, black coat and hat and then the rest of the staff wore white aprons and caps."

Woughton House had been chosen by the Captain from a proximity to favourable hunting country whilst having ready access to London, and therein his business interests. Nevertheless he maintained an enthusiastic interest in the village life. Not least on Saturday, August 22nd 1925, when from having taken an active part in the preliminary arrangements he placed the grounds, or park, of Woughton House at the disposal of the committee organising the first annual show of the Woughton and District Horticultural Society. This, intended as an allotment and cottage garden horticultural society, had been formed for the parishes of Woughton, the Woolstones, Simpson, Walton and Milton Keynes, and with Captain Hudson as the President a flower show was held in January 1926. Indeed that month the Captain and his wife had been the principal organisers when the villagers performed plays to clear the debt on the churchyard drainage.

However the Captain's financial fortunes suffered a deficit in July 1929, when for dangerous driving he was fined £5 with his licence endorsed. In politics in 1931 he was amongst those nominating Sir George Bowyer, and it was from that year until 1933 that he held the joint mastership of the Oakley Hunt with Captain Arkwright. Seemingly around the autumn of 1934 the family left Woughton, since being stated of Worton, Wiltshire, in October 1934 he was fined £1 for driving with a licence 3 months out of date. As for Woughton House the next occupants would be the Baillies, resident there at least in December 1935. In August 1936 at Shipton Moyne the sale arose of Pond Farm, 'a modernised Tudor House and 50 acres, near the polo ground at Westonbirt and in the heart of the Duke of Beaufort's country.'

This became the residence of Captain Hudson and his family, and not least from being situated in good hunting country. However in February the following year it was whilst riding with the hunt that he took a fall. His horse in stumbling had kicked him, causing injuries to include a broken arm. Fortunately two doctors were on the field, and having received medical attention the Captain was carried some distance to the road, to be taken home by car. In business life he was joint managing director of Morgan Bros (Publishers) Ltd., of Essex Street, WC, whilst, with his wife being an ARP Warden, in military matters at the outbreak of WW2 he was listed on the Territorial Army Reserve of Officers. He duly became a Home Guard Commander, and it was perhaps especially for members of the Home Guard that in 1941 a booklet was produced by Morgan Bros (Publishers) Ltd. entitled 'Facts about the Rifle.'

During his military service in WW1 the Captain had suffered dysentery, and in enduring epi-gastric spasms had for some time been in ill health. In fact it was perhaps alcohol that provided a measure of relief, for in 1942 on Tuesday, February 24th he was charged with being drunk in charge of a car in Wood Street, Bristol. Giving evidence, Detective Inspective T. Coles said that about noon on the day in question police constable Dancey on hearing a crash saw a car being driven erratically along Wood Street, towards Queen's Square. It was stated that the Captain was a Home Guard Platoon Commander, and in view of his need for a vehicle for Home Guard duties his licence, although endorsed, wasn't suspended. Yet this was on condition that he abstained from intoxicating liquors for 10 months. A fine of £10 was imposed with £3 2s 9d special costs.

However the following year on March 5th he was found dead in the stables of his residence at Pond Farm from a self inflicted rifle wound to the head. He left £54,119 1s gross, net personalty £42, 611 14s 9d, with probate granted to his brother Sir Austin Uvedale Morgan Hudson MP, baronet, and Sir Felix John Morgan Brunner, baronet. Captain Hudson was buried on March 9th at Shipton Moyne, where in 1948 his widow was living with her son Martin. She died in 1991 at Netherfield, Ashdown Road, Forest Row.

CAPTAIN THE HON. ARTHUR MALCOLM AUGUSTUS BAILLIE

In residence at Woughton House in 1935 was Captain the Hon. Arthur Malcolm Augustus Baillie, the second son of the second Baroness Burton Baillie. He was born in 1896 on July 4th, and following education at Eton joined the Royal Artillery in 1914. He fought in many of the major battles, and after the war in 1919 transferred to the Life Guards. At East Retford in 1927 he married Rosemary Laycock (born in 1905 on September 27th) on March 17th, and when at Woughton from having been 'four years instructor at equitation school,' established in conjunction with Commander Maurice Arthur Brind the 'Woughton Stables,' the contemporary advert stating 'horses sent for trial' and 'horses taken to school and manner.' Indeed it was in 1935 on June 15th that the new company of Baillie, Brind & Co. Ltd. was registered, 'To take over the business of horse dealers carried on at Melton Mowbray and elsewhere in Leicester by the executors of the will of the late H. Beeby, and also the business of a hay, corn, and coal merchant, carried on at Fenny Compton Wharf, Leamington Spa, by J.L. Hall as "Henry Beeby and J.L. Hall.' 'Permanent directors Captain the Hon. A.M.A. Baillie, Woughton House, Bletchley, Bucks., Hon. Mrs. R. Baillie, of Fenny Compton Wharf, Leamington Spa, and Mrs. O.A.M. Brind, same address.' However on Wednesday, November 27th 1935 at the Mansion House, London, Commander Brind, 'RN retired', appeared on a charge at the instance of the Commissioners of Customs and Excise. The details were undisclosed but he was stated to be aged 42 and a horse dealer. Bail was allowed on the personal sum of £4,000 and two sureties of £2,000 each, with it understood that he had been arrested on the Tuesday at Fenny Compton, where he and his partner, the Hon. Arthur Baillie, carried on the hunting stables formerly conducted by Mr. J.L. Hall, a well known trainer.

Then at the Mansion House on Tuesday, December 17th 1935 charges regarding the importation of horses from Ireland was the basis before the Lord Mayor against three defendants. Of these Captain the Hon. Arthur Malcolm Augustus Baillie, of Woughton House, was charged on four summonses of having been concerned in alleged fraudulent attempts to evade duties. The following year charges were brought against Commander Brind. However the case was dismissed against Baillie, who in 1937 left Woughton House.

By December he was resident at Horley Manor, Banbury, and at the outbreak of WW2 was appointed from the Reserve to be a Major in the Life Guards. He died in 1963 on February 14th aged 66 at Manor Farm, Bridgham, Norfolk, and from family heritage is commemorated in the churchyard of All Saints Church, Rangemore, Staffs., together with his wife Rosemary, who died on May 31st in 1987.

THE BLOUNT FAMILY

A FAMILY BACKGROUND

George Bouverie Blount was born at Malta in 1838 on December

7th, one of the children of William Simpson Blount, a lieutenant in the Royal Navy, 'now commanding HMS Hermes', and his wife Leonora Ann Clavell. Born in 1809 at Paignton, Devon, she was the daughter of John Clavell and had married William at Falmouth in 1836 on October 12th. Included amongst his various naval service, apart from command of HMS Hermes ('a Mediterranean mail packet') he had additionally been associated with the Royal yachts. However in June 1843 making sensational news he shot himself in his water closet at his home of 6, Woodland Terrace, Trafalgar Road, Greenwich. This was whilst his wife and their children were visiting Leonora's father, Captain Clavell, at the Naval Hospital, but since Leonora was nearing the birth of another of their children, the tragedy was not immediately conveyed to her. By 1861 Leonora was resident as a housekeeper at Westminster, Whitehall, with her son George, now employed as an Admiralty clerk. She died in 1863 and in 1866 at the church of St. Nicholas, Nottingham, on September 19th George married Annie Christina Attenburrow, born in 1844. With ages as per the census, in 1871 attended by domestic staff they were living at 28, The Terrace, Barnes, with the family comprised of himself and his wife and their children Rose Leonora, 3, Edith Ann, 2, and George Hugh, 10 months. Also resident was George's sister Leonora, an 'annuitant,' born at Chatham. By 1874 the family had moved to Erith in Kent, where a son, Oswald, was born in 1879 on October 7th. In 1880 George was initiated into the Freemasons in the Royal Naval College Lodge on December 14th. He was now a Senior Clerk at the Admiralty resident with his wife at Woodside, Lessness Heath, where their children George Percy Cosmo, Minna Bertha and George Ronald Beddard were born. By 1880 the family were residing at 31, Picardy Road, Belvedere, Erith, where in 1881 on October 11th a son, Harold, was born. Then in 1891 the family residence was at St. Ann's Lodge in the village of Stanwell in the district of Staines. George, 'civil service supernumerary clerk admiralty,' was the head with the family comprising his wife Annie, their unmarried daughters Rose Leonora, Edith Annie, and Minna Bertha, and their unmarried sons. In 1901 the family were living at The Rectory, Northchurch, Berkhamsted, Berks., with George, now retired, his wife, their unmarried daughter Rose Leonora, and sons, also unmarried, George Hugh, a solicitor on his own account, and Oswald, a member of the Stock Exchange. George Bouverie Blount died in 1910 on July 13th. Probate was granted to his widow Annie Christina & son George Hugh Blount, with effects of £3,950 19s 8d. Annie died at The Rectory in 1916 on October 9th.

GENERAL HAROLD BLOUNT

Harold Blount, one of the several children of George Bouverie Blount and his wife Annie Christina, was born on October 11th 1881, baptised on November 13th. The family, with his father employed as a clerk in the Admiralty, were resident in Picardy Road, Belvedere, Erith, Kent. Then in 1891 both Harold and his brother Oswald were pupils in Eastbourne at the preparatory school of 'The Grange,' St. Anne's Road, where the education prepared boys for Public Schools and the Royal Navy. (The premises later became Eastbourne College but have since been demolished.) In September 1898 Harold was commissioned as a Second Lieutenant in the Royal Marines Artillery, being stationed in 1901 at Eastney Barracks, Royal Marine Artillery Quarters, Eastney, Southsea. In 1907 he was appointed as assistant professor of fortifications at the Royal Naval College, Greenwich, and on promotion to Captain in 1909 went to the Royal Naval College at Dartmouth. There he had charge of a term of cadets, with his home address now being The Rectory, Northchurch, Berkhamsted.

In 1912 on November 19th he joined HMS New Zealand, a ship gifted to Britain from New Zealand, which in 1913 under Captain Lionel Halsey made a cruise to the Dominions, receiving, on arrival at New Zealand as a thank you, a rousing welcome during April and May. Throughout WW1 the ship saw action at Heligoland, Dogger Bank and Jutland, and primarily for the latter in the 1917 New Years Honours list Harold was awarded the DSO; 'Captain Harold Blount. Performed excellent service as officer of "Q" Turret on 31st May, as well as in the action off Heligoland in August, 1914, and at the Dogger Bank in January 1915.'

As for another decoration, the Russian Government awarded him the Order of St. Stanislas 2nd Class (with swords) for distinguished service at the Battle of Jutland. Harold continued to serve in the vessel until February 10th 1919, when next appointed as instructor in musketry for the Marines. Then from 1922 until 1924 he served as Fleet Royal Marines Officer, Mediterranean, and from 1924 until 1928 as Brigadier Major Royal Marines at Portsmouth. In 1928 he was again appointed as Fleet Royal Marines Officer, Mediterranean, and in 1930 aboard the vessel 'Rajputhna' returned from Malta to land at Plymouth, with his proposed address listed as HM Barracks Plymouth. From 1931 until 1934 he was Colonel Second Commandant, Chatham, and then Commandant Depot Royal Marines until 1937, when he became Major General.

Early in 1937 he, his brother Oswald, and sister Minna, removed their home address from Tring to Woughton House. (Seemingly it had been sometime between 1916 & 1919 that the family had transferred from The Rectory, Northchurch, to The Wolds, Tring, situated between the railway and the canal at Tring Station, a hamlet in the parish of Aldbury.) At his own request Harold retired from military service in March 1939, and as such at the outbreak of WW2 was resident with his brother Oswald at Woughton House, where the domestic staff comprised a cook, two housemaids, a parlour maid, and a kitchen maid. Also accommodated, possibly as part of the contingent for Bletchley Park, or the other secret organisations removed to the rural safety of North Bucks, were two secretaries - 'Civilian Admiralty NI.' Nearby at Woughton Cottage lived the Blount's chauffeur Patrick O'Reilly with his wife and their schoolboy son. With hostilities declared, in 1940 for a long while General Blount would command A Company of Bletchley's Home Guard, and with the headquarters being at the police station in Simpson Road one police inspector would later recall; "You could tell to the minute what time it was by his comings and goings."

As for Woughton, as a member of the Home Guard unit in the village Mr. Garratt, who died in 1980, having lived most of his life in the village, would recall; "The General at Woughton House he was so keen on the Home Guard and so was his brother, Mr. Oswald. The General used to drill us in Woughton Park near the cricket pavilion. We used to practise attacking Milton Keynes, we used to climb the church tower and then Mr. Oswald used to order breakfast for us at the Swan and we used to have fried eggs."

Woughton's Home Guard - probably taken in 1945. General Blount and Oswald Blount are seated in the front row in civilian dress.

Regarding Bletchley, the General was appointed as Town Commander and on the National Day of Prayer in early September 1941 led over 100 men of the Home Guard to the service at St. Martin's Church. Also he undertook duties of public service, and that year under the wartime powers was appointed by resolution of the Newport Pagnell Rural Council as the councillor for the combined parishes of Walton and Woughton. The continued spectre of invasion was the topic at a meeting on Thursday, March 5th 1942 of the ARP Committee in the Council Offices, Bletchley. Here a letter dated February 24th from General Blount asked permission to use - 'in case of necessity' - the Council Chamber as a local defence battle headquarters, and this was duly agreed.

It was then at the Council Offices that as the Senior Military Representative on Friday, March 13th 1942 he attended a meeting of the Local Defence Committee. This commenced at 2.30pm to include amongst the several considerations the appointment of a small executive committee to function under the conditions of blitz or invasion. A large committee was deemed to 'be useless and possibly ineffective under such conditions,' and in consequence it was agreed to form such a body to consist of the chairman (Councillor Flack), General Blount, the Superintendent of Police, plus the ARP

Officer and Clerk. During the pre invasion period this would cover all 'minor matters,' such as the arranging of lectures, the considering of circulars received, and imparting information to the present and larger committee.

In measures to support the armed forces, in 1943 Bletchley accepted a challenge from Buckingham Borough Council to raise, on a percentage basis, a larger sum per head of the population during Wings for Victory Week. The Week was officially opened in Leon Recreation Ground, where under General Blount a parade assembled to include the WRNS, Army, ATS, Home Guard, Army Cadet Force, RAF, WAAF, ATC, police, ARP Red Cross, NFS, and St. John's Nurses. In succession to the late Brigadier J.P. Whiteley, in February 1944 General Blount became president of the Bletchley branch of the British Legion, and in December on Tuesday 5th at a meeting of A Company (Bletchley) Home Guard the formation of a rifle club was discussed. This would be known as 'The Bletchley Home Guard Rifle & Social Club' and in consequence General Blount was appointed as President. With the war finally over, as the first Sunday of Thanksgiving Week in 1945 on November 11th large crowds attended the open-air services, and on behalf of the British Legion at the Armistice Day ceremony at the Bletchley Road memorial a wreath was laid by General Blount. Then in 1946 on Sunday, June 30th about 300 representatives of various branches in the North Bucks group of the British Legion attended the group rally at Bletchley. As the first since the war this coincided with the silver jubilee of the foundation of the British Legion, and under the command of General Blount, as President of the Bletchley Branch, many veterans from World War One were included. They assembled in the market field, and 'it would have been difficult to find a wrong-footer amongst them.'

At a public meeting held on November 7th 1946 it was decided to add to the Old Bletchley war memorial the names of all those from the parishes of Bletchley, and also Water Eaton, who had been killed in World War Two. This was regardless of religious denominations, and a committee would be appointed to organise the necessary appeal. It was hoped to be able to clean and permanently illuminate the memorial but permission for adding the names would need to

be obtained from Bucks County Council. When this was granted
General Blount would finance the cost of renovating the memorial,
re-blacking the existing names, and adding the inscription. As for
the Bletchley Home Guard Rifle Club this General Blount, as the
President, described as having had a 'phenomenally successful year'
at the annual meeting in 1947 on January 2nd. Many competitions
had been won, to include not least the Bucks County Championship
and the Astor County Cup. As for domestic matters, in October
1947 a girl aged about 16 was needed at Woughton House; 'Live in,
other staff kept. Comfortable place, good wages, plenty of free time.
Bicycle provided. Apply General Blount.'

In 1954 on March 29th the death occurred of General Blount's
sister, Edith Annie Blount of The Old House, The Mint, Rye, Sussex.
(This was formerly The Foresters public house.) She died at Little
Fowlers Nursing Home, Hawkhurst, Kent, and with effects of £19,093
10s 3d General Blount was granted probate. (She had been born in
1868 on December 6th.) At this time General Blount was chairman
of Newport Pagnell Rural District Council and indeed served on
most of the committees, as well as on the Birchmoor Water Supply

Grave of General Harold Blount

and Drainage Committee. In other activities he was President of the Bletchley branch of the British Legion. However at the annual meeting in October he announced his retirement. The chairman, Charles Head, said he was sorry to lose such an excellent President, and when he asked how long he'd held the position the General said "It was when Mr. Callaway was Chairman. I think it was during the war, about 18 or 19 years. I followed Captain Mells as President." Actually he was elected in 1944, and Major V. Goldsworthy, of Rickley Lane, Bletchley, who would be the next President, presented him with the Legion's highest honour, the gold badge, saying that the General had attended each of the three Remembrance services every year during his 15 years. Yet the General still continued as chairman of the governors of Leon Secondary School, Bletchley, going in every week to see the children, talk to them and the staff, and to keep in touch after they left school. This he continued until his death at Woughton House in 1967 on Sunday, August 13th. He was 85. That morning he told his brother Oswald that he wasn't feeling too good, and subsequently staying in bed he died peacefully at 4pm. He was cremated at Milton on Wednesday afternoon, with the private mourners - who travelled there directly from Woughton House - being his brother Oswald Blount, Clive Blount, Dr. B.K. Blount, Mr. and Mrs. Charles Blount, nephews and niece, Mr. and Mrs. J. Holloway, Miss Porter-Hargreaves, and Major V. and Mrs. Goldsworthy. Interment was in Woughton churchyard, as also had been those of his sisters Minna and Edith Annie. At a memorial service held at St. Mary's Parish Church he was described by Canon C. Elliot Wigg as a very great Christian gentleman. Also taking part in the service were the Reverend K. Wright, Rural Dean of Bletchley, and the Reverend Allan Campbell, rector of Amersham and a former rector of St. Mary's Church, Bletchley. Due to an unavoidable circumstance the Bishop couldn't be present. However from the General having been chairman of the Leon School governors in attendance were Miss D. Tofield, the music mistress, who shared the duties of organist with John Rose, and, accompanied by three ladies from the church (Mrs. K. Beckett, Mrs. J. Hughes, and Mrs. H. Coles) a choir of girls from the school. During his address Canon Wigg included; "When a few days ago we laid to rest the ashes of

Harold Blount in this peaceful country churchyard of Woughton on the Green we placed beside them in the earth the well worn Bible which had been his companion throughout his long and eventful life and which he read daily every evening before committing himself to rest." "I think his garden was his very great delight in his later years and he worked in it with enthusiasm right up to the end of his life." The lesson was read by the Reverend Campbell, and among the congregation Mr. and Mrs. Rissip represented Blount & Co., with Mr. D. Bradshaw representing Leon School. Probate was granted to Clive Ronald Blount, retired stockbroker, with the effects totalling £44,066.

MINNA BERTHA BLOUNT

Minna Blount

Baptised at All Saints Church, Belvedere, Kent, Minna Bertha Blount was born in 1875 on October 13th to George Bouverie Blount, an Admiralty clerk, and his wife, Annie Christina. In 1881 the family were resident at 31, Picardy Road, comprised of her father, who was a senior Admiralty clerk, born at Malta, her mother, born at Nottingham, and siblings (ages as per the census) George Percy Cosmo, 7, George Ronald Beddard Blount, 3, and Oswald Blount, 1. In 1891 with a domestic staff of four servants the family were living at Stanwell comprised of Minna, her parents and unmarried siblings Rose Leonora, 23, Edith Annie, born in 1868, George Hugh, 20, an undergraduate at Oxford, George Bertie, 19, a medical student, and George Percy Cosmo, 17, an Army pupil. George Bouverie Blount died in 1910 and with four servants in 1911 Minna was resident at The Rectory, Northchurch, with her widowed mother and unmarried siblings Edith Annie, George Hugh, who was now a solicitor, and Oswald, who was now a stockbroker. From January 1910 Minna became involved, 'class secretary,' with the British Red Cross, and when a Red Cross Detachment was formed in the district in 1912 she was appointed Commandant. Indeed it was as Commandant that following the outbreak of World War One she supervised the running of a VAD Hospital at Ashridge House, the residence of Lord and Lady Brownlow. This served until 1915, in March of which year a VAD Hospital opened at Bancroft. Subsequently this moved to The Beeches at Berkhamsted and until its closure in July 1919 was successively overseen by Miss Minna Blount, Mrs. Porter and Mrs. Haygarth Brown. It seems the period overseen by Minna ended in February 1917, for that year she was appointed Executive Officer for the Local Food Control Office (advertising in March 1919 that she had rabbits and hutches for sale at her home of The Wolds!) Then after the war she sought election on the Tring Division of Hertfordshire County Council, and as per her election appeal in October 1920 she wrote;

"LADIES AND Gentlemen, I am offering myself as a candidate for the County Council chiefly on the ground that I believe there is endless work to be done on bodies such as this by women, and I see no reason why you should not be as well served in this work by a woman as by a man. I am and always have been very much interested in local affairs, and my war work brought me into close touch with Tring, and its surrounding neighbourhood. For many years I have had a good deal to do with hospital work, and should watch your interests in this respect, and also with regard to child welfare very closely. I am strongly in favour of smallholdings for those capable of working them, and am thoroughly interested in matters connected with housing. I am always in favour of economy, and believe in keeping expenses down to the lowest possible point, bearing in mind that the best is usually the cheapest in the end. I ask you, Ladies and Gentlemen of Tring, to give me your votes, and I assure you that if you do me the honour of electing me your member I will serve your interests to the very best of my ability.

Yours faithfully,

MINNA BLOUNT

The Wolds, Tring."

She was duly elected unopposed, being one of the first two women members. During her time of public service she would become a JP and perform good work on the Old Age Pension Committee, be involved with the Tring branch of the NSPCC, the Girls' Friendly Society in Tring, the Aldbury Nursing Association, the Tring Women's Section of the British Legion, and the National Council of Women. Also from its inception in 1924 she would be chairman of the Tring Fuschia Club, and for 16 years would serve on the Tring Local Education Sub Committee. Her residence throughout was The Wolds, living there in 1923 with her siblings Harold, Edith and Oswald, and in August 1926 with 'two in family' she advertised the need for a house parlour maid; 'three maids kept.' In 1931 she was again elected unopposed for the Tring Division of Herts. County Council but in early 1937 she relinquished her various roles when she moved from Tring with her brothers Harold and Oswald to Woughton House. However having only been resident in the village for a few months she died that year on Sunday, July 4th in a London nursing home at 20, Devonshire Place, London, W1. She had been taken critically ill the previous week and following this tragic news the members of

Grave of Minna Blount

Herts. County Council stood for a moment in silence before their meeting, with the chairman moving that a letter expressing the deep sympathy of the Council should be sent to the relatives. The funeral took place at Woughton Church on Wednesday, July 7th, at which representatives of Herts County Council and the many organisations with which she had been associated at Tring attended. With John Rose at the organ the rector of Woughton, the Rev. L.V. Lean, conducted the service and at the interment in the churchyard the committal sentences were read by the Reverend Prebendary R.H. Pope of Northchurch. An appropriate inscription on the gravestone informed that she had been Justice of the Peace for Hertfordshire and represented Tring Urban District on the Hertfordshire Council from 1922 to 1937. Administration was granted to Harold Blount, with effects of £8,559 12s 5d.

OSWALD BLOUNT

Born in 1879 on October 7th, Oswald Blount, a son of George Bouverie Blount and his wife, Annie Christina, was baptised at the church of St. John the Baptist, Erith, Kent, on November 6th. In 1881 the family were living at 31, Picardy Road, Belvedere, Erith, and in 1891 Oswald was a pupil, together with his brother Harold, at the preparatory school of 'The Grange,' St. Anne's Road, Eastbourne. By 1901 his home address had become The Rectory, Northchurch, Berkhamsted, resident with his retired father, his mother, and siblings George Hugh, and Rose Leonora. He was now a member of the Stock Exchange and indeed in 1903 is listed as a jobber at the Stock Exchange in partnership with three others. The commercial address was 9, Old Broad Street, London, with his bankers being Paris Bank Ltd. In fact Oswald would spend his working life at the Stock Exchange and formed his own company, Blount & Co. In domestic life his father died in 1910 on July 13th, with probate granted to his widow and sons George Hugh Blount and Oswald. However the family address remained the same, and in 1911 Oswald was living at The Rectory, Northchurch, Berkhamsted, with his widowed mother, Annie Christine, and unmarried siblings Edith Annie, George Hugh, and Minna Bertha. During WW1 Oswald served in the Royal Army Service Corps, attaining the ranks of Second Lieutenant and then

Captain, and was subsequently a special constable. It was during this period, sometime between 1915 and 1919, that the family moved from The Rectory, Northchurch, to The Wolds, Tring, where Oswald would become very much involved with the Tring Draghounds. In fact it was in 1920 on Monday, July 5th that a meeting of farmers and others at the Rose and Crown Hotel at Tring decided to revive the pack of drag hounds, which before the war had used to hunt in the Tring District. This would now be called The Tring and District Farmers' Draghounds, and with Oswald appointed as treasurer would meet once a week. Then as reported in a local newspaper of January 8th 1937; 'Through the agency of Mr. Wallace A. Foll and Messrs. Brown & Co. of Tring, Woughton House, where Capt. The Hon. Arthur Baillie has resided for the past few years, has been sold to Mr. O. Blount of Tring.' Consequently in early 1937 Oswald, his brother Harold and sister Minna, moved to their new residence but sadly Minna died shortly afterwards. Here in this rural location Oswald would become much involved with farming, and at the Conservative Club, Bletchley, in 1943 on Wednesday, September 8th purchased for £7,500 the freehold Tattenhoe Hall Farm, with vacant possession. On the instructions of John Ridgway Monk this had been auctioned by Wigley and Johnson, and comprised an area of about 260 acres 'with a fine farmhouse, two cottages, ranges of buildings and a Dutch Barn.' Having moved to North Bucks from Northumberland, from 1953 this would be managed for many years by Tom Humble, who recently celebrated his 100th birthday. As for the associated farming families, as one member would later recall Woughton House "was filled with memorabilia, animals heads from darkest Africa and it's where I was first introduced to the wafer thin cucumber sandwiches. Blount's used to have a cook called Connie who was famous for her shortcake, out of this world, even Mother was impressed." Having been in poor health for a couple of years in 1971 Oswald died aged 91 on July 22nd. Often to be seen at Bletchley Market he had continued his interest in hunting and farming, and even until shortly before his death had farmed some 240 acres at Tattenhoe, a strip of which is now part of Windmill Hill golf course. A Friday funeral service was held at noon at St. Mary's Church, Woughton, with interment adjoining the graves of Oswald's siblings Harold,

Minna, and Edith. He left £221,798 gross, bequeathing £500 to Dr. B. Furber of Aspley Guise; £5,000 to May P. Hargreaves; £500, an annuity of £200 and some effects to Connie Guess; an annuity of £200 and a pair of cottages to Herbert Wilson; £300, an annuity of £100 and, 'if he is in his service at his death and not under notice,' a cottage to Geoffrey Pulley; £200 to Mrs. J.C. Beckett 'if in his service at his death'; and £500 to George V. Kenyon. The remainder of his property was mainly distributed to relatives, with probate granted to his nephews Bertie K. Blount, of Tarrant Rushton House, Blandford, and Clive R. Blount of 1, The Woodlands, Stanmore Hill, Middlesex.

In 1974 plans were proceeding to convert Woughton House into a high class hotel and restaurant. The scheme was in line with proposals contained in the Woughton Village Plan published by Milton Keynes Development Corporation in 1972, and Mr. L. Blair, hotel executive for Otmer Place Developments Ltd., of Amersham, said a preliminary survey to test local demand had been carried out;. "Most of the companies in the Milton Keynes district were approached and we had an encouraging response." However he wouldn't say on whose behalf the survey was made; "The whole thing is in a very preliminary stage."

Grave of Oswald Blount

Woughton House. Platinum Jubilee fete, June 2022

THE WOUGHTON SMALLPOX ISOLATION HOSPITAL

This section concentrates only on the early years. Further information is held at Bucks Archives in the following references:

The records of the North Bucks Joint Hospital Board include records of the North Bucks Smallpox Isolation Hospital minute books, 1901 to 1934 (AR65/1974/2-4), account book, 1905 to 1929 (AR65/1974/17), ledger, 1914-1934 (AR65/1944/18), and financial statements, 1914-1934 (AR65/1974/19-20).

'The Isolation Hospital Act of 1893 gave a County Council power to provide in any district within their county an isolation hospital, this being on petition from a local authority (ie an Urban or Rural District Council) of not less than 25 ratepayers. Under Section 6 similar power was given to a County Council if their County Medical Officer of Health reported that a hospital ought to be established

for the use of the inhabitants of a district. In either case a local enquiry by a committee of the County Council would follow. On the conclusion of such an enquiry the County Council would make an order either dismissing the petition, or constituting a hospital district and directing an isolation hospital for such district to be established. The County Council would also have power to constitute a joint hospital district, comprising two or more local areas.'

In December 1900 various suggestions were under consideration by Bucks County Council towards providing an Isolation Hospital for infectious diseases. Indeed locally emphasised when in August that year a young woman named Ada Mcdermott when staying at the Swan, Woughton, was taken ill with typhoid three days after arriving in the village. Then in the offices of the Newport UDC in 1901 on November 30th a meeting of the District Councils in the Newport Pagnell Union was held to consider the matter. Here it was resolved that combined action should be taken for providing accommodation for smallpox cases, and to provide a hospital as near as possible to the centre of the combined district. For such provision the initial expenses would be borne by the various authorities; namely Newport Pagnell Rural District Council, one half; Newport Pagnell Urban District Council, one quarter; Fenny Stratford Urban District Council, one quarter. Mr. G.W. Branson was tasked to make the necessary enquiries but in December 1901 he had to report having been unable to find a suitable site with a cottage or other building. He therefore suggested a field situated off Little Woolstone lane between Woolstone and Great Linford, and at a cost of £63 the provision of hospital tents was made. Railway saloons were purchased in March 1902 and that year a Smallpox Committee was appointed. Then in July two cases of smallpox at Newport Pagnell were transferred to the new hospital and also two cases at Great Linford. In 1902 on November 12th the Rural District of Stony Stratford and Wolverton applied to have patients from their area admitted. Including representation on the Committee, terms were agreed, and under Section 57 of the Local Government Act 1894, on June 8th 1904 the committee was constituted as a Joint Smallpox Hospital Committee. The expenses were to be proportioned as Newport Pagnell Rural District Council, one third; Stratford and

Wolverton Rural District Council, one third; Newport Pagnell Urban District Council, one sixth; Fenny Stratford Urban District Council, one sixth. Each authority would be represented by three members, four to form a quorum. On October 21st 1904 near Bleak Hall in the parish of Woughton the provisional purchase was confirmed of 2¼ acres of land. This was at £40 per acre, with the freehold vested in the four authorities. In consequence in 1905 on May 10th a tender of £305 12s 6d was accepted for the construction of a wood and iron hospital of 12 beds. Also the sinking of a well. However on completion this was unfortunately found to have water that "turned out bad." In 1905 on Tuesday, May 23rd at a meeting of the Fenny Stratford Council a report was read from the joint committee in charge of the smallpox hospital. Enclosed were the plans and tenders for the new buildings on this Bleak Hall site, and with the cost to the Fenny Stratford council being £50 acceptance was asked for as soon as possible. This was because the committee had agreed with the tenant of the site of the old hospital at Woughton, Mr. Adams, to take over some of the old railway carriage bodies etc. for £10. The tender of Mr. H.A. Lee of Fenny Stratford was accepted, with the need emphasised that month by an outbreak of smallpox in the town. Then at the meeting of Fenny Stratford UDC on Tuesday, June 20th 1905 the clerk read a report of the proceedings at a meeting of the Joint Small Pox Hospital Committee held on June 7th. Correspondence between the committee and the contractor, Mr. H.A. Lee was read, in which he asked permission to withdraw from the contract on the ground that mistakes had been made in the tender. However he would be informed that they had no alternative but to request that he carried out his contract. In an update on proceedings, on Tuesday, October 24th 1905 at a meeting of the Fenny Stratford council the report of the joint committee in charge of the Isolation Hospital was read. This confirmed the removal of the old temporary buildings at Woughton to the new site at Bleak Hall, and the report was duly adopted. In 1906 on May 9th an application was received from the Potterspury Rural District Council to send patients from their area to the hospital. Also to have representation on the Committee. This was duly considered and agreed on the following terms:-

1. Payment of £12 10s per annum towards the capital charges of

building (ie., quarter of £1,000 at 5 per cent.)

2. Representatives on the Committee to be three members.

3. An annual contribution of quarter the expenses of upkeep and establishment charges.

4. The expenses of all patients sent into the hospital from their district to be borne by them pro rata.

5. The arrangement to be determined by three months on either side, notice to end on 31st March in any year.

6. The above terms to be subject to the approval of the various appointing Councils.

Dated May 18th 1906 a letter was received from Potterspury Council accepting the terms, with letters of approval received from the various component Councils. As a further development a tender from Mr. Taylor of Fenny Stratford for the erection of a cottage (£173 7s 0d) was accepted in 1906 on June 20th, with arrangements made for the appointment of a permanent caretaker. Of the combined scheme the establishment and other charges were now apportioned as 'Potterspury Rural, establishment one quarter, construction £12 10s; Newport Pagnell Rural one quarter and one third; Stratford and Wolverton Rural one quarter and one third; Newport Pagnell Urban one eighth and one sixth; Fenny Stratford Urban one eighth and one sixth.' In June 1910 at a meeting of the Small Pox Joint Hospital Committee a caretaker was appointed subject to his getting married as soon as possible. He had since got married and was now in residence. With there having been no further incidence of disease within the hospital's area, complying with their instructions in May 1911 the County Medical Officer presented the Public Health and Housing Committee of Buckingham RDC with a detailed report on the county's isolation accommodation. In view of this report the Committee instructed that suggestions be made to the Buckingham Urban and Rural District Councils, Wing RDC, and the Joint Isolation Hospital Committee (which managed the Smallpox Hospital at Woughton) towards holding a conference of their representatives. Here collaborative means would be considered towards providing sufficient isolation accommodation for the whole of the northern portion of the county. Thus consisting of the nominated representatives and officers of the public bodies this was held at the Woughton smallpox hospital on Wednesday July 19th 1911. Mr. Chantler, of Newport Pagnell, presided over the large attendance, and following full discussions it was decided to refer the matter to a committee composed of the chairmen of the respective authorities, or a representative of the same, and the Medical Officers of Health. Such committee would consider the cost of additional buildings, land etc., should it be decided to enlarge the hospital for the needs of the stated population. In conclusion a vote of thanks was afforded to Col. Broome Giles for having kindly provided tea and refreshments. At the meeting of Winslow RDC on Friday, July 28th 1911 the chairman and vice chairman reported on their attendance at the recent Woughton conference. They reaffirmed the purpose as being to establish a joint small pox hospital for Newport Pagnell, Wing, Winslow and Buckingham Rural District Councils, and it was resolved that Mr. Hughes, the chairman, should represent the Council at the next conference in September. Whilst there seemed a general willingness to subscribe a small annual amount towards maintaining the building, there was disagreement amongst the members about paying anything with regard to its enlargement or other large expenses.

As for Buckingham RDC, at their meeting on Saturday, August 5th 1911 Dr. Benson, in reporting on his attendance at the Woughton conference, said that in his opinion the existing facility would be sufficient to meet the needs of the immediate future. Additional expenditure had been mentioned but this he thought unnecessary, and he considered it would be to the Council's advantage to join with the other councils in the proposed matter. This was assuming any expense was reasonable. Mr. Denchfield explained that the matter had arisen due to a recent Act of Parliament, with it being pointed out by the County Medical Officer of Health that unless 'something of the nature' of a joint small pox hospital was established, then each council would have to provide its own building. From the financial aspect it would therefore be advantageous for the councils of the district to combine. By the resolution passed at the recent conference another conference would now be held, at which the Medical Officers of the Councils would attend with (Mr. Denchfield being chosen as theirs) one representative of each body. In continuing debriefs, at the meeting of Buckingham Town Council on Monday, August 14th 1911 the Mayor gave his short account of the recent meeting. Councillor Osborne hoped the council would in no way be committed in this matter, especially since in the event of an outbreak a member of the Corporation had offered to allow tents to be erected in one of his fields. Therefore he would strongly oppose the Borough going to any great expense regarding this projected joint small pox hospital. The rates in the Borough were already heavy, and now owing to improved sanitation and arrangements for water there was little incidence of the disease in the country. He thought being burdened with the significant cost of providing a hospital was unnecessary. However the Mayor said the County Council had called upon the Corporation to make some provision, and thus it was his opinion that the matter should go forward. After the next Conference the council could then decide what to do. This was carried. As agreed the committee appointed by the Woughton conference met on September 6th, at which it was emphasised by Mr. Chantler, the chairman of the existing Joint Committee, that the latter had in no way sought or desired an enlargement of the area. The initiative had been solely that of the County Council through their Medical Officer and Chairman of the Public Health Committee. However, should the County Council conclude that a scheme encompassing all the authorities would best serve North Bucks, then the Joint Committee would offer no objection. This was provided it could be done on a fair and equitable basis, and with this view accepted several suggestions were forwarded, with the following resolutions passed:

1) That the expenses incurred by the Joint Committee to date viz £1,543 be apportioned over the whole on the nine authorities on a proportional basis, the four councils to be admitted (with the present authorities) as joint owners of the hospital property, and as members of the Committee, and construction and establishment being met in the future by contributions on a proportional basis.

2) That the cost of obtaining a good and adequate supply of water be borne by the 9 authorities, and that the existing committee hand over the hospital, cottage, saloons etc. in a good and substantial condition.

3) That it be understood that the foregoing proposals are provisional only, and subject to confirmation or rejection by the various authorities.

4) That a copy of this report signed by the chairman and clerk to be sent to the clerks of the various councils concerned.

5) That the expenses of treatments of cases be continued as at present, viz; that all expenses of medical attendance, nursing, medicine, provisions, necessaries, attendance, and all expenses incidental to the treatment of any case or cases, be borne by the authority or authorities in whose district the cases occur pro rata.

The Joint Isolation Hospital Committee then referred the matter to the constituent District Councils. Three of these were willing to extend the site and to receive the new districts into combination. Two, Bletchley Urban, and Stratford and Wolverton Rural, were against. As for Mr. Osborne, a councillor of the Buckingham Town Council, he said at their meeting on Monday, October 2nd 1911 that the estimated grant of £43 to the joint small pox hospital at Woughton was excessive. Indeed it was high time the ratepayers made 'a bold stand' in these expensive projects. The Mayor, Councillor R.E. Bennett, said the deputy mayor and the Medical Officer of Health, Dr. Pemberton, had attended the recent conference at Woughton, on September 6th, and in consequence had drawn up a report. This had now been printed and circulated amongst the members:

"GENTLEMEN, - In accordance with your instructions we attended the Committee Meeting at Woughton, on September 6th, 1911, on the Proposed Joint Small Pox Hospital, and we beg to report as follows:-

1. It was pointed out by the Chairman, that the Original Conference originated solely from the County Council, through their Medical Officer of Health and Chairman of the Public Health Committee. That it was through the above Council that the Committee of the present Hospital were asked to consider the question of allowing other districts to join in.

2. At present the districts concerned in the Hospital are the following:- Newport Pagnell Rural, Potterspury Rural, Stony Stratford Rural, Fenny Stratford Urban, Newport Pagnell Urban. The fresh districts it is proposed to add to this number are:- Buckingham Urban, Buckingham Rural, Wing, Winslow. The increase in the number of Districts will necessitate enlargement of the area of the Hospital Site as now constituted. The enlargement of the present Caretaker's Cottage or the building of a new one, for accommodation of Nurses in the event of an epidemic of Small Pox, and a proper

Water Supply. In order to meet the expenses of the above and to render the proportion of each District fair, the following scheme was proposed and seconded and carried unanimously by the meeting. It was pointed out that the present building and site etc., had cost the present Districts £1,543. It was proposed therefore to divide this same in proper proportions amongst all the Districts (old and new), according to their Area, Population, and rateable value as follows:-

Newport Pagnell Rural, area 67,060; population 19,026; rateable value £117,039; proportion 1-4.

Potterspury Rural, 18,778; 5189; £33,543; 1-18.

Stratford Rural, 4,218; 10,427; £70,454; 1-6.

Fenny Stratford Urban, 3,684; 5,172; £30,296; 1-36.

Newport Pagnell Urban, 3,432; 4,239; £17,189; 1-36.

Buckingham Town, 5,007; 3,282; £17,308; 1-36.

Buckingham Rural, 52,216; 8,322; £83,615; 1-6.

Wing, 25,867; 6080; £86,922; 1-6.

Winslow, 33,413; 6,995; £55,643; 1-9.

This will effectively divide the original cost of the building in fair proportions amongst all the districts. The four new districts will pay in their shares to the Common Fund, and the amount will give a total of £730. (It will be noticed that Buckingham Urban's share amounts to about £43 (1-36 of £1,543.) By this means all the districts will be placed on a level basis, and the £730 will go to defray the expenses of the extra area, enlargement of Cottage and Water Supply necessary. This seemed to the meeting the fairest method of division, the original districts having already sunk their money in the present building and site, and then in future years should any further expenses be incurred, they will be shared by all the districts in the same proportions as above.

3. Annual upkeep expenses of hospital. The present charges are:- Salaries, £30; caretaker, £10; necessaries, £15. Extra charges under new scheme:- Salaries, £34; necessaries, £15; total, £104. These charges will again be divided up amongst all districts in the same proportion, giving Buckingham Urban an annual expenditure of £3 (1-36 of £104).

4. Expenses of treatment of cases in hospital. All expenses of Medical attendance, Nursing, medicine, and necessaries and all expenses incidental to the treatment of any case or cases to be borne

by the Authority or Authorities in whose districts the cases occur. Dr. Bradbrook, of Bletchley, is under agreement with the present Committee to attend cases in the hospital. A caretaker lives in the cottage on the site, and looks after the hospital. He is in the employ of the County Council, but during an epidemic he gives his full time to the hospital, and is paid his full wages and 10s a week. An ambulance is kept at the hospital, and can be had at any moment by applying to Mr. J. Thomas, Newport Pagnell. In conclusion, we urge the Council to give this report their earnest consideration. There is an initial outlay of about £43, and an annual expenditure of £3. This will enable any case of small pox to be promptly removed from the neighbourhood of the Borough to this hospital, and all dangers and difficulties promptly removed, and the chances of an epidemic of this terrible disease in the Borough of Buckingham considerably lessened.

F. ADCOCK,

Deputy Mayor, Member of Conference.

T. EBEN PEMBERTON,

Medical Officer of Health to the Borough of Buckingham."

In conclusion, due to discussions including concerns of finance an amendment that the question should be deferred for three months was seconded and passed. At their meeting on the evening of Tuesday, October 10th the Bletchley council decided to reject the scheme (which, to remind, had originated from Bucks County Council proposing to extend the Joint Small-pox Hospital at Woughton, at present open to Bletchley UDC, Newport Pagnell RDC and Newport Pagnell UDC, Potterspury Rural, and Stony Stratford RDC, to take in Buckingham Town and Rural, Wing and Winslow Councils.) The Bletchley argument was that whenever an outbreak occurred at any other town the cases would be brought to Bletchley.

Regarding Winslow RDC it had been at their meeting on Friday, October 6th 1911 that the decision was made not to take part in the scheme. In a letter Dr. T.F. Vaisey had advised against joining, and the Sanitary Inspector said there hadn't been a case in the whole of the Winslow Union since he held the office, a period of 19 years. It was the general opinion that it would be very expensive, not only with the initial share of the cost of £172, but with no idea of what future claims might be. Dr. Hogarth, the County Medical Officer, in company with Dr. T.F. Vaisey (their Medical Officer) attended a meeting of the Winslow RDC on Friday, November 17th 1911. Here the question of the proposed scheme was discussed, and replying to questions he said that due to the alteration made in the vaccination laws, whereby a large proportion of the population was now unvaccinated, it was felt that isolation hospitals should be provided to deal with cases whenever they occurred. In his opinion it would prove more economic and more satisfactory to the Winslow council if they joined with the other councils in North Bucks. The facility had a cottage occupied by a caretaker, and an extent of some 2 acres of land. In consequence on Friday, December 1st 1911 at the meeting of Winslow RDC the chairman said he thought they couldn't do better than adopt the proposed scheme. However various concerns were raised about the cost, including that of the land to be added, and in the opinion of one member tents would be quite adequate in the event of a minor outbreak. He didn't think they should go to the expense of the £172 which would be the initial amount. Also there was £3 a year for the upkeep of the facility. The chairman pointed out that if they decided to buy two acres and erect a cottage that would cost them money, but in response Mr. Colgrove said if they purchased 2 acres of land at about £35 per acre, and built a cottage for about £200, it would be their own. If they joined the Woughton scheme they would have to pay all that money and have only one voice in its management. The chairman then asked where they could put up the tents, to which Mr. Young replied he would allow them on his land for nothing. Also during the meeting one member remarked that in the Woughton district the area known as 'No Man's Land' would shortly be sold.

At the meeting of Buckingham RDC on Saturday, December 9th 1911, with regard to the Joint Small-Pox Hospital Scheme the chairman moved the adoption of the following recommendation of the General Purposes Committee; "That the Council accept the terms contained in the report, provided the Rural District Councils of Wing and Winslow also agree." This was seconded by Mr. Chapman, with Mr. Gough's proposal that it be adjourned for a fortnight also seconded. In the absence of Mr. Denchfield, who was away from home, the clerk then read a letter sent by him stating that Wing had adopted the proposed scheme, and the meeting now did likewise. As for the Stratford and Wolverton Rural District Council, the reason for their unwillingness to admit the new authorities seemed unclear, except for a statement made by their representative at the meeting of the Joint Isolation Committee on November 6th 1912. This was to the effect that the Joint Isolation Hospital Committee had provided for their own needs, and that other authorities ought to make independent provision. Thus due to the unwillingness of these two constituent authorities, the Joint Isolation Hospital Committee, despite having a majority in favour of extension, had no power to proceed with any further action. However on November 28th 1912 the County Council directed that an enquiry 'in accordance with Section 6 of the Isolation Hospitals Act 1893,' should be made by the Medical Officer of Health for the County. This regarded the need to establish an isolation hospital for the use of the inhabitants of the district comprising the Borough of Buckingham, the Urban Districts of Bletchley and Newport Pagnell, and the Rural Districts of Buckingham, Newport Pagnell, Stratford and Wolverton, and Winslow. In consequence on December 6th 1912 he wrote to the clerks of the relevant District Councils informing them of the County Council's directive, stating, as far as he knew, the present position of affairs regarding each of the councils concerned. He asked for further information to be furnished in writing within the ensuing 6 weeks, and for the purpose of holding an enquiry, and for receiving any verbal information which the several clerks, or medical officers of health, desired to give, informed them of his intention to be present at the Bletchley Station Hotel on Wednesday, December 18th 1912 at 2pm.

Meanwhile in 1912 on December 10th a resolution was passed by Bletchley Urban District Council stating; "That after having heard the letter read from Dr. Nicholson, this Council is of the opinion that there is no necessity to enlarge the existing small pox hospital and it does not favour buying any more land for future requirements, particularly as it would be easy on emergency to hire enough land which might be required for immediate use. Moreover it considers that the safety of the public is fully ensured by the existence of the present premises should unfortunately an outbreak of smallpox occur."

As for the letter mentioned, in responding to the Council's enquiry Dr. Nicholson had written; "In reply to your request as to whether in my opinion more land is necessary for present requirements, I beg to say that in my opinion, the present accommodation is sufficient for the present requirement, ie as long as smallpox is not prevalent in the district. As I understand it, the intention of the Committee is, and always has been, to have some provision at hand for the purpose of receiving and isolating the first cases occurring in the district, but if there were to be an outbreak of smallpox, and in view of the fact that so many children in the district are now protected by vaccination, then I expect we should find the existing provision inadequate to meet the demands which might be made upon us. The present may be a favourable opportunity for the Council to acquire land to meet future requirements, especially so seeing that the report of the Committee intimates that there is the possibility that the land may at some future time have to be acquired compulsorily, when the price of land would probably be enhanced. I am dear sir, Yours faithfully, Edgar Nicholson, M.O.H. The Clerk to the Bletchley Urban Council."

As scheduled, on Wednesday, December 18th 1912 the County Medical Officer of Health attended the meeting at the Bletchley Station Hotel, with the presence of Messrs. Tarver and Young, with Mr. Stapleton, assistant clerk, representing the Newport Rural District, and Mr. Ward representing both the Newport Pagnell Urban District and the Joint Small Pox Hospital Committee. Here a suggestion was put forward that in the event of the present site being extended and improved it might, when small pox was not present in the district, also serve as an isolation hospital for other infectious diseases. From the meeting, as from previous occasions, he duly obtained all the information necessary for the purpose of his report, and wrote; "I am therefore of the opinion that a small-pox isolation hospital ought to be established for the use of the inhabitants of the district named. There appear to be two possible alternatives: (1) The various District Councils concerned may come to some agreement on a voluntary basis, or (2) the County Council have power, after inquiry, to constitute a joint isolation hospital district under Section 9 of the Isolation Hospital Act, 1893."

As for the details of the present facility, the hospital was situated on a narrow strip of land 2¼ acres in extent in the Newport Pagnell Rural District in the parish of Woughton on the Green. It lay close to Watling Street 3 miles north of Bletchley, and although the site was satisfactory for the isolation of smallpox cases the area was meagre in extent, and would need to be extended laterally to ensure satisfactory provision in the event of a large outbreak. The existing buildings consisted of a brick and slated caretaker's cottage; a wooden and iron building on brick foundations containing 2 wards, with accommodation for 6 male and 6 female patients, a nurse's bedroom, a sitting room and a kitchen. If the Local Government Board's standard of 2,000 cu. ft. per bed was applied, then each ward had accommodation for 4 beds and 1 cot. Three railway carriages were estimated to accommodate three patients in each. One marquee was estimated to accommodate six to eight patients, and there was also a bell tent. As for the accommodation for nurses and domestic staff, this would be totally inadequate. The marquee would have to be used as a mortuary, one of the railway carriages would have to serve as a discharging block, and the ambulance shed, which contained an old four wheel covered cart, would have to function as a laundry. On the present site for dealing with an outbreak of more than 15 patients at a time it would scarcely be possible to erect any additional temporary buildings. Even for dealing with a limited outbreak the present provision was inadequate in 3 respects - insufficient area, want of proper water supply, inadequate accommodation for nursing and domestic staff. Nevertheless, for the reception of occasional isolated cases the present provision was perfectly adequate, and during the initial stage of an outbreak the nurses could be accommodated in the caretaker's cottage. In 1901 and 1902 there had been a few isolated cases in the district, in 1909 one isolated case at Buckingham, whilst in England and Wales in 1912 there had been 115 reported cases.

In 1913 on Saturday, April 26th at a meeting of Buckingham RDC unanimous resolve at the recent Bletchley conference was reported by Mr. Denchfield. The council had already agreed to join the scheme, and now all that was needed was their approval, as decided upon at the conference. He therefore proposed that this should be done, and being seconded by the Rev. Norman Ramsay such was agreed. Then at a meeting of Winslow RDC on Friday, May 9th 1913 a letter was read from the County Council. In this the RDC was asked to approve an increase in the expenditure limit at the Woughton hospital from £150 to £250. However Mr. Missenden voiced disapproval of such increases, saying that since representatives had now been appointed to meet regularly at Bletchley, why couldn't these proposed increases be deferred until the committee met. The matter could then be discussed there. The chairman was of the same opinion, whilst Mr. Young said it would have been better if they'd had nothing to do with the scheme at all. Mr. Dickens proposed that the council shouldn't approve the increase; Mr. Missenden seconded, and it was carried. As for other related matters, at the meeting of Buckingham Town Council on the night of Monday, August 11th 1913 a cheque for £36 15s was signed as their first instalment. Maintenance of the Woughton facility was an obvious and ongoing necessity, and in October 1913 an advert appeared;

'North Bucks Small-Pox Hospital Joint Committee.

To building contractors. The committee invite tenders for repainting and repairs of hospital buildings etc at their hospital, No Man's Land, Woughton. Specifications and particulars on application to the Hospital Superintendent.' In December 1913 at the meeting of Buckingham RDC the clerk produced the precept for £165, being the second instalment to the Joint Smallpox Hospital at Woughton, and it was agreed to pay. Then in January 1914 it was announced that a piece of freehold land in the parish of Woughton had been acquired from Mr. J.L. Shirley as an addition to the North Bucks Smallpox Hospital. Thus the facility continued, and in 1919 at the Hospital Cottage, Woughton, the occupants were Henry Knopp and Louisa Knopp. In late 1931 an inspection of the Isolation Hospital was made with a view to its value 'between a willing seller and willing buyer,' this being in connection with the proposed transfer 'to another Authority' under Section 63 of the local Government Act 1929. In the subsequent report was stated that the property was situate in the parish of Woughton on the Green, 'at a point just off Watling Street where the parishes of Shenley Brook End, Fenny Stratford, Simpson all converge.' The area comprised 4a 2r 21p, fenced in on the north west side by a four rail creosoted deal fence 5ft high. By a boundary fence on the south east side which belonged to the adjoining owner. The buildings were a brick and cement faced and slated caretaker's cottage, 'of very bad construction,' containing one sitting room, kitchen, scullery and two bedrooms. Adjoining was a boarded and corrugated iron roofed earth closet, coal barn and store room. The cottage walls were braced by iron ties, several settlements were evident, 'whilst the roof is not at all satisfactory.' North of the cottage was the isolation hospital. This was of timber construction on a brick foundation, with the outer walls and roof covered on the outside with corrugated iron sheets. Inside the whole was match boarded, and 'This building comprises two main wards measuring 30ft 2in x 20ft 4in. The centre part, which projects on either side from the main wards, is occupied by a nurse's bedroom, sitting room, kitchen etc., the projection at either end comprising E.C.s, stores etc. The whole has boarded floors and is ventilated through the roof.' 'The whole of this building is in very good order, except for a little pointing and repair required to the brick ground pin. Additional buildings comprise a corrugated iron garage with a concrete floor, and three old railway carriages.' A well in the garden of the cottage sufficed as the water supply, with another well at the extreme north 'of the spot of land.' Rainfall from the Hospital roof supplemented the wells with the water treated through a Roberts Separator and a sand and gravel filter. As for tenure, "We are instructed that the whole property is Freehold and free from Land Tax and Tithe." As for value (independent of certain furniture and equipment) "We estimate the Freehold value of the property as on a transfer from one Council to another, to be SEVEN HUNDRED AND FIFTY POUNDS (£750) and shall be happy to supplement this report, if required, in any way necessary." Possibly the Isolation Hospital was transferred to the North Bucks Hospital Board and in early 1946 was declared a waste of ratepayers' money by Mr. H.E. Meacham JP, of Stony Stratford. As chairman he had been speaking at a meeting of the North Bucks Hospital Board, where the clerk, Mr. M.C. Clifford, reported on the efforts of the Board to have the hospital discontinued. Showing that it was the Board's responsibility to make arrangements for smallpox cases letters were read from the County Medical Officer and the Ministry. Also that the agreement with Oxford Hospital to take patients was only temporary. Mr. Meacham said that even if 'the place at Woughton' was kept open it would be too problematic to get a nurse should a case arise. At a hospital like Northampton the matron was desperate for nursing staff, and in his opinion there wasn't the slightest chance of getting a nurse at Woughton; "It would be best to pack up the whole thing, it was a waste of ratepayers' money." The clerk said the Woughton hospital had been erected 29 years ago. There had been 7 or 8 cases and in reply to a question about costs he said the Woughton hospital rates were small. They paid the caretaker a retaining fee of 1s a week, plus National Health, and he lived there rent free. In conclusion, on the suggestion of Col. Byam-Grounds the County would be asked if one hospital could be retained for the nursing of all cases arising within the county. Then in 1947 on Thursday, March 27th the fate of the Woughton Smallpox Hospital was again discussed by members of the North Bucks Joint Hospital Board. Here it was reported that from damage caused by frost and wet some of the walls of the hospital were breaking apart. The brickwork was in danger of falling away, and in the report of the Board's Architect two systems of repair were suggested. However Mr. Meacham said the Board had repeatedly tried to have the hospital closed. Ever since they took it over there had only been one patient, and doubtless they would be encumbered with the liability when the Health Act came into force next year. He didn't think they should spend a lot of money on the facility, and many members thought that to keep it going was a waste of time. One member asked if it would go to the Ministry of Health but Mr. Meacham thought it would be taken over by the county. If this was in the next year then it was safe to assume they would close it down. Whilst there was another hospital in the south of the county, whenever the Board suggested sending any case from this area to that hospital, and closing Woughton, it had been tabooed by the Ministry. However it was agreed to put the necessary work in hand. Then in early 1949 it was announced that the hospital was to be sold. The sale of the site and buildings duly took place, and in 1950 as part of the proceeds on Friday, November 24th, £99 18s 7d was approved by Winslow RDC towards providing a public convenience at Winslow.

MEDICAL MISCELLANY.

In 1856 at noon on Wednesday, March 19th, the Guardians of the Newport Pagnell Union held a meeting to appoint a medical officer. This was in accordance with the order of the Poor Law Board for the Fenny Stratford District, comprising the parishes of Bletchley, Bow Brickhill, Great Brickhill, Little Brickhill, Newton Longville,

Simpson, Fenny Stratford, Walton, Water Eaton, and Woughton. The salary would be £49 10s, exclusive of the charges allowed by the order of the Poor Law Board for cases of midwifery and surgical operations.

In 1905 on Saturday, June 25th, the 6th annual competition of the various corps of the St. John Ambulance Association, North Bucks., was held for the challenge cup and silver medals. By kind invitation of the Levi family the venue was the grounds of Woughton House, where tents were erected and music provided by the Bletchley Station Band. Colonel and Mrs. Levi supplied luncheon in the morning and tea in the afternoon, and included amongst the large invited company were the president, Mr. W.W. Carlile MP, Lt. Col. P.B. Giles and his wife, Surgeon Captain C.J. Deyns, Lt. Col. Bull, Captain and Mrs. J. Chadwick, and Dr. Buxton of Fenny Stratford. Only 4 teams entered, not as many as before, being Bletchley Station (Loco), Olney, Stony Stratford, and Wolverton. Each was subjected to a searching examination by the adjudicators - Dr. Square of Leighton Buzzard, and Surgeon Captain Baker of Aylesbury. The former took theory (viva voce) and practical bandage work, and the latter the stretcher drill and the various methods of carrying wounded, and of artificial respiration. The competition finished at nearly 6pm, when the teams with Col. and Mrs. Levi and the remaining guests removed to the committee's tent on the lawn. Here the awards were declared and the cup and medals presented. With Bletchley being the winners, with 438 points out of 500, Mrs. Levi presented the cup to the winning captain, Mr. W.J. Brown. A silver medal was presented to each of the members, and running up medals to the 2nd team.

In May 1920 a Motor Ambulance scheme for North Bucks was instituted.

From Village Memories by Ouida Rice:

> "Old Mrs. Beckett, she used to make lace and she used to live in the thatched cottage called Laurel Cottage, where the Lavenders is now and she had lots of children. Now old Tom Beckett he used to cure warts and he used to cut a twig from the hedge and he marked the top of your wart with a cross and then you buried the twig and the wart would be gone in a month and it worked, well it worked for me anyhow."

RELIGION

RELIGIOUS NOTES
1866

After a thorough restoration the church opened for divine service on Sunday, September 2nd. The lesson was read by the rector, the Reverend Maurice Farrell, and the Archdeacon of Buckingham preached in the morning. In draining the churchyard an ancient stone coffin was raised. It seemed of great antiquity, with faint tracings of a cross, and intersecting circles at the head.

1867

On the afternoon of Wednesday, July 24th in fine weather the foundation stone of the Wesleyan Chapel was laid by James Harman esq., of London. A large number of friends from various parts of the circuit attended the ceremony, and also to contribute to the building fund. The superintendent of the Newport Pagnell circuit, the Reverend John Danks, commenced the service, after which the 6th chapter of 2nd Chronicles was read by the Reverend J.H. Taylor of Wolverton. The Reverend G. Walker, Baptist minister of Fenny Stratford, then engaged in prayer, and following the devotional services remarks regarding the need and purpose of the building were made by the Superintendent. He then presented a suitably inscribed trowel, and a mallet, to Mr. Harman, who having laid the stone handed the treasurer a cheque for £20 as his contribution towards the costs of the chapel. A second stone was laid by William Grimes of Castlethorpe, who contributed a gift of 10 guineas. After a collection had been made the service closed with the singing of the Doxology and the pronouncing of the Benediction. Loaned for the day by Mr. Sheppard, of Newport Pagnell, a large tent accommodated a tea, to which a large company sat down at 4.30pm. Lady friends had supplied the provisions, and afterwards Mr. Harman presided at a public meeting, with addresses given by the Reverends B. Bartlett and G. Watkins, the circuit ministers, and Messrs. Grimes, Rodwell, J. and R. Stevens, Armstrong, Irons and Whiting. The proceeds of the day amounted to £55, with the total required for the building estimated at about £200.

The Salvation Army arrives, to mixed reviews! As per a letter from 'A LOOKER ON.'

"For some little time the villagers of Woughton, and more particularly those residing near to the Jubilee Oak, have been enlivened for an hour in the evening by choice strains of music, three young men, viz., Thomas Gayley, Walter Biggs, and Thomas Dytham, all belonging to the Salvation Army, having purchased, the two former a cornet each, and the latter a trombone. And considering, sir, the short time they are able to give to practice, play remarkably well. The following are some of the pieces their fellow young men are regaled with, "What can wash away my sin," "Nothing but the blood of Jesus," "Come and join our army," "Now I can read my title clear," "Sinner whither will you wander." The sole and only object of these young men is to keep their companions from the ale bench, and it appears that most of my neighbours, if not delighted, do not interfere. But what do you think, sir, "Oh tell it not in Gath." There lives a gentleman on the village green who evidently has no ear for music, unless it is "Rule Britannia," especially for such elevating songs as above named. Well, this said gentleman, who I believe is not troubled with corns, actually made the journey from our village to the Town Hall at Fenny on Thursday, the 9th, and appealed to the Bench to know if this nuisance could be put a stop to. When the superintendent very properly asked if they stood in his field to play, "Oh, no," said the stern looking old gentleman. "Do they impede the traffic? "No, not that I am aware of." "Well, then, we can't interfere with them. We have the same thing - and that continually - at Fenny Stratford." I do not happen to know this sage old gentleman's politics, but really one is driven to put him down as a Tory of the old school, who evidently believes in no change, always to be as we were. If he were a father and I his child I fear I should get more frowns than smiles, for I happen to be of a very mirthful turn, would much rather sing and would much rather dance than mope about as if there were no sunshine at all. My friend and neighbour, let me advise you to listen attentively and next time our young friends play "Come and join our army," accept the invitation. You will then be a much happier man, casting sunshine around you, singing to your cattle, &c., as you traverse the fields, causing even the brute creation to say - "Why Thomas has got converted!" Complaints from this quarter will then be heard of no more."

Held at Oxford in the first week of May, at the quarterly meeting of the Board representing the four Diocesan Societies, the Church Building Society granted £30 towards restoring Woughton Church. The estimated total cost, exclusive of the chancel, was £450.

With the Lord Bishop of Oxford as the preacher, on Thursday, November 5th the church re-opened after a restoration, with a lunch held in the schoolroom. The rector had financed the cost of repairing the chancel, and a new organ had been presented by Mr. and Mrs. W. J. Levi. Restoration of the nave had been undertaken by general subscriptions and contributions from the parishioners.

1893

In March the debt due to the Bank on the restoration of the nave was still over £200. However in the following month Mr. Levi would give £100 towards reducing this sum, such that just over £100 remained.

1894

In November 1893 the Sunday School had re-opened, and in February 1894 there were 61 names on the register.

In March 'a friend' paid the balance due on the debt of the 1891 restoration of the nave. The offertories would now be devoted partly to re-glazing the nave windows, presently in a bad state of repair, 'and partly to various good objects outside the parish of which notice will be given from time to time.'

By November about £9 had been raised from the offertories towards re-glazing the nave windows. Mrs. Levi then kindly provided the balance, 'a considerable sum,' and 'We hope our people will show their appreciation of our beautiful church and its bright services by an increased and reverent attendance.'

1896

On Easter Eve the dedication of the chancel screen took place, with Heber's hymn 'Holy, Holy, Holy' sung unaccompanied during the procession of the clergy. Then while the rector read the prayer of dedication the clergy and choir remained standing at the west of the screen. Afterwards the rector opened the chancel gates and the clergy and choir proceeded to their places. The screen was a replacement for one removed some 300 years ago, and had been the idea of the renowned architect Mr. J. Oldrid Scott who, in reporting on the condition of the church six years ago, had said "Nothing would add to the beauty of the whole building more than the erection of a Chancel Screen. It is easy to see where the old one stood. Doubtless, with its gallery above, it must have been a most conspicuous feature in the Church. A very much simpler one is all that is needed now. It should be extremely light and open, and should not rise much above the capital of the chancel arch. Such a screen would be a most notable improvement, and I greatly hope it may be adopted." In consequence such a feature was included in the faculty obtained from the Bishop for restoring the church. The work was that of Mr. Bridgeman of Litchfield (who also carved the pulpit) with the iron gates wrought by Mr. Barford of Maidenhead.

1897

With Charles Warnes as foreman of the workers, in May work was about to be undertaken on the considerable alteration of the Rectory House and cottage.

In late October, a Church Army Van belonging to the Diocese of Oxford arrived under the charge of Captain Bennett and his two assistants, Mr. J. Sykes and Mr. G. Parsons. They stayed for three days, during which daytime visits were made to the houses, with evening services held in the school. Illustrated by Magic Lantern these were well attended.

1899

Causing much amusement (and confusion) the church clock only had one hand.

1905

'To let at Michaelmas, the old rectory, Woughton: 3 sitting rooms, 5 bedrooms, hot and cold water, bath, good garden. £40 apply rector.'

1906

On the evening of Wednesday, July 18th during a violent thunderstorm lightning struck and completely demolished a chimney stack of the rectory. Entering the rector's study the bolt blew out the grate of the fireplace and ripped up a portion of the floor. Tiles were broken and the walls of plaster around the electric bell torn and damaged. The rector although present in his study was fortunately uninjured.

1926

During January the villagers performed plays at Newport Pagnell to clear the debt on the churchyard drainage. Captain Barton Hudson and his wife of Woughton House were the principal organisers.

1927

On August 21st 1927 at St John's, Haslemere, High Wycombe, the death occurred at the age of 84 of the Reverend Frederick Francis Field. He had been the rector of Woughton from 1884-1913, and following its foundation in 1900 was the first initiate of the Freemason's St. Martin's Lodge, Fenny Stratford. He became the 6th Worshipful Master in 1905.

1931

In October a memorial was placed in the church to Canon Whitaker, rector from 1917 to 1930.

1934

On Sunday, December 9th the death occurred at Woughton at the age of 75 of the Reverend Arnold Theophilus Biddulph Pinchard

1935

The Reverend Leslie Victor George Siddian Lean was appointed rector of Woughton.

1937

On Saturday, July 31st the Hon. Francis Hubbard, of Addington, opened the Woughton on the Green Church fete in the Rectory Gardens. During the afternoon the boys of St. Mary of the Angels Song School, London - 'The Cockney Sparrows with Nightingale Voices' - gave two programs of song. The Rector, the Rev. Lean, said that £88 of the £100 required for the village hall had now been raised, and he believed that, 'at long last,' electric light was coming to Woughton. They wanted to have it installed in the church before winter, with the estimated cost being about £65.

1942

In March the Reverend C.A.M. Roberts accepted the living of Woughton, vacant for some time.

1952

In 1952 on the afternoon of Saturday, December 27th a portable oil stove was accidentally knocked over at the Rectory, and Mrs. Lilian Blumenau had to run through flames to escape from a blazing room. Sustaining burns to her hands and face she was admitted to Northampton General Hospital. Her husband, Dr. E. Blumenau, president of the Wolverton Photographic Society, said that after the stove was knocked over he rushed to the bathroom for water, but when he got back his wife had run through the flames. Newport Pagnell fire brigade were called but were delayed by having at times to be guided through the dense fog by torches. Fortunately Dr. Blumenau had managed to extinguish the blaze by then.

1953

Thomas Dytham who played the organ at Woughton Methodist Church for many years died in January aged 82. A carpenter by trade he was employed at Wolverton Works for 34 years. As a self taught musician he founded the orchestra for the New Bradwell Pleasant Sunday Afternoon Society.

The Old Methodist Chapel.

1958

On March 1st the Reverend Robert A. Law was instituted as rector of Woughton. Ordained as a deacon in June 1954 he became curate at St. Luke's, Newport Pagnell, then leaving in March 1956 for St. Saviour's, Reading. On June 2nd that year the Church of England Men's Society together with wives and friends left Newport Pagnell to visit Salisbury and its Cathedral. On the way back they stopped at St. Saviour's to call in on the Reverend Law, who entertained them to tea and showed them around the church.

1959

In October large splits became apparent along two of the main walls of the Rectory, possibly caused by subsidence.

1974

In September great dissatisfaction was voiced in the village regarding internal alterations to the church. Not least from 81 year old John Rose of The Close, the organist for over 60 years;

"Pews have been torn out, hymn books and Bibles burned, so I've heard, and the whole character of the place destroyed. In a village like ours the church is and always has been the focal point of our activities. And obviously, from time to time some repairs and improvements are necessary. But what they are doing is sacrilege. They will completely destroy the one beautiful thing we have left in this village"

(He died in 1979 and a brass plaque mounted on oak would be placed in the church inscribed, "In memory of John Davies Rose 1883-1979. Organist of the church for over 60 years. Also his wife Emily Rosenee Hillman 1892-1980.")

It seems the pews were removed to the church of St. Michael the Archangel, West Retford, Nottinghamshire, and were taken out in 2007. By kind information supplied by Pat Bloodworth, churchwarden, "a small number went to private purchase and the majority of them went to St. Martin's Church at Bole, which is in the Clays group of parishes."

1975

In April two men were arrested on a charge of stealing a £200 pedal organ from Woughton Parochial Church Council. Awaiting appearance at Bletchley Magistrates Court they were held in the cells of the former Bletchley police station, but when the time for their court appearance arrived it was found that the lock had jammed. A fire engine with senior officer and crew came to force the lock with a screwdriver to free the men, and as the fire officer said; It was an old fashioned lock with an old fashioned key and we had to use a bit of brute force."The council had considered renovating the cells but with the new Milton Keynes court pending it wasn't deemed worthwhile. The men were remanded for a week - one on bail and the other in custody.

1979

On the evening of Tuesday, July 17th the Reverend Timothy Whiffen, a former missionary in India, was inducted as the new rector of Woughton by the Bishop of Buckingham, the Rt. Rev. Simon Burrows. A special guest at the ceremony, at which Mr. Whiffen was also commissioned as a member of the Ecumenical Ministerial Team, was Bishop Solomon, a former Bishop in the United Church in South India. On his return from India Mr. Whiffen first became the vicar of Clay Cross in Derbyshire.

1983

In June thieves broke into the church at Woughton and drank a bottle of communion wine. They threw a paving slab to enter the vestry and made an untidy search, but according to the rector, the Rev. Whiffen, nothing else was stolen.

In September, 34 year old Dick Chamberlain would be leaving as co-director of Inter Action at the Old Rectory, Woughton. Seeking a new challenge he would now be assistant director at the Eastern Arts office in Cambridge, with the family home for himself, his wife, and children Zoe, aged 10, and Joe, 2, and dog Rosie, being in the village of Swavesey, in Cambridgeshire. A former youth and community worker, in 1978 from being 'attracted by the energy of a new city' he came from Manchester to be involved with the Peartree Bridge based community. The premises had been established as a base by the London based organisation in 1975, and although the Old Rectory had been renovated, the outbuildings and grounds still had to be developed. Also there were ideas for a community farm, which was commenced following his arrival. In the subsequent years in company with co-director Roger Kitchen and a team of experienced workers, to include his wife Jen, a successful programme of activities was developed.

RELIGIOUS RECOLLECTIONS.

Peoples' memories, with acknowledgment to the book 'Village Memories' by Ouida Rice.

Mrs. Sinfield

'Rectory Stud down the road to Simpson, a large Victorian house, used to be the Rectory. "It used to be a very well kept place down there. They used to have splendid parties there and the village fete used to be held on the big lawn."'

John Rose

"We always kept up Woughton feast, the dedication of the church in August, and we used to dance in the pub loft just opposite the church."

Mr. Shirley

"The Levis brought all their servants, the Harleys from Walton used to come with all their servants, and we brought what we had."

Mrs. Sinfield

"But the church itself used to be run more by the old ladies of the village; they loved their bit of church, the old ladies did. They cleaned the brasses, they put flowers in the pots. But with the coming of the city the old ladies didn't like the newcomers and the old ladies no longer take an interest in the church and the church itself is run by the newcomers."

Miss King

"The Sunday school was held in a proper brick built building just behind the church near Church House. It even had its own organ and we used to walk in a crocodile from the Sunday school to the church."

Mrs. Coles

"What I don't like about Milton Keynes is the way they've altered the church, everything's gone to pot. They used to have a good Mother's Union at one time, we used to have outings and all sorts of things. Well there's nothing like that now. I don't agree with the church being done the way it's done. It's alright for the new people because they've known nothing different, but to us it's not our old church, it's lost all the sacredness."

Mrs. King

"The church wouldn't have been changed like this if the General had still been there."

(This was General Harold Blount of Woughton House, who had been commandant of the Royal Marines.)

Mr. Coles

"We had a rector down there that followed Parsons Field and Dunlop, Canon Whitaker was his name, and we used to have Bible classes down there and after these classes we had a good feed. Behind the rectory there was a piece of land and it was all strawberries and we went and picked the strawberries and went into Bible classes eating them. And there used to be a gardener down there, a rum old kettle of fish, old Sumner. He came tearing in and told the old Canon and the Canon said, 'I wished I'd known, I'd have given them summat to eat with them.'"

Mrs. Beckett

"We had Bible classes at the Rectory two or three times a week, lovely they were, we had refreshments and everything. We always had to take our shoes off and put plimsolls on. There used to be a set of little bells in the kitchen and we'd ring them and the cook used to say that we'd have no bread and jam if we didn't stop. After I left school I worked for the Canon for seven years with Mrs. Bates and I lived in there."

Mrs. Garratt.

"You'll see a little summer house in the garden at the Rectory, by the road. In the summer house we used to have lovely tea parties and they used to hide pieces of chocolate and all sorts of things in the garden because it was a huge garden and you had to go and find them. And I found a bar of chocolate in that summer house and it's exactly the same now as it was then."

Mrs. Kathleen Beckett

She had been the cleaner at the church for many years.

"I think it is disgusting. Every Saturday afternoon for the past 38 years I've cleaned the church and polished the woodwork ... only to see those beautiful old pews ripped out and discarded. The fairest thing would have been to hold a meeting and let the people of the village decide what was going to happen. I was baptised and married in that church. Every one of my 6 children has been baptised there. But I won't go there again. I know they have got to cater for new people moving into the village. And I'm sure most of us older residents will do our best to make them welcome. But no one has any right to destroy the character of a church which has meant so much for most of our lives."

(Kathleen Maud Beckett of 7, The Close, Woughton, died in 2003, buried at Woughton July 2nd; 'In loving memory of Kathleen Maude Beckett 1914-2003. Loved and sadly missed Mother, Grandmother and Great Grandmother. Forever in our thoughts.')

THE RECTORS

REV. DAVID JAMES

The Reverend David James was born in 1681 and in the parish register for Hambleden for each page of baptisms after the entry for May 13th, 1706, he signs as the curate. (His last signing in the baptism register was in 1713 on October 28th.) Indeed as curate of the parish in 1709 on November 28th he married 'Mrs' Martha Keck of London with a licence. (In the Bishops Transcript he is described as the Rev. Mr. Daved Jeames of this parish and she as Mrs. Martha Keeck.) Martha was the daughter of Anthony Keck of London, a noted money scrivener, and his wife Mary, and in 1711 a son, Anthony, was born (d1786). An entry for Hambleden on September 9th 1712 records 'the baptism of John, 'son to Mr. Daved and Martha Jeames,' and in 1713 on October 12th 'Daved son to Mr. Daved and Martha Jeames, baptized.' Then Thomas in 1715 (d1754), and a daughter, Mary, born in 1717 on September 23rd, baptised on October 3rd at St. Dunstan in the West London. (She married Henry Pye of Farringdon and their eldest son, Henry James Pye, would become Poet Laureate. She died aged 88 on May 13th 1806 at Devonshire Street, Bloomsbury.) In 1713 David had become rector of Woughton, instituted on September 22nd. Thus it was from Woughton of July 6th 1729 that he sent a letter to Thomas Cockman of University College, Oxford, congratulating him on his successful installation as Master of University College. Also he mentioned that his brother in law, Robert Keck (matriculated 1702) had left £500 to the College. In 1720 this money had been offered to Arthur Charlett, who suggested investing the sum with the interest paid to the College. However David now suggested that the principal should be paid as well. Then in a further letter to Thomas of 1729 July 27th he gave more details of Robert Keck's bequest. This included an extract which showed that in a will dated December 6th 1718 (Keck died at Paris in 1719 on September 16th, aged 34) he bequeathed the £500 to University College for the benefit of the Master. Additionally in the letter he hinted a request that his son's name might be put down for University College, in the hope of getting him a Bennet Scholarship! As for Robert's demise, the executrix was his sister Martha, the wife of David James. She died in 1735 on May 7th and in Woughton church on the floor of the tower chamber is a slab to her memory. Also on the south wall of the sanctuary is a large marble memorial to Martha James, 'sole surviving child of Anthony Keck of London, gent, and Mary his wife who died 1735 May 7th age 47.' 'This monument was erected by her sorrowfull husband the Rev'd David James, Rector of this parish, near whom lyeth the aforesaid Rev'd Mr. David James, who departed this life January the 8th 1746, aged 65.' 'Immensely rich,' being possessed of an estate of £5,000pa, he was succeeded as rector of Woughton by Thomas Troutbeck, and in his lengthy will included 'I give to the poor of the parish of Woughton on the Green ten pounds to be disposed of amongst them at the discretion of my executor.' Amongst many other bequests was that to his sister Margaret Evans, wife of Thomas Evans, then resident at Pengwern in the parish of Kennarth (ie Cenarth) in the county of Carmarthen. Also to her son the Reverend Mr. James Evans, of Great Linford in the County of Bucks, and her daughters Margaret and Martha Evans. To his only daughter Mary and her husband Henry Pye, of Farringdon, he gave £50 each and to their sons £100 each. His namesake son was bequeathed all his interests in the parish of Woughton on the Green, Great Woolstone and Little Woolstone, and also at Ampthill and elsewhere. In Woughton church in the sanctuary is a marble memorial to his wife Catherine, who died in 1780 on December 13th aged 50. Also to her husband who died in 1789 on June 26th aged 76. Also Ann, widow of David James, who died in 1791 on October 31st aged 45. Their bodies lie interred under the floor of the tower, wherein a memorial stone is set.

Memorial to Rev. David James and his wife. (above)

Memorial to Martha James (right)

REV. FRANCIS ROSE

'Born in Scotland, his family was descended from the ancient House of Rose of Kilravock, County Moray, and maternally from the House of Fraser of Lovat.'

Francis Rose was born in 1792, the second son of David Rose Esq., of Ardlach, and his wife Emilia. She was the daughter of James Laing Esq., of Boyndie, County Banff, and Elizabeth Fraser of Lovat, Inverness. In 1819 Francis married Ann Frances, born at Belstead, Suffolk, the second daughter of John Josselyn Esq., of Copdock Lodge, Suffolk. Francis was educated at the University of Aberdeen (Marischall College) and gained an MA in 1813. (Towards the end of his life he set up bursaries for the University, which are still evident today.) On his own presentation he became rector of Woughton and Woolstone in August 1823, and in 1829 in September advertised a country residence to let; 'A Genteel, modern-built House, pleasantly situated at WOUGHTON on the GREEN, within an Hundred

Yards of the Grand Junction Canal, along which Boats are constantly passing to and from London; within two Miles of Fenny Stratford …Nine rooms, outbuildings, garden enclosed by brick wall, and an orchard." In 1837 he was made a magistrate for Bucks and Northants, being resident with his wife at Woughton rectory, and in 1841 was made a Doctor of Divinity. At Woughton in 1849 on being accused of detaining parish documents he was summoned to appear at Newport Pagnell Petty Sessions. However in clarification of the facts he wrote from Woughton Rectory on December 1st 1849;

> "Reports had been industriously circulated, to my prejudice, that various writings, title deeds, and documents relating to charities belonging to the poor were in my custody. It was, therefore, material to me to have an opportunity of publicly stating what writings really did remain with me as the Incumbent of this parish, and of publicly surrendering the same to the parochial authorities."

In his letter he stated that just after divine service on November 15th the churchwardens and a clergyman called at his house demanding the parish documents; "I had reasons for declining to see them. It had been well if my wife also had declined seeing them, for one of them has, since then, affirmed on oath that she attempted to snatch a letter from the hands of the clergyman. I am requested by her to state that this is utterly false."

On the evening of the same day he stated that 'a body of labouring men' came to consult with him as to the best means of obtaining, 'in the shape of allotments for gardens,' what was locally referred to as the Poors' Common.

> "I embraced the opportunity of their presence and sent for the overseers."

One of them attended, and the Reverend then produced all the parochial documents that he held. These he handed over to the parties and duly received the acknowledgment;

> 'We, the undersigned, have received of the Rev. Dr. Rose the following documents, to be by us given to the churchwardens to be deposited in the wooden or the iron chest of Woughton, viz.:
>
> 1. A Feoffment Deed, dated 1707, in which are the words, 'Six small tenements, 13 acres and 1 rood of arable land, in trust to and for the repairs of the Parish Church and benefit of the poor people of

Woughton for ever.'

2. An Inventory, dated May 3, 1782, in which are these words - A charity of about £6 6s 0d per year for the poor, but applied to the overseers' book, and not known by whom it was given; and a house let to Widow Fowler, at £5 0s 0d, for the poor also. Ordered at the same time that the above charity be properly applied for the future. - Luke Heslop, Archdeacon.'

3. An Inclosure Award on parchment.

> John Chapman, Overseer.
> John Hedge.
> William Marshall.

Nov. 15, 1849.'

The Reverend said that on November 21st, six days after he had parted with them, a summons was issued calling him to show cause why he had refused to give them up. "I was happy to appear at Newport Pagnell on the 28th of November, when the above receipt was produced. The overseer delivered up the foregoing documents, and I was fined £2 and costs."

As for another matter, the following year on August 8th he wrote to a newspaper editor;

"Sir - In consequence of a paragraph which appeared in your number on the 3rd inst., I beg to state that I am not one of the Secretaries of the Wickliffe Club. I may at the same time observe, that I should be happy to see some wise, temperate, and judicious system of Church Reform, which would not separate the Church from the State."

In 1851 the domestic staff at the rectory comprised one servant but shortly afterwards Francis faced an accusation of having committed adultery with a parishioner. With the Bishop saying that Dr. Rose was "delated (sic) to me as guilty of adultery with a parishioner," a Commission duly found there was a prima facie case, ie despite an absence of evidence, guilt was assumed until proved otherwise. Francis firmly denied the charge, but in view of the "ruinous expenses of the Arches Court" submitted to the judgment of the Bishop, who sentenced him to three years suspension. However since there was no proof the Bishop later came to disbelieve the charge, and in a 'most private' letter of 1854 wrote to Mr. Charles Eyre, of Welford Park, Berks., asking if, as the patron, he could see fit to nominate Dr. Rose to the perpetual curacy of Baulking, near Uffington, Berks. This had become a separate ecclesiastical parish in 1846. (By marriage Welford Park had passed in 1706 to William Eyre, on condition that he changed his name to Archer. Then in 1800 John Houblon MP acquired the interest and changed his name to John Archer-Houblon. On acquiring the property his younger son, Charles, then re-adopted the surname Eyre.) As for the Bishop's reasons; "For first the crime was not proved: secondly the Rev. T. Athawes, a very good man and one of the commissioners, has since become convinced of his innocence, and the Rev. H. Bellairs, father to the Queen's Inspector, in whose town he long lived, is equally convinced." (The Rev. Athawes was rector of Loughton 1833-64, practising as a barrister before his ordination.) In the letter the Bishop acknowledged that for Dr. Rose to resume duty at Woughton "would be most injurious," but he felt it hard that he should be "permanently set aside." In consequence Francis became Perpetual Curate of Baulking and Woolstone, resident with two servants at Uffington, in Broad Street. There his wife died aged 91 in 1865 on September 17th. Francis died in 1870 on May 4th, and in the church of St. Nicholas at Baulking may be seen a marble wall tablet to their commemoration, with the inscription:

'On the outside of this chancel and opposite the middle window are interred the mortal remains of Ann Frances Josselyn: who entered into that rest which remained to the people of God Sept. 17th 1865 aged 91 years. She was the well beloved wife of the Revd. Francis Rose AM,DD, JP for the counties of Bucks and Northampton, and incumbent of Baulking cum Woolstone, who also departed this life May 4th 1870, aged 77 years.'

REV. LESLIE VICTOR GEORGE FIDDIAN LEAN

Leslie Victor George Fiddian Lean was born on March 6th 1898, baptised on April 10th at Kensington. His father, Victor Cumming Lean, was an officer in the mercantile marine, who in 1896 at the age of 30 had married Clara Fiddian, born in 1866 on July 19th. In 1911 the family were living at 79, Lansdowne Road, Notting Hill, with Victor - having now retired as a mariner - employed with the

National Telephone Company. Following school education Leslie became a bank clerk but in 1922 was ordained as a deacon and (being ordained priest in 1923) served from that year until 1926 at the church of St. Luke, Paddington. As per the ecclesiastical records he was permitted to officiate at the church of St. Alban, Teddington, from 1926 to 1927, and from 1928 until 1929 was curate of the church of St. Andrew and St. Philip in Golborne Road, North Kensington, adjoining Kensal Green. Then in 1930 he was granted permission to officiate at St. Mary, Paddington Green. In 1931 his father died, and he and his mother continued to live at 79, Lansdowne Road. In 1932 he was the author of 'Good Manners in Church & Out. A Guide to Church Customs for the Laity,' becoming that year curate at St. Mary. In 1933 he published 'The Drama of the Holy Mass' and that year in October was appointed a manager of Group No. 3 North Paddington (Amberley Road and Campbell Street) Provided Schools. This was for the period ending 30th June 1934, in which year he published 'The Voice of Undivided Christendom.' He remained as curate of St. Mary until 1935, when on his appointment as rector of the parish church he and his mother, 'of private means,' moved to Woughton, where he would also become a member of Newport Pagnell RDC. Then in 1941 at a special police court on Thursday, July 17th he appeared on 7 charges of alleged indecent assault on boys under the age of 16. With a short break for lunch the proceedings lasted from 10.30am to 4.30pm, during which all the alleged victims gave evidence. In court were the Bishop of Buckingham plus clergy from many parishes in the Bletchley rural deanery. John Robey in speaking for the Director of Public Prosecutions said the boys were members of the choir. The alleged offences had occurred with boys aged 9 to 16 between September 1940 and May 1941 in the church vestry, the rectory greenhouse, and the rectory summer house. Giving evidence Inspector W. Merry said the rector when told of the accusation on May 29th was in emphatic denial. He had been arrested on July 2nd at East Twickenham, and regarding the accusations made several statements to include; "The whole thing is a fabrication, I have never been in such a place in my life as this village. The whole moral outlook is corrupt among certain people." As for one particular boy, "He is a vile little liar, which sums up the whole lot of them." On three charges the defence submitted no case to answer. On the others the rector proposed making no statement at present. Allowing bail of £50 in his own surety, and £50 of the Hon. Francis Hubbard, of Addington, the Bletchley Magistrates then sent him for trial at Aylesbury at the next Bucks Assizes. Thus on Tuesday, October 14th he duly appeared on charges of improper assault upon choir boys of his church under 16 years of age. On 2 charges of indecent assault on 2 boys aged 12 he pleaded guilty. However not guilty to the other charges, which were not proceeded with. Giving evidence, Dr. John Barnes, of Harley Street, said the rector had consulted him in December of the previous year, saying he had suffered sexual tendencies all his life. On examination the Dr. diagnosed that from the point of mental health his personality was abnormally unstable. There was a history of insanity in the family and, with the rector expressing willingness to undergo the associated treatment, he considered the case to be relevant under the Mental Health Act 1930. The judge, the Hon. Sir Wintringham Norton Stable Kt, MC, was told that having been of previous exemplary service the rector had irretrievably ruined himself. His homosexual tendencies had been lifelong, but these he suppressed until his mind had been weakened due to the war and the evacuation of slum children. As for insanity in the family this was apparent on both sides - 4 on 1, and 3 on the other. After hearing the evidence the judge remarked that "Perhaps had this man not been held by the inhibition more peculiar to the clergy than those of baser clay this calamity might never have happened." In conclusion, and in accordance with the 1930 Act, the rector was bound over for 12 months, dependent upon his entry for that period as a voluntary patient at the hospital at St. Andrew's, Northampton, for special treatment. His mother moved back to Kensington and died in 1942. As for Leslie, as per the electoral roll he was resident at The Old Manor, Bradenstoke, Chippenham, Wilts., between 1947 and 1951, in which year regarding the property a sale notice for an auction on July 18th states 'by direction of L. V. Lean Esq with vacant possession.' This was to be followed on July 26th by an auction of the antique and modern contents of the residence, to interestingly include three oil paintings by Thomas Fiddian. However it seems the residence didn't sell, for in December 1951 it was still offered 'For immediate sale at low price.' Despite being an 'extremely attractive' early 18th century residence, with 6 bedrooms, outbuildings, a garage, stable and garden, in all about 1 acre, it was still on offer in December 1952 at £3,250, and then in September 1953 at £2,500. Then with perhaps a hint of desperation in November 1953 'This property can now be purchased for under £2,000 … the outstanding bargain of the year.' However this was no longer a concern for Leslie, since presumably for reasons of health he had moved to Italy, where in 1953 on January 3rd he died at Beda College, Rome, where he is commemorated.

REV. MAURICE FARRELL

Maurice Farrell was born in 1807 in County Longford, Ireland, the son of James Farrell, a clergyman of the United Church of England and Ireland. He was early educated by his father and then aged 15 in 1822 on January 7th he entered Trinity College, Dublin, as a pensioner (ie he paid a fixed annual fee for his education). He obtained a BA in the spring of 1828 and an MA in November 1832. (His brother James, born in 1803 on November 26th at Longford, and early educated by his father, entered the college in 1818 on November 2nd, gained a BA in 1823 and an MA in 1832. He became Dean of Adelaide, and there is much information about him on the Internet.) In religious matters, in 1833 at St. Nicholas Church, Leicester, on Monday, August 5th Maurice gave an evening sermon in aid of the British Reformation Society 'for promoting the Religious Principles of the Reformation'. Then as the acting secretary in 1834 on May 2nd he gave the Society's annual report in Exeter Hall, London. The following month on June 9th in a convocation at Oxford he was admitted ad eundem - 'the Reverend Maurice Farrell MA Trinity College Dublin.' It seems he became rector of Sherborne, Dorset, for a marriage allegation states 'Maurice Farrell bachelor and clerk of the parish of Sherborne, Dorset, to marry Margaret Foster spinster of parish of Biddenham at the parish church of Biddenham. Signed Maurice Farrell and George Cardale, surrogate. 1836 April 27th.' Indeed in 1836 on Thursday, April 28th at the parish church of Biddenham, Beds., he married the said Miss Margaret Foster, eldest daughter of the late thrice married John Foster of Brickhill Hall, Bedford.[23] Born in 1795 on August 7th she was baptised at the

Fulneck Moravian Church, Yorks., on September 6th 1795 - 'They live upon their Estate in Beycrly.' (She was the daughter of his first wife Margaret, daughter of Thomas Bosville Place, Recorder of York, and by her mother had three male siblings.) With the Rev. Farrell now as curate of the parish church, in 1838 on December 13th a son, Maurice Foster Farrell, was born at Cardington, baptised in 1839 on January 20th. Then in 1841 a daughter, Margaret Maria, baptised on December 21st. However she sadly died in 1853 and in Cardington church at the west end of the north aisle is a tablet to her memory. In April 1855 the Rev. Farrell was instituted to the living of Woughton by the Bishop of Oxford. As for his son, in 1857 on June 2nd he matriculated at Exeter College, gained a BA in June 1861 and that year became a student of the Middle Temple. Then in November 1864 he was called to the degree of the utter Bar by the Hon. Society of the Middle Temple, being holder of the Exhibition awarded by the Council of Legal Education, Michaelmas term, 1864. Also the Certificate of Honour First Class awarded in Trinity term 1864, this as a result of the general examinations of the students of the Inns of Court held at Lincoln's Inn Hall. Meanwhile at Woughton, following a restoration the church was reopened for public worship in 1866 on Sunday, September 30th. The service was read by the Rev. Farrell who had defrayed the cost of restoring the chancel. In March 1880 the old rectory house at Woughton, 'with garden and orchard,' was advertised for let with possession. Persons were to apply to the Rev. Farrell, who with relevant domestic staff was resident in April 1881 at Woughton rectory with his wife, who was now partly deaf. Then on October 8th that year at Woughton Rectory she died, and in Woughton church on the north wall of the sanctuary a commemorative tablet would be placed: 'In memory of Margaret, wife of Maurice Farrell, Rector of Woughton, and daughter of John Foster Esquire, QB, of Brickhill House, Bedford, and The Bogue, Jamaica. Died October 8th 1881, at Woughton Rectory. This tablet was erected by her husband, Maurice Farrell of Woughton, and her son, Maurice Foster Farrell; Barrister at Law, in the Middle Temple. A record of their fond affection, and grateful sense of the rare qualities of her mind and character. "Her ways were ways of pleasantness, and all her paths were peace."' Following the death of his mother Maurice Foster Farrell gave up his practice of barrister in London and moved from 4, Essex Place, to live with his father at Woughton. Then on the Reverend Farrell's retirement in 1884 they moved to The Hoo, Wootton Green, near Bedford. In 1888 on Friday, January 20th having dined with Sir Philip Payne, a resident in the locality, Maurice Foster Farrell - 'of eccentric habits' - set off at 11pm to walk the three miles home. He was carrying a lantern and on the way called at the cottage of James Devereux, who gave him directions from his bedroom window. Thinking that he might have misheard or mistaken his instructions he then called after him but received no reply. When Maurice failed to return home a search was made, it being thought that in the dark he might have wandered into the fields and stumbled into the river Ouse, a distance of about half a mile from the cottage. Eventually on the Tuesday morning his hat was found in rushes at the river side near Kempston church, and shortly afterwards a body was dragged out of the river near the same spot, where the water was some 20 feet deep. There was no sign of the lantern and there were no indications of foul play or intoxication. An inquest was held at the Half Moon Inn on Wednesday 25th, at which the jury returned a verdict of found drowned. Being aged over 80 and now in ill health the Reverend Farrell was overcome with grief, and died on June 28th 1888. On Tuesday, July 24th at The Hoo, Wootton Green, an auction by the direction of his executors took place of household furniture, 400 volumes of books, a brougham 'in beautiful condition,' a bay mare, a set of carriage harness, garden utensils etc. He left personal estate of £4,085 8s 4d, and in his will, proved in London on August 2nd 1888, he bequeathed amongst other charitable legacies, one for the poor of Cardington parish, to be applied in the distribution of clothing.

After the death of the Reverend Farrell, in 1890 John Wootton and Joseph Newman, guardians of the poor for Cardington and Eastcotts, respectively applied to the charity commissioner of England and Wales for an order of future regulation and management of Farrell's charity, called 'The Charity of the Reverend Maurice Farrell.' The charity apparently operated in the parishes of Marston, Cardington, Wootton in Bedfordshire, the parish of Woughton on the Green in Buckinghamshire, and Rathcline in Longford County in Ireland, since seemingly these were parishes where the Reverend had variously ministered.

The Vicar and Churchwardens of Cardington were proposed to be the trustees overseeing the running of the charity in Cardington. The provisions of the charity were recorded by the Charity Commission as: "Subscriptions or donation in aid of the funds of any duly registered Provident or Friendly Society accessible to such inhabitants (in this case, inhabitants of the Parish of Cardington) and the supply of clothes, linen, bedding, medical or other aid in sickness, food or other articles in kind." The same provisions were true in Wootton and Marston. By August 1891 new trustees were in place, to include the new Reverend of the Parish the Rev. Hillier.

The charities seem to have carried on throughout the 20th century, with the parishes being removed from the Charity Commission between 1992-2000, according to the parish of operation. (No doubt the Rathcline branch was removed earlier with the independence of Ireland.)

REV. HAROLD FRANCOME PAINTER

Harold Francome Painter was born in 1895 on August 5th at Teddington, the eldest son of Henry Francome Painter (d1954), a clerk in the Admiralty, and his wife Bessie Belinda (nee Seymour) (d1959.) With Henry in occupation as 'a staff clerk, Admiralty,' in 1901 Harold was resident in Kingston Lane, Teddington, with his parents and, all born at Teddington, his two brothers and a sister. A cook and a nurse comprised the domestic staff. Then by 1906 the family address was 62, Castletown Road, Fulham, where at the church of St. Alban the Martyr he was confirmed that year on December 16th. In 1911 Harold was attending Felstead School, Dunmow, and in the first month of WW1 he enlisted in the 4th Dragoon Guards. Serving in France, from the rank of private in the 4th Reserve Cavalry Regiment in 1915 on February 21st he was commissioned as 2nd Lt. in the Northumberland Hussars. Then in 1918 when attached to the French Army with the rank of Staff Captain he was awarded the Croix de Guerre, and mentioned in despatches. In 1919 his rank was Lieutenant, temporary Captain, but on demobilisation

Rev. H F Painter

he studied for the Church of England ministry at New College and St. Stephen's House, Oxford (the Oxford theological college), resident at 17, Norham Gardens. In 1922 he graduated BA and that year on October 1st was ordained deacon in the diocese of London. Then as priest in 1923 on October 7th. In 1926 he gained an MA, being appointed that year (until 1934) as domestic chaplain to Lord Halifax, 'with whom he travelled extensively in the cause of Catholic reunion.' His first curacy was at St. Mary Magdalene, Paddington, under the Rev. C.P. Shaw, a former vicar of Goldthorpe, and he later became a curate at Chard, in Somerset. In 1928 (until 1950) he was appointed Chaplain to the Forces (reserve of officers) and on December 28th that year relinquished his rank as Captain in the Northumberland Yeomanry. In 1929 on the death of Canon Kingsley, the vicar of Hickleton, he was presented to the vacancy by Viscount Halifax, retaining his position as domestic chaplain. In consequence at the crowded parish church of Hickleton on the evening of Monday, April 29th he was duly instituted by the Bishop of Sheffield. During this incumbency in 1932 on the afternoon of Sunday, March 20th he performed, in the absence of Lord Halifax, the dedication at the opening of the first aid post erected by the Dearne Valley Corps of the John Ambulance Brigade. In 1934 he resigned from the Hickleton living and left Goldthorpe on Tuesday, June 19th. Whilst at Hickleton apart from performing valuable work in the parish he had also undertaken extra parochial appointments, to include that of chaplain to the Doncaster home of the Diocesan Rescue and Preventative Association. Also he played an important role in the amalgamation of the Anglo Catholic Congress and the English Church Union, and would now undertake work of organising and lecturing for the Church Union in the north of England. Then in May 1936 he was appointed as vicar of Cowley St. Mary and St. John, Oxford, inviting Doris Barham, the housekeeper at Hickleton vicarage, and her parents to join him. Resident at The Vicarage, he remained until 1946. From 1947 until 1952 he was Chaplain of St. Mary's Convent and St. Joseph's Hospice, Chiswick, and was then appointed rector of Gresham with Bessingham, Norfolk. That year in a quiet ceremony at North Walsham he married Mabel Barnett, the eldest daughter of Mr. and Mrs. Leonard Barnett, of 50, Divinity Road, Oxford. In 1954 a daughter, Clare, was born and in 1955 a son, Luke, the year in which Harold was appointed as rector at Woughton. There he remained until appointed in September 1957 as perpetual curate at St. Mary's, Stony Stratford, being presented to the Bishop for institution by the People's Warden, Mr. L. Cooper. During the induction escort was provided by the Rural Dean, the Reverend C. Hutchings, and also taking part was the Vicar's Warden, Mr. A.W. Dillow. Afterwards tea was provided in the church schools. Remembered as a kindly man, the Reverend Francome Painter retired from the active ministry as vicar of St. Mary's, Stony Stratford, in 1967. In retirement he lived at Little Milton, Oxfordshire, and there he died in 1973, with the funeral held at St. James', Little Milton.

REV. ROBIN HENRY BAKER

The Reverend Robin Henry Baker was born in 1931 on August 11th, the son of Harry Baker (born 1901) and his wife Charlotte (nee Moores, born 1905). They married at Manchester in 1929, and with Harry employed as a wholesale representative for an electrical manufacturer, in 1939 the family were living in Prestwich at 17, Maple Grove. On leaving school Robin attended university at Manchester and then from theological college came as curate to St. Peter's Church, Swinton, Lancs., with his home address as 26, Laburnham Avenue. From Swinton, after serving a brief second curacy he became the incumbent at All Saint's Church, Stretford, Trafford, Greater Manchester He then served for 6 years as a full time chaplain of a large psychiatric hospital in Yorkshire and in 1972 moved to Milton Keynes. Taking up his duties on May 1st his first appointment was Team Rector of Woughton, forming the first new major parish of Milton Keynes by bringing the villages of Simpson, the Woolstones, and Woughton on the Green into one parish. It would be whilst at Woughton that he made a major contribution to the restoration of St. Mary's Church. The work began in mid August 1974, intending to make the church 'a drier, warmer, brighter and more cheerful church.' The floor would be completely relaid to curb rising damp, the roof made water tight, the heating and lighting overhauled, and a great deal of new painting undertaken. The dampness had been caused by a primitive concrete floor laid at the last restoration of the church in 1896. As for the present work the bulk of the money was from the Oxford Diocese. Also a grant from Milton Keynes Development Corporation and the Bucks Historic Churches Trust. Additionally local people had agreed to raise £2,500 as a contribution over the next 5 years. In the words of the Rev. Baker, "Colour can make a vast difference to the 'feel' of the church. A group of people from the church have said they would like to have a go at tapestry, applique, collage and embroidery – to add that sort of colour to the building. If there are people who would like to work on this project from anywhere in the new city area, they will be welcomed." However not welcome by many of the older residents were certain aspects of the restoration, not least the 'ripping out' and discarding of the old pews. Yet although plans for the modernisation had been drawn up before his arrival he said; "The main aim is to make the church more flexible. The chancel will be used only for worship, but the nave could then be used for all kinds of activities like drama, concerts, music, meetings or exhibitions. Far from bringing in revolutionary new ideas, this merely means we are going back a few hundred years to medieval times when the church really was a centre for community activity." The work was being carried out by a team of workers from T. and M. Contractors, Old Stratford, and in addition to this activity he was looking for a group of local people to make a tapestry as an altar frontal for the church; "We shall get some help from St. Andrew's Church, Bedford, and will probably use the services of a professional designer. But the actual work itself will be done by local people." Then in 1979 he was appointed to set up a parish at Central Milton Keynes. Winning the competition for the naming, he became Team Leader and vicar of Christ the Cornerstone Church, and for his work in bringing various denominations together, and contributing largely to the forming of new parishes in the city, in 1984 he was made an honorary Canon of Christ Church Cathedral, Oxford. Whilst resident at Kindleton, Great Linford, Milton Keynes, it was announced in April 1986 that he was to become rector at Banbury. As for his departure he said, "I'm very sad at leaving Milton Keynes. It was a tremendous privilege to be the first Church of England priest appointed in Milton Keynes... It's a great experience to see a city built from absolutely nothing." He served at Banbury for 5 years and then in 1991 became parish priest at Scorton, near Preston. He retired in 1996 and moved to Milton Keynes, where he died in 2004 at the age of 72 on January 27th. He was buried in the churchyard at Woughton, in the church of which is an oval stone plaque inscribed; "Christ is the Cornerstone. ROBIN HENRY BAKER 1931-2004. Team Rector of this parish 1972-1979. Ecumenical Pioneer and Visionary."

CANON GEORGE HERBERT WHITAKER

Baptised on July 18th, George Herbert Whitaker was born in 1847 at Oakington, Cambridgeshire. He was the son of the local rector the Rev. George Whitaker (b1829 d1882), born at Westbury, Wilts., and his 28 year old wife Arundel Charlotte (nee Burton), a clergyman's daughter, born in Sumatra. In 1851 the family, including George's three siblings, were resident at Church End, Oakington, attended by three servants. Then the following year in 1852 the family moved to Canada, on the Reverend Whitaker's appointment as Provost and Professor of Divinity at the new Toronto University. (As King's College this had originally been founded by Royal charter in 1827 under the Church of England. Then in 1850 it became a secular institution, when the name became the University of Toronto.) In Canada more children would be born, to make their subsequent lives in Canada and America. In 1861 George was still living with his family at Toronto, but returned to England to undertake education as a boarder at Shrewsbury School. In 1866 on May 4th he was admitted as a pensioner at St. John's College, Cambridge, and matriculated that year at Michaelmas. He was Bell Scholar in 1867 and gained a BA in 1870, taking a first in the Classical Tripos. In 1871 as a Fellow of St. John's College, Cambridge, (he would be a

Fellow for 22 years, from 1870-92,) he was living at Hurst, Berks., with his uncle (a solicitor) and his family. George was Assistant Master at Wellington College, Berkshire, from 1871 until 1874, having in 1873 on May 3rd at a Congregation (at which the vice chancellor Dr. Cookson, Master of St. Peter's College, presided) been awarded an MA. In 1875 on Sunday, September 19th he was ordained deacon at Ely by the Bishop of Ely, and became curate that year of St. Michael's, Cambridge. In 1877 he became curate of All Saints Cambridge, and that year on Trinity Sunday was ordained as priest by the Bishop of Ely. In 1878 he was appointed head of the Theological College at Truro, and in other positions the Bishop of Truro appointed him as his examining chaplain in 1883. Then with the Bishop as patron in May 1885 he received the appointment of residentiary canon in Truro Cathedral. He remained as head of the Theological College until 1885, and in February 1888 was appointed by the Right Rev. Dr. Walsham How, Bishop designate of Wakefield, as his examining chaplain - this 'from having formerly been chancellor and a residentiary canon of Truro Cathedral.' In May 1889 the Bishop of Hereford signified his intention of collating the Rev. George Herbert Whitaker, 'Fellow of St. John's College, Cambridge, and Canon of Truro,' to the vacant residentiary canonry in Hereford Cathedral. Thus in 1889 on the morning of Saturday, May 25th he was formally installed, in a ceremony which, after the second lesson at matins, consisted of the whole of the clergy moving in procession round the cathedral. He was then led by the hand by the Dean and Canon Lidderdale Smith to his stall, and after a special prayer the usual morning service then commenced. He would be Canon of Hereford from 1889 until 1892. In 1891 he was resident with his sister Bertha in Eastbourne at the lodging house of Emma Bull at 1, Bourne Street. Then in November 1893 it was announced that the vacant canonry at Truro Cathedral had now been filled by the Rev. George Herbert Whitaker, 'Junior Dean and Divinity Lecturer of St. John's College, Cambridge.' Indeed it was at Cambridge that he would be Select Preacher in 1896. Resident with his sister Bertha, in 1894 he became curate of All Saints Church at Eastbourne, from where he moved in 1904 to become curate at Burwash, in Sussex. There he remained until 1910, next moving with Bertha to Meinheniot, in

IN · MEMORY · OF · GEORGE · HERBERT
WHITAKER · SOMETIME · CANON · OF
TRURO · & · HEREFORD · RECTOR · OF · THIS
PARISH · 1917-1930 · A · DISTINGUISHED
SCHOLAR · A · HOLY · & · HUMBLE · SERVANT
OF · GOD · LOVING · AND · GENEROUS · TO
CHURCH · AND · PEOPLE · HE · DIED · 23rd
MAY · 1930 · AGED · 84 · YEARS · AND · IS
BURIED · AT · BRASTED · KENT

Canon Whittaker memorial plaque.

Cornwall. Then the following year they sailed for a visit to their family in Canada, returning to Bristol from Montreal in September. George remained as curate of Meinheniot, Cornwall until 1915, when he was appointed rector of Souldern, Oxon. In 1917 he was appointed as rector of Woughton where his sister Bertha, born in 1845, died in 1924. She was buried in Woughton churchyard, with the gravestone inscribed 'God is Love.' There was profound sympathy for him, from being renowned for his kindness and benevolence. As exemplified the following year, when, one Saturday in November, through his generosity the junior members of the Woughton church choir were taken by car to Northampton to see the English Cup tie between the Cobblers and Barnsley. This was under the supervision of John Rose, the organist and choirmaster, and afterwards they enjoyed a sumptuous tea, followed by two hours at a picture palace. A joyous occasion, although for George life was now lonely and depressing at the Rectory, and so he asked John Rose if he could come and live with him at Church House, near to the church. As John would recall; "It was his house and so he came in 1928 and they lived together. He had a mental attack and he had a brother in law who had a living in Kent and I got in touch with him and told him the Canon wasn't very well and he came down and said he'd take him back with him. So he took the Canon to Brastead and the next thing I heard a day or two later, he was dead so that was terrible and we all went down to the funeral. We left there at four in the morning because the funeral was a seven and then we came back." As for the circumstance of the Canon's death, in 1930 at the age of 83 he was on the point of retiring. However, having occasioned two stays in a mental home, and having been manifest not least in 1892, when he had to be restrained, he had long suffered 'a bitter religious depression.' By this he had the delusion of being the incarnation of wickedness, 'whereas he was one of the best men living,' and thought that in his early days he had been guilty of some heinous sin that now imperilled his salvation. The malaise had also occurred in 1915 when the nursing was undertaken by his sister Bertha. With the condition having now worsened on Sunday, May 18th 1930 his brother in law, the Reverend Edward Venn Eustace Bryan, rector of Brasted, near Westerham, Kent, decided to collect him by car to stay for awhile at Brasted Rectory. Dr. William Symes of Brasted was called in to attend him, and in consequence measures were taken to have him treated at an appropriate institution. Then on Friday, May 23rd he was found drowned in a pond near the Rectory in Moorcocks Field (sometimes Moorcocks Mead). The inquest was held on Saturday, May 24th 1930 at Brasted, at which it was stated that on the Friday morning he had been found missing from his bedroom. It seemed the bed had been slept in, and in consequence of the alarm being raised a search of the grounds was made, with the body discovered some three hours later in only a few inches of water in the pond. The beard was above the level but the clothes were muddy, his walking stick was upright in the mud, and his hat was on the bank. When recovered the body had the coat buttoned tightly, and a slipper was found to be under each armpit. This was thought from his intending to look for other shelter, as he imagined himself to be a burden to everyone. Dr. Symes said the Canon had told him that he was afraid of death, so although he might have gone to the pond with thoughts of suicide it could well have been an accident. In his opinion he wouldn't have been able to climb down the bank without assistance, and therefore might have slipped. The Coroner returned a verdict of 'found drowned,' and with the interment made early on the Tuesday morning many parishioners from Woughton attended the funeral at St. Martin's Church, Brasted. In his will the Canon left £592, with probate granted to the Rev. Edward Venn Eustace Bryan of Brasted Rectory, Sevenoaks, as the sole executor. As for his association with Woughton, a tablet was placed in the church to include the appropriate words 'A distinguished scholar. A Holy and humble servant of God. Loving and generous to church and people.'

REV. ARNOLD THEOPHILUS BIDDULPH PINCHARD
Boxing clever with the 'peaky blinders'

"Years ago, while Vicar of St. Jude's, Birmingham, the reverend gentleman was the pioneer of working men's clubs in connection with churches, and many an hour has been enjoyed by Birmingham men who joined in a game of draughts, dominoes, cards, etc., in the room attached to his church. Boxing, too, was also an attraction, and the Rev. Arnold Pinchard was always ready to accommodate any rival in an exhibition spar. He was a clever boxer."

Born in 1859 to John Henry Biddulph Pinchard, a solicitor, and his wife Laura, Arnold Theophilus Biddulph Pinchard was baptised on July 28th at the church of St. Mary Magdalene, Taunton. In 1861, with John as an 'attorney and solicitor,' the family was resident at The Mound, Taunton. Then in 1871 as one of the pupils of the vicar of Shaw, Arnold was at the vicarage at Corsham Road, in the village of Shaw, in the parish of Melksham. In 1881 he was attending Allhallows School in the High Street, Honiton, and was further educated at the London College of Divinity, Highbury, London, (St. John's Hall, Highbury). In 1885 on Sunday, December 20th at Worcester Cathedral he was ordained by the Lord Bishop of Worcester as deacon, and then in 1886 on Sunday, December 19th as priest. In 1887 he attended University College, Durham, and his first curacy was with the Rev. Alan Watts at Holy Trinity, Bordesley, Birmingham. Then when the Rev. Watts removed in 1887 to Dartford the Reverend Pinchard accompanied him, and had charge of a mission district. In 1888 on April 11th at St. Augustine's, Honor Oak Park, Forest Hill, London, he married Maud Sophia Julia Butler, daughter of the late

John M. Butler 'MD, FRCS, Eng., etc.,' of Woolwich, and Mrs. Butler, of Eythorne, Honor Oak. In 1889 the newly weds left England for the Argentine, where Arnold would take up the post of vicar of Holy Trinity, Lomas-de-Zamosa, Buenos Ayres, and Chaplain at Barracas-al-Norte, Buenos Ayres. With his parish extending some 500 miles long by 200 miles wide he was an expert horseman, and during one of the country's frequent revolutions he had to abandon his sermon due to the deafening noise of the bombarding artillery. In 1892 he was appointed Canon of Stanley, in the Falkland Islands, and in 1894 a daughter, Betty Mary Veronica Pinchard, was born at Lomas de Zamora on May 24th. (She became a talented actress and died at The Lawn, Holybourne, Alton, Hants., in 1984 on April 25th.) In 1895 Arnold and his family returned to England, and for almost a year he assisted the Rev. G. Cameron in the parish of St. Stephen, Newton Row, Birmingham. Then in May 1896 he was appointed by the Crown to the living of St. Jude's, Hill Street, Birmingham, vacant since the death in January last of the vicar, the Reverend W. Lewis. The patronage was jointly vested in the Crown and the Bishop of Worcester, with alternate rights to present, and since 'wherein dwelt those who are the despair of the clergy,' and being a parish where the church had ceased to have any social or religious influence, the appointment was hardly a promising prospect. Not least from being the home of the notorious 'peaky blinders,' so named from the type of cap worn with a peak, which was pulled down to shade the upper part of the face. Indeed, as described in a sermon by the Rev. David Simpson in 2020; 'the Peaky Blinders were angry anarchists who were guilty of murdering not just local people but Officers of the Law.' However the Reverend understood the nature of his 'flock,' and, by methods 'which did not perhaps entirely commend themselves to the more orthodox members of the community,' he gained their respect, and introduced into the church those who would have never otherwise entertained such a course. In fact in November 1896 it was written, 'Our comrade, Arnold Pinchard, has somewhat startled the good, conventional people of Birmingham by the Socialistic manner in which he is dealing with the slum people by trying to bring a little light into their otherwise miserable lives.' (The slums were known as 'The Rookeries.') Having been a middleweight boxing champion he began a Boxing Club, and in founding a girls' club in January 1897 he began to discover some depressing details of their plight; "In the cases of thirteen girls, taken at random, in the room one evening, it was found that they worked at very heavy work, for the most part for ten to eleven hours a day (allowing the dinner hour), and that their wages varied from 8s down to 4s per week. How can they keep body and soul together under such circumstances?"The following year with the help of the Women's Trade Union League he then undertook the challenging task of organising the pen making girls and women of Birmingham. Some 200 members were represented but with this being only about 1 in 150 of the workforce he was endeavouring to raise £50 to retain a woman organiser in position. Consequently in an appeal for funds he wrote; 'I may mention, by the way, that young as the Pen-makers' Union is, it has already been instrumental in inducing one firm to abolish the 2d per week charged to each employee for gas, and in securing promises that other fines and deductions will soon be things of the past.' Perhaps not immediately however, for some employers were victimising those workers who had signed. Taking a break from all this, in 1899 on November 25th Arnold sailed from Liverpool for South America, there to visit some of his former parishioners at Lomas. In 1901 he was resident at 99, Bristol Road, Edgbaston, with his wife Maud, and (ages as per the census) daughters Betty 6, Joan 2, and son Patrick, 3 months. Then in May he was inhibited by the Bishop of Worcester from preaching anywhere in the diocese except at his own church, with additionally the license revoked of his curate, the Rev. C.E. Armitage. Seemingly this was due to his ceremonial use of incense, for the Bishop, 'who never misses an opportunity of fighting the ritualists,' had a month ago expressed himself strongly on the subject. He asked the vicar to refrain from its ceremonial use, and regarding ordinary services the Reverend Pinchard complied. However he reserved the right for its introduction on special occasions. Accordingly, just before Palm Sunday he informed the Bishop that he intended to use incense on that occasion, and also on Easter Sunday. He received no reply but the Bishop later wired to notify that he would be inhibited, saying "One act of disobedience is as bad as fifty." The issue aroused much indignation amongst the parishioners, as both the Reverend and the curate were very popular, but in November came the appointment of a new bishop, and the inhibition was removed. In 1902 Arnold became associated with a movement to establish a stage society in Birmingham, the object being 'to secure the production, from time to time, of some of the many ancient and modern plays which cannot be produced successfully from a financial point of view, under ordinary conditions.' In consequence in September of that year as 'a Ritualist clergyman and social reformer' he engaged Mr. Ben Greet's company to perform 'Everyman', an old morality play, in the theatre of the Midland Institute at Birmingham This was solely to enable the people of Birmingham to witness the play, with any profits to be directed to the mission of the Good Shepherd. Indeed from initially being the 'Pilgrim Players' the company would eventually become the Birmingham Repertory Theatre. As for matters of education, in the wake of the 1902 Education Act in April 1904 he commenced an experiment to support his Church Schools purely by voluntary help. Thus he would dispense with Government influence, for "They, as Church people, had their grievances in regard to it, for they had sold their schools for a mess of pottage; they would never get back what they had sacrificed. The alliance of the Church with a pagan State had brought about many anomalies, and now they had sold all they should have kept for money." Despite this meaning diminished salaries the teachers were happy to remain. Prominent in the fight for improved social conditions, in March 1904 he attended a mass meeting of Birmingham working men in the Town Hall. Organised to protest against the contracting of Chinese labour in the South African mines, 'as being degrading to the Chinese labour, dangerous to the welfare of South Africa, and opposed to the best interests of labour throughout the Empire,' he was the chief speaker, and moved a resolution that the British Government had in this matter sold its birthright 'at the bidding of a horde of Polish and German-Jewish financiers, who devised the policy entirely for their own greed.' In recreational involvements, the first public performance of the Pilgrim Players was 'The Interlude of Youth' in 1907 on October 2nd. This was staged in St. Jude's Mission Hall, Inge Street, and when the Birmingham Repertory Theatre opened in 1913 he produced 5 plays, with the music arranged by his half brother the Reverend Lester Pinchard. Following the outbreak of WW1 Arnold began working in consort with the Belgian Consul, Adolph Myers, for the relief of Belgian refugees. Indeed by his efforts a fair sum was collected, and with funds and garments needed he could be contacted at St. Jude's Vicarage, Station Street, Birmingham. Additionally in September 1914 he sent £128 to the Birmingham and District War Refugees Fund, a sum principally collected in the theatres of Birmingham. As the war progressed, at various meetings he advocated the need for conscription, 'however distasteful that might be.' Indeed the mounting casualties brought sadness to many families, including, as would soon prove to be, his own. On the afternoon of Saturday, January 6th 1917 at St. Jude's with the ceremony conducted by her brother, the Rev. Lester Pinchard, his daughter Betty Mary Veronica Pinchard, of 101, Station Road, Birmingham, married Adolphus Broadfield Cohen. He was serving as a Lieutenant in the West Warwickshire Regiment but the marriage would tragically prove short, for he died from wounds in France in 1917 on July 22nd. The Rev. Arnold Pinchard was now secretary to the Birmingham Lord Mayor's Committee for Organising Hospitality for Refugees, and for his work was awarded an OBE in 1918. Also he was created a Chevalier de l'Ordre de la Couronne by the King of the Belgians. After the war at St. Stephen's Church, South Kensington, in 1919 on September 10th he conducted the marriage of his now widowed daughter Betty to Forbes Lankester McNaughton, aged 28, a Captain in the Royal Artillery. He was resident at 19, Queen's Gate Place, with Betty resident at 35, Beaufort Road, Edgbaston, Birmingham. With her father being chaplain of the Actors' Union, Betty had been in the cast of the Birmingham Repertory Company for the past four years, and previous to that for many years with the Pilgrim Players, who performed at Edgbaston Assembly Rooms, Francis Road, Edgbaston. (In 1938 she married John Henry Leather, manager of Bromley Little Theatre.) With the headquarters situated in London, in November 1919 Arnold was elected secretary of the English Church Union upon the commendation; 'Mr. Pinchard has gifts, appreciated in the civic as in the ecclesiastical life of Birmingham, which make him eminently suited to the post.' In 1930 his residence was 56, Belsize Park Gardens, London, NW3, but at the beginning of 1933 after 13 years as secretary he indicated his wish to resign at the end of July. He would receive a pension of £500pa, and then, having been presented by Henry Bowles as patron, in 1933 on Monday, October 23rd he was installed as rector of Woughton by the Bishop of Oxford. However the next year on Sunday, December 9th he died at Woughton rectory at the age of 75. Probate with effects of £734 10s 10d was granted to his widow, who died in 1939 on October 25th at 21, Northcourt Road, Worthing. As for his early pioneering work at Birmingham, a memorial at St. Jude's was dedicated in July 1936 by the Rev. Lester Pinchard.

REV. FREDERICK FRANCIS FIELD

Born in 1843 on April 1st, Frederick Francis Field was baptised at the church of St. Peter and St. Paul at Mansfield, Notts., on April 23rd. The son of William Field and his wife Jane (nee Millnes), the family's address was Church Street but by 1861 Francis was an assistant master at College House, Fore Street, Edmonton. In 1867 on October 11th he was admitted as a sizar at St. John's College, Cambridge, matriculating in 1868. Then as an undergraduate lodging in Lambeth he gained a BA in 1871, the year in which on St. Thomas's Day he was ordained deacon at Winchester by the Bishop of Winchester, and appointed as curate of St. Stephen's, South Lambeth, Surrey. In 1872 on Saturday, December 21st within the episcopal palace at Ripon he was ordained priest by the Bishop of Ripon, and licensed to the curacy of Gilling, near Richmond, Yorks. In 1874 on Saturday, September 5th the Lord Bishop of Ripon licensed him to the curacy of Kirk Deighton, near Wetherby and subsequently in February 1878 to the curacy of St. Mary, Leeds. Next he was appointed in 1880 as lecturer at Watford, Herts., and that year on July 14th at the parish church of St. John, Roundhay, Leeds, married Henrietta Frances, the youngest daughter of a wine merchant, William Collett Myers esq., of Grove House, Roundhay. In 1881 with the Rev. Field as the senior curate and lecturer at Watford parish church, the couple, with one servant, were resident in St. Albans Road, Watford. However in October 1884 Frederick was presented to the living of Woughton by the patron, Mr. H.C. Bowles Bowles, of Myddleton House, Waltham

Cross, Hertford. The estimated value was £300pa with the population of the parish numbering about 230. With domestic needs attended by two servants, in 1891 he and his wife were living at the rectory, and apart from his ecclesiastical duties during his incumbency at Woughton the Rev. Field would be a member of Newport Pagnell RDC and a candidate for the Woughton on the Green and Simpson School Board Election. He remained at Woughton as rector until 1913, being that year licensed to preach in the diocese of Oxford. Also that year in February he purchased the prominent property of St. John's, Hazelmere, which, having been the residence of the late Mr. R.D. Wheeler, was sold by Messrs. Vernon and Son, Land Agents, High Wycombe. Built in 1854 on the edge of Hazelmere, 'on the hill behind the Beech Tree pub,' it adjoined the main road from Wycombe to Amersham, about 1½ miles from Amersham, and apart from the residence also included was a small park, woodlands, plantations, an orchard, two cottages, and outbuildings - in total some 18 acres. Here the Reverend and his wife intended to spend their days in retirement but world events would soon dictate otherwise. In 1914 WW1 broke out, and when the vicar of Hazlemere, the Rev. Henry Clissold, volunteered for the Forces, to become an Army Chaplain, the Rev. Field found himself having to handle much of the daily running of the parish, to include St. Andrew's, Totteridge. Also the Church Hall at Terriers, where in 1916 he proposed the building of a church. For the present this was prevented by the wartime limits on the construction industry, and excepting discussions regarding the land needed for a proposed site little could be done. Then in 1924 when the Terriers returned from the parish of Hazlemere to High Wycombe he gave £1,000 as an endowment to finance a resident curate at Terriers. Additionally his idea to provide a proper church building was reconsidered, to be constructed on land promised by Lord Lincolnshire. However the intended architect died in 1926 and the death of the Rev. Field occurred at St. John's on August 21st 1927. Probate was granted to his widow, who in deciding to continue the project chose the eminent Sir Giles Gilbert Scott as architect. On June 10th 1929 she laid the foundation stone, and during a service conducted by the Bishop of Buckingham the church, complete with a massive central tower, was opened in 1930 on Saturday, October

St. Mary's Church. Causing much local resentment the pews were removed to create an area for 'community events.'

St Mary's Church at Woughton

11th. In 1935 the church would then be the venue for her funeral service on October 30th. She left gross estate of £49,059 13s 1d, and dependent on their matching her endowment her bequests included additional money to the Ecclesiastical Commissioners; 'Meeting the condition set in motion a train of events which lead to the separation of St. Francis' from the parish of High Wycombe and the creation of the new parish of Terriers in 1937.' In other bequests she left £100 to the vicar and churchwardens of Roundhay Church, Leeds, upon trust for the upkeep of certain family graves - 'whom failing to St. Francis Church, High Wycombe, for parish purposes.' Her interest in freehold property at Woodlesford, near Leeds, she left to Charles Coad (great nephew), and her interest at Merrion Street, Leeds, to her great nephew George E. Stock for life, with remainder to Mary Frances Stock. Dedicated on November 3rd by the Bishop of Buckingham, in 1938 a memorial tablet to Mrs. Field was placed above the font on the west wall of the church, which was the subject of an extensive restoration funded mainly by the Heritage Lottery Fund in 2013/14. As for Woughton, in 1936 on August 15th a tribute was presented 'by past and present parishioners' worded; 'In grateful remembrance of the Reverend Frederick Francis Field, Rector 1884-1913, and Henrietta Frances his wife, benefactors of this church and parish. This statue and altar, were erected by past and present parishioners of Woughton-on-the-Green, August 15th, 1936. Rest eternal grant to them, O Lord. Let light perpetual shine upon them.'

REV. CHARLES ROBERTS

The Reverend Charles Aldersey Morley Roberts was born in 1893 on August 28th, baptised on October 8th at St. Clement Church, West Thurrock. His father, Charles, born at Manchester, was a clergyman, and his mother, born at Pendleton, Lancashire, was Emily Mary (nee Morley). Attended by two servants in 1901 the family was living at The Vicarage in the village of Balking, near Farringdon, Oxfordshire, together with Emily's 76 year old father, Thomas. Charles was educated at Keble College and Pusey House, Oxford, and was ordained deacon in September 1918 by the Bishop of Buckingham in Oxford Cathedral. His first curacy was at Bracknell, Berks., and in 1920 he became curate at South Ascot. There he remained until 1923 when he went to South Africa to take up work in the church at East London, Grahamstown. There in 1926 on February 1st he married at St. Saviour's, East London, Hilda Kathleen Pemberton, born in 1898 on November 1st. In 1926 they returned to England and to Sunningdale, resident in 1928 at Garden Cottage in Priory Road. At a time when the rector was the Venerable R.W. Legge, Archdeacon of Berkshire, in 1930 Charles went as assistant priest to Sonning, where in 1931 he and his wife were resident at 'Taberna,' Butts Hill Road. There they were resident at the outbreak of WW2, with Hilda as an ARP driver. The position having been vacant for some time, in March 1942 Charles accepted the living of Woughton, and before a large congregation on the morning of Sunday, April 26th he was instituted as rector by the Bishop of Buckingham. The presentation had been due to Sir Henry Bowles, as the patron, who aged 83, and still active, had motored down especially from Enfield to perform the duty. As for the new rector's recreational pursuits, his chief occupations were bee keeping and cricket. In 1952 on June 21st at Woughton Rectory his wife died, and then aged 61 the Reverend Roberts died in 1955 on January 2nd. Having suffered a short illness he had been transferred on the previous Wednesday to Northampton General Hospital, where his death occurred. Well known amongst the local clergy he had for many years been the Chapter Clerk and Secretary of the Bletchley Ruri-decanal Conference, and with an interest in all the village activities was school correspondent for the Simpson and Woughton schools. The funeral service was conducted by Canon C.A. Wheeler. Clergy from many local parishes attended, and amongst the many mourners was included Mrs. Blumenau. Probate was granted to Barclays Bank with effects of £16, 946 3s 4d.

An old postcard view of The Swan at Woughton

THE SWAN

The Swan, variously Ye Olde Swan, and The Old Swan, dates from the 17th century, and a deed records that in 1696 the Old Swan at Woughton on the Greeen changed hands for £15. Of the early licensees in July 1782 mention is made of a widow Mrs. Hillyer, and in January 1785 of a Mr. Pinkard. Indeed some of the surnames are recalled among the modern developments. Of a farming family in the village, Richard Watts is mentioned in May 1786 and a Mrs. Churchill in February 1796. In this section is told the story of some of the subsequent publicans.

JOHN CHAPMAN

John Chapman, was born at Cogenoe (sometimes known as Cooknoe), Northants., in 1797, baptised on August 6th. His namesake father had married Elizabeth Sibley in 1791 on November 20th at Cogenhoe. She was the daughter of Edward Sibley and his wife Sarah. Possibly their second daughter of that name, for the registers record the baptism of an Elizabeth Sibley in 1764 on May 15th but a burial of the same name on September 1st. Therefore they probably had a subsequent daughter named Elizabeth. However the relevant baptism records no longer exist. Edward was a man of substantial wealth, and when 'weak of body' made his will on September 7th 1791.[24] This included for Elizabeth to be a major beneficiary, and by her marriage it was shortly before Edward's death in 1793 that, John, as his son in law, had already acquired his land before the proving of the will on October 12th 1793.[25] Elizabeth died at Cogenhoe in 1798, buried on July 13th, and now as a widower in 1800 at Cogenhoe on September 1st John married Sarah Norton. However this proved concerning to the Sibleys, since it meant their land ownership, which Elizabeth had brought with her marriage, would pass out of their control. Thus at this second marriage they took back the land. John's second marriage produced several children but Sarah died in 1812, buried on June 28th. By 1823 his son John had moved to Woughton, where that year on December 4th he married Elizabeth Battison, daughter of William and Mary Battison. She was born in 1796 at Little Houghton, baptised on September 3rd, and present at the marriage as first witness was John's brother, Edward Sibley Chapman, baptised at Cogenhoe in 1795 on May 31st. At Woughton on March 26th 1827 a son, John, was born, baptised in 1829 on September 16th, and in 1831 John is recorded as a freeholder in the village, owning land and tenements.[26] Then in 1837 on January 29th the death occurred of his father, 'a kind husband, a loving father, a good neighbour, and was benevolent to the poor.'[27] By 1841 John was landlord at the Swan, recorded as a maltster, with his family now comprised of himself and his wife Elizabeth and their children (ages as per the census, and all born at Woughton) John 15, Ann 11, Adelaide 9, Jane 6, and William 4. Also accommodated was John Fountaine, 60, a brewer. Whilst continuing at the Swan, in 1851 John was also farming 200 acres, resident with his wife and children John, Adelaide, Jane, and William. Also mentioned, no doubt associated with the inn, was a servant, John French, maltster, aged 70, born at Drayton Parslow. In 1857 on November 12th John's son, John, married Hannah Hazlewood at the church of St. Mary le Bow, City of London. Born at Simpson and baptised in 1828 on Christmas Day she was the daughter of Richard Hazelwood, publican, and his wife Mary. With his occupation as a farmer, at the time of his marriage John was residing in Lawrence Lane, City of London, as was Hannah. In 1858 a daughter was born, Annie Elizabeth, baptised at Woughton on December 27th. In 1861 John (senior) was still a farmer/employer in the village, resident with his wife and unmarried offspring Adelaide and William. Also a lodger and maltster George Benbow, single, age 20, born at Loughton. In 1871 John, farming 200 acres and employing 6 men and 2 boys, was resident in the village with his wife and unmarried son William. Elizabeth died at Woughton in 1880 on January 11th aged 84, and as a farmer and innkeeper John died at Woughton in 1880 on January 19th, being buried in the churchyard. Subsequently that year on Thursday, April 22nd at the Swan Hotel, Fenny Stratford, with regard to Woughton Mr. Geo. Wigley, on instructions from the executors of the late John Chapman, auctioned the freehold and fully licensed Swan; two freehold closes of accommodation land adjoining, with house and premises; 4 brick and slate cottages and gardens; and a grass paddock 'with a malting standing thereon.' Also, at the village of Swanbourne, the Boot Inn and two cottages. The whole was offered in 7 lots and with bidding commencing at £600 the Swan was bought in at £855. In 1880 on Wednesday, June 16th at Newport Pagnell Petty Sessions Mr. W.B. Bull, of Newport Pagnell, applied for the transfer of the license of the 'Old Swan', Woughton, from the late John Chapman to his son William Edward Chapman. Mr. Bull presented a numerously signed testimonial as to character, but the license was endorsed until enquiries could be made, and the usual notices served. Subsequently at the Sessions on Wednesday, July 14th Mr. Bull again applied for the transfer. However this was refused due to the opposition of Superintendent Hedley, on the grounds that the applicant was not a fit and proper person to conduct the house. This was allegedly due not least to his addiction to drink, and from being in the habit of associating with persons of bad character. Giving evidence, police constable Lawdon said that when he visited the Swan on June 26th at midnight, long after the time for closing, he heard people talking about betting. Then on trying the door two or three times he heard Chapman say "there is someone at the door." At this P.C. Lawdon said it was the police, and he wished to see who was in the house. He then heard three or four footsteps going across the house, and when he went round to the rear the door was opened by Mrs. Druce. He then looked around the premises and saw a man who they called 'Bob.' However the constable then saw Mr. Chapman coming from the rear of the house. He was seemingly wiping sweat from his face, and the constable heard him tell Mrs. Druce not to open the door. The application for the transfer was duly refused and in August 1880 the pub - 'with good outbuildings and 2 acres of grassland, lately carried on by John Chapman' - was put up for let; 'Apply to Mr. Hipwell, brewer, Olney.' In 1881, now as 'a retired farmer' John was living at Woughton with his wife Hannah, unmarried daughter Annie Elizabeth, and John's brother William, single and, due to the recent events, described as 'a retired publican.' Then in 1888 on April 28th at the church of St. Mary, Hornsey, Annie married Thomas German Redfern. A widower, he was the son of German Redfern, a colliery agent, and was in occupation as a hotel keeper in Wightman Road, Hornsey. As for Annie, her residence at the time of her marriage was stated as being Fenny Stratford. By 1891 John was living at Kingsthorpe, Northampton. However in the census his wife, Hannah, was resident with her daughter Annie Elizabeth Redfern and her family in the parish of All Saints, Northampton, with Thomas in occupation as a hotel keeper. Of 89, Oliver Street, Kingsley Park, Northampton, John died in 1898 on September 4th, with probate granted to his widow, Hannah. By 1911 Annie and her family were living in Leicester, with Thomas now employed as a commercial traveller. However Hannah was living at 30, Cowper Street, Northampton, with her 20 year old unmarried granddaughter Gladys Redfern, who as a shorthand typist was employed at a shoe factory. Then aged 85 Hannah died the following year.

FREDERICK BARKER

Baptised on October 10th, Frederick Barker was born at Great Linford in 1847 to Charles Barker, an agricultural labourer, baptised on May 28th at Great Linford in 1826, and Maria (nee Hancock), born at Great Linford in 1827. The couple had married at Great Linford in 1846 on November 5th, and in 1851 at Great Linford the family comprised Charles, his wife, and their children Frederick and Sophia. By 1861 their progeny had increased and, with his mother now as a lace maker, Frederick was an agricultural labourer. Then in

1868 on September 20th at Christ Church, Fenton, Staffordshire, Frederick married Mary Sutton, born at Little Houghton in 1848 to William Sutton and his wife Mary Ann, baptised in 1821 at Denton, Northants. (Mary Ann's maiden name was Barker, and the couple had married in 1843.) In 1869 Frederick and Mary were living at Park Street, Fenton, and shortly afterwards a son, Thomas, was born. Sadly he died in his early months, and then baptised in 1870 on July 17th a daughter, Florence, was born at Fenton. Frederick was now employed as a carter, and by 1871 the family were living in Fenton at 77, Market Street, 'Private House.' Here the head of the household was Mary's father William Sutton. Born at Little Houghton he was working as a carter, and the household comprised himself and his wife Mary Ann, their unmarried daughter Elizabeth aged 17, born at Little Houghton, in occupation as a potter, and Frederick and Mary. Also their daughter Florence, who died at Fenton in 1872 on April 8th. However that year at Fenton on December 14th a son, William Harry Barker (usually known as Harry) was born. He was baptised in 1873 on January 12th, and in 1880 a daughter, Mary Jane, was born at Longton on December 11th, baptised on January 9th at St. James, Longton. There the family were now living at 8, Sutherland Road, where again the head of the household was Frederick's father in law, William Sutton, resident with his wife. He was now employed as a brewer's horse keeper whilst Frederick, resident with his wife Mary and their children - William Harry and Mary Jane - was employed as a gentleman's coachman, being also a groom. In 1888 Frederick became the publican at Woughton, living with his wife Mary and their unmarried son William Harry, employed as a gardener and domestic servant, and daughter, Mary Jane. However in 1889 at Fenny Stratford Petty Sessions on Thursday, January 10th Frederick was charged with having allowed a lottery, or draw, for two ducks to take place at the Old Swan. A fine of 2s 6d and £1 1s 6d costs was imposed. In 1901 Mary Jane was in occupation 'at home' as a dressmaker/employer. Her brother was still employed as a gardener and domestic worker, and in 1902 he married Louise Jane Flude. Born in 1882 she was the daughter of George Flude, a tailor, and his wife Elizabeth. Then after the death of George, Louise continued living at the family address of 5, Bury Avenue, Newport Pagnell, as a 'tailoress,' resident with her widowed mother and a 25 year old boarder Alf Dawson, a butcher. As for Mary Jane, in 1903 on August 19th at St. John the Evangelist, Westminster, she married Albert Edward Eastment, born in 1876 on June 18th at Camberwell. He was the son of Joseph Eastment, a bank steward, born at Walton (only a few miles from Woughton), and his wife Martha (nee Freeman.) In occupation as a clerk, Albert was resident at 12, St. John Street, SW, and in 1904 a daughter, Kathleen was born. Sadly she died the following year and by 1911 Mary Jane and Albert were living at 26, Ashburnham Road, Luton, where he was employed as a clerk to a straw hat manufacturer. At this time William Harry was still at Woughton as a gardener, while his wife Louise (at least on the day of the census) was living as a tailoress with her widowed mother at Newport Pagnell. Also resident was her widowed brother Joseph, who was also a tailor 'working at home.' As for Albert and Mary Jane, in 1915 a daughter, Madge, was born. (She died in 1988.) Meanwhile, at Woughton, Frederick continued as the publican at the Swan, and as recalled by a resident of the village, who later became landlord of the Swan;

Grave of Mary Barker

186

"Old Barker, the landlord of the pub, he used to have his beer in twice a year in great big 36 gallon barrels and it was very strong ale in those days. They used to bring it in on a big trolley from a horse drawn dray. He used to have some very specially strong ale, and he was a very hot Conservative, old Barker, and if his customers would run down the Liberals, he'd let them have another pint. They'd say 'that Lloyd George, Mr. Barker, he wants shooting,' and Barker would say 'quite right, Enoch, have another pint.' And he'd let them have another pint of the very strong ale." "The pub was opened on Sundays, but the landlord he never opened the door until the parson had gone down the road to the rectory at mid-day. The pub was supposed to be open at twelve, but if there was late celebration perhaps it would be quarter past or nearly half past, but he wouldn't open that door until Mr. Field had walked down to the rectory. 'Knocker' Pursell used to be the one who usually knocked on the door when the Rector had gone by."

In 1918 Frederick's wife, Mary, died on October 8th, being buried in the churchyard. Then in 1919 the death occurred of Louise on March 28th with probate granted to Francis Littleboy, bank director. Continuing such bereavements, in 1923 Mary Jane died at Luton, and in 1928 on December 21st at 1, Alexander Place, Old Bradwell, the death occurred of Frederick, with probate granted to Emma Arrowsmith, wife of Oliver Arrowsmith, 'and one other.' Now as a widower, at the outbreak of WW2 Albert, employed as head cashier at a hotel, was resident at 9, Canning Road, Croydon, with his unmarried sister Emily Louise Sylvia Eastment, born in 1874 on September 20th. Together with her sister she had been early employed as a short hand writer and typist. Albert died in 1962 on June 14th when resident at 'Tainui,' 71, Victoria Road, Shoreham, being buried in Mill Lane Cemetery, Shoreham. Probate of £2,050 was granted to his sister Emily, who died at Worthing in 1963.

GEORGE GREEN

In 1880 at the Newport Pagnell Petty Sessions on Wednesday, August 25th a new license was applied for by George Green. George came from the Stony Stratford district and Supt. Hedley said it was his duty to mention that he had been twice convicted there. However George promised to keep good conduct, and the license was granted. Not that his promise was kept for long, for he was back at the Petty Sessions in 1882 on Wednesday, October 4th, charged with permitting drunkenness on his licensed premises on September 22nd. His previous offences were mentioned, and for the latest transgression he was fined £10 and 13s 6d costs, or 6 weeks in prison, with the license to be endorsed. Then in September the following year the Swan was advertised to be let with immediate possession, 'Apply to Hipwell and Co., Olney.'

(In September 1885 as the contemporary landlord George Matthew Mead appeared at Newport Pagnell Petty Sessions on Wednesday 16th for the renewal of the license. The hearing had been adjourned from the last bench while two cases of drunkenness on the premises were again considered. The license was granted, with Mr. Hipwell, the owner of the premises, undertaking to give Mead six months notice to quit.)

JOHN JAMES HUGHES

John James Hughes was born in Camden Town in April 1868 to Bernard Hughes, a railway signalman, born in County Down, Ireland, in 1839, and his wife Mary Ann (nee Mitten), born the same year. In 1881 he was living with his parents and his 10 year old sister Rose at Hammersmith, the place of her birth. Having previously served in the army in the Royal Field Artillery, in 1898 around May he joined the Bucks Constabulary with the collar number 50 and was posted to Great Missenden, being promoted to 2nd Class Constable in 1899 on May 29th. That year when resident as a police constable at Great Missenden on November 23rd he married at Emmanuel Church, Hampstead, Edith Alice Hobbs of 25, Hillfield Road. Born in 1877 on November 22nd she was the daughter of George Hobbs, a carpenter. Having been called to rejoin the Army, John was discharged from the police force in 1900 on February 12th and would be paid up to that date inclusive. When his army service was no longer required he would then be allowed to rejoin the police as soon as a vacancy occurred, and resume his former position. A daughter, Mary Louisa, was born at Kensall Rise, London, in 1900 on November 3rd, and in 1900 on December 17th he was reappointed to the police force with the collar number 146. In April 1901 he was living at Great Missenden with his wife and daughter, and that month earned the written commendation; 'the Chief Constable is much pleased with the conduct of PC 146 John Hughes in a case of house breaking at Missenden on the 13th February last.' The Constable displayed great promptitude and energy in tracing and arresting 3 men for this offence and recovering the stolen property.' He was promoted to 3rd Class Sergeant in 1901 on October 28th and on November 2nd was posted to Buckingham, where a son, Reginald George, was born in 1903 on January 13th. From October 26th 1903 his police pay was now 31s per week, then 32s per week from October 29th 1906. In 1907 on September 11th at Wendover a son, Horace James, was born. However on September 30th 1908 from the Chief Constable's office at Aylesbury came the reprimand; 'Sergeant John Hughes, having been found quite unsuited for his position, and having been under the influence of drink when on duty on the 23rd inst, is reduced to the rank of Merit Class Constable at 27/6 per week from this date inclusive.' He was appointed to Woughton where a son, Alfred William, was born in 1909 on March 19th. Then in 1910 on October 11th a daughter, Hilda May. At Woughton in 1911 the family comprised John and his wife, and their children Mary Louisa, Reginald George, Horace James, Alfred William and Hilda May. From October 2nd that year he was credited with pay of 28s 6d per week, being on October 27th awarded the George V Coronation Medal. Then in a further accolade in 1912 on May 9th from the Chief Constables Office, Aylesbury, was noted 'Police Constable 146 John Hughes is commended for having arrested at Harlington, Bedfordshire, a man who had stolen a pony and cart at Newport Pagnell, on the 1st inst.' At Newport Pagnell Petty Sessions on May 8th the prisoner was sentenced to three months hard labour, with police constable Hughes commended by the Chairman of the Bench. At Woughton another daughter, Winifred Edith, was born on June 24th 1912 and that year John resigned from the police force on December 16th, being paid up to December 15th. In recognition of his five years' of police service at Woughton, in early 1913 as a token of their esteem the villagers raised £13 for him by subscription. Now in need of new employment in February 1913 he advertised 'Wanted, situation, any capacity, such as night watchman, storekeeper, caretaker, etc. Fourteen years' references. Hughes, Woughton, Bletchley.' With his occupation indeed stated as a storekeeper, following the outbreak of WW1 he attested at Oxford on February 15th 1915 - '45 years 9 months, store keeper, married, previous military experience in Royal Field Artillery' - and was appointed to the Royal Regiment of Artillery. That year in May a son, Henry John, was born, and after the war John resumed residence at Woughton, becoming landlord of the village pub in 1920. In 1922 on August 4th a son, Lawrence, was born, and at the outbreak of WW2 at 'Ye Old Swan' the family comprised John and his wife, with Henry John Hughes, single, a brickworks general labourer; Hilda Mary Hughes, incapacitated; and Lawrence Frank Hughes, a brickworks general labourer. (In December 1936 Winifred Edith Hughes, his youngest daughter, had married Oliver Bubb, only son of the late Mr. J. Bubb and Mrs. Bubb of Bugbrooke, Northants.) Around 1940 John left to live at Little Woolstone, where he took an active interest in the social life of the village. Aged 82 he died in 1949 on Wednesday, May 18th, the funeral being conducted at Little Woolstone church on the Saturday by the rector, the Rev. Berry.

JOHN DAVIES ROSE

The Rose family and the village of Woughton on the Green have been associated for generations, with John Rose having been the landlord of the Swan for some 45 years until 1972. He was also organist at the church for some 50 years, and clerk to the parish council for 45 years.

John Rose was born at Woughton in 1893 on August 8th to Joseph Rose and his second wife Hannah, nee Davies. A farmer's daughter, she was born in 1867 at Llangler, Carmarthenshire, and in 1881 was living with her parents and siblings at Penboyr, Blaenbargrd. Following her marriage to Joseph, by April 1891 the couple, and Joseph's daughter by his first marriage, were living at Woughton with his brother in law and family. That year on August 16th a daughter, Ann Jane Rose, was born at Woughton, baptised in 1892 on January 3rd. John was the next child, and then in 1895 on March 15th William (d1925), baptised on May 26th. However in 1901 the children were resident with their uncle in the village. It seems Hannah died sometime before 1908, for in December that year Joseph married a widow, Sarah Butcher (nee Ansell), born at

Houghton Conquest in 1864. She had firstly married John Butcher, an agricultural labourer, and as a pillow lace maker on her own account was resident with him at Wavendon. He died in January 1905 and in 1911 Sarah was living in married life at Woughton with Joseph, now employed as a general labourer with the district council, and his two unmarried sons; William, occupied as 'assisting in the garden,' and John, 'assisting in bakehouse.' Previously, from around 1905 John had been working on a farm, and would recall in later life;

"We all left school and I went to work at Green Farm. I was only 12 and I went milking at 6am until 8am. Then I had a bit of breakfast and then up to the fields to drive the plough till 2 o'clock. I walked down home for a bit of dinner and then went across to milk the cows at 4 o'clock and fed the cows and after tea I had to go back again. We used to take the horse and carts down Bury Lane and across the river to Walton church and then to the mill and it was a proper cart way. Everybody was very poor really, the wages for a farm labourer was fourteen shillings a week and we had to work all the days of the week, there were no days off, Saturday was just the same as another day. I lived with my grandmother, we were lucky we always kept cows at home, we kept three or four and I milked them before I went to school."

As for working at the bakery;

"After two years on the farm, the baker at Simpson asked my father if I would come and work with him. I went to work at Simpson bakehouse, 5s a week he gave me, and I worked there for 9 years. Seemingly from a family trait, John possessed musical ability; "I was brought up as a Weslyan Methodist, my mother was a great Welsh Methodist singer, and I suppose I inherited her talent. When the Chapel Sunday School closed they sent me to the Church Sunday school. The squire heard me sing at a school concert and he asked me to sing in the choir. He made a fuss of me, but I didn't appreciate it fully. He taught me the organ and piano and I went to King's College Oxford with him. The squire, Colonel Levi, he ran the Bletchley Musical Society for 21 years. When the squire died he left me £1 a week as long as I played the organ." When the First World War broke out John then left the bakery;

"I spoke to the squire and the parson about going to war. There were not many drivers in those days, so unbeknown to anyone I went to London to learn driving and mechanisms and all that sort of thing. When Colonel Levi heard about it he met me at Bletchley station with the horse and groom. I passed the RAC exam and then I joined the army as a motor driver. An officer came to see Colonel Levi and checked upon my driving. I had six shillings a day, which was marvellous in those days. Colonel Levi saved all the money for me until the end of the war. I just missed the draft to Africa because I had smashed my toe, but the next draft was to Salonika. I was there for four years, driving an ambulance. After the Armistice was signed in 1918 we had to move a lot of evacuees and we left Salonika in 1919 and went to the Dardanelles and then across the Alps by train to Boulogne."

John returned to Woughton, and in 1919 on September 3rd at St. Michael's Church, Bromley, married Emily Hillman who, born in 1892 on April 21st, was living at 204, Brunswick Road. At this time John's father, Joseph, was an engine driver whilst Emily's father, Henry John James Hillman, was a fireman with the London Fire Brigade. In 1921 on January 28th a daughter, Joan Mary Rose (later Mrs. Marks) was born, and now with the war over John became valet and chauffeur to Colonel Levi, driving the Colonel's Rover car. John also operated a taxi service, with the fare to Bletchley station charged at 2s 6d. In 1925 his brother William died and then his father in 1926. In 1924 when Woughton House was sold Mrs. Levi moved elsewhere, which meant John and his family had to seek new accommodation;

"When Mrs. Levi went away I hadn't got a house to live in because I lived in a tied house belonging to the squire's property. I'd been a chauffeur there and looking after him when he was ill, and I was more or less lodging with my father. I was married at the time and I said to Canon Whitaker (who had come to Woughton in 1917) "There's a bit of spare ground up there by the church and I think I can afford to build a house there" and he said to me, "I think I can do something to help with that. He used the proceeds from selling the second supplement of Hymns Ancient and Modern to build that house up by the church, Church House. It was really the organist's house, it was built for me anyway and of course I lived there from

1926 until 1940." Canon Whitaker lived at the Rectory with his sister Bertha, and when she died he lived there on his own. He had some women in to help but wasn't very happy with them and said to Mr. Rose "Can I come and live with you." It was his house and so he came in 1928 and they lived together. He had a mental attack and he had a brother in law who had a living in Kent and I got in touch with him and told him the Canon wasn't very well and he came down and said he'd take him back with him. So he took the Canon to Brastead and the next thing I heard a day or two later, he was dead so that was terrible and we all went down to the funeral. We left there at four in the morning because the funeral was a seven and then we came back. I carried on living there and we had different parsons, some were good and some were no good. Some were high church, some were low church and we were all used to moderation."

John and his wife remained in the village and at the outbreak of WW2 were living at 'The Mystery,' Newport Road, Woughton, where John was now engaged by the War Office as a motor driver. Also living in the village, accommodated in Newport Road at Charity Cottages, was Emily's father, Henry, who, born in 1866 on January 8th, had retired from the London Fire Brigade. With her parents now resident at the Old Swan, Woughton, in 1942 their only daughter, Joan, married Robert Austin Marks (1913-1993). Born in 1913 on May 18th he was resident at Hill View, Bulbourne, Tring, and at the time of his marriage was in occupation as a 'pig and bee farmer.' At Woughton, John after many years as licensee of the Swan retired at the end of the first week of March 1972. This was when the premises closed for renovation and alterations by the brewers Watney Mann (Midlands) Ltd., and of his years as landlord John said;

"I've enjoyed it all, in a village pub. But I would not like to be starting now, even as a young man, with this new city and everything going on. It will need a different sort of man altogether now."

For many years Mrs. Kath Beckett had been a barmaid at the pub, and now in retirement John and Emily would be her neighbours in the village at The Close. However as principal guest at the re-opening of the pub John returned to the Swan and pulled the first pint. The pub would now remain as a one bar pub, albeit with the bar considerably larger, with the new landlord to be 23 year old Stephen Kalton. John continued to live in Woughton where he died in 1979. His wife died the following year.

CALLING TIME

Apart from the legend of Dick Turpin there was another mystery at 'Ye Olde Swan' in February 1986, when having been mine hosts for the past 2½ years Alan and Margaret Williams were suddenly replaced by a relief manager. The locks of the pub had been changed but together with their two sons the couple were still living in the upstairs flat! David Geddes, managing director of the owning company, Hamden Hosts, refused to reveal if they had been sacked, dismissed or suspended, merely saying "A new, permanent manager will start as soon as possible." As for Mr. Williams, he said he was "in the middle of delicate negotiations" with Hamden Hosts; "We are still living in the flat … we have nowhere else to go. The company has asked us not to go into the pub itself." During their tenancy, by organising numerous charity events the couple together with the regulars had raised thousands of pounds, and just a few days before the change of landlord had thrown a special party for 35 pensioners. 'The regulars are baffled.'

THE LEGEND OF DICK TURPIN

The Swan is well known from having supposedly been frequented by the highwayman Dick Turpin, when he came from his previous hunting ground of the Great North Road for the spoils to be had on Watling Street. In reminding of the legend, in 1985 on Sunday, February 24th following the re-opening of the Swan after a major renovation (which was marked on the Wednesday by firing a cannon in front of the pub!) there was a 'Stand and Deliver Appeal.' This commenced at noon, when outside the pub many little 'highwaymen' from the riding stables at 'Interaction,' based at the Old Rectory, collected money for a special outing for the old people of the village. At the Wednesday opening John Fleming, general operations manager at Hamden Hosts, said "The first hour's takings are to be donated to Interaction, a local community centre, providing a variety of facilities including a community arts project, interest groups for young mothers and a riding stable for children and adults where special classes are also held during the week for handicapped children." A cheque was presented on the night to the Director of Interaction, Roger Kitchen. As for the legend of Dick Turpin, to confuse his pursuers he allegedly paid a local blacksmith to reverse the horseshoes of his famous steed Black Bess. The stone from which he climbed onto her back is said to be cursed, and indeed when Margaret Williams ran the pub with her husband Alan, she said "Nobody in the village will move it. And the regulars wouldn't tackle it even if you offered them £100. We had builders in to renovate the pub recently and I told them about the curse. They didn't shift it an inch - they painted around it." Published in 1934 by Blandford, in H. Harman's book 'Sketches of the Bucks Countryside,' he refers to the connection of the Swan to Dick Turpin, also writing about a secret hideout inside the pub; 'It looks like some old dungeon - no light enters. By the old inhabitants it was known as the 'prison room' where malefactors and fugitives from justice hid with the collusion of the landlord.'

MODERN TIMES

With the coming of the new city, successive proprietors of the Swan variously changed the premises to adapt to the new clientele. Villagers who had lived in Woughton for years were of mixed opinions, with Mrs. Sinfield saying "Of course, but the pub was modernised from being an old stone floored pub with a cellar with the beer drawn straight from the barrels. It's not the pub it used to be and the skittle table and all that sort of thing has disappeared. The locals don't go there much now." In the early years of the city's development, in 1972 the brewers Watney Mann (Midlands) Ltd. undertook extensive renovations and alterations, and with 23 year old Stephen Kalton as the landlord the pub re-opened on Wednesday, March 8th. All the old oak beams had been retained and the bar was now considerably larger, with three separate areas. A dairy and cheese room had been converted into a comfortable lounge, and there was an extension for the playing of pub games. At the rear of the pub was a modern kitchen for the preparation of luncheons and speciality evening dishes. With the provision of a large car park, externally the appearance of the premises was little altered, with the principal change being a large bay window to replace the old cellar doors. As for the new landlord, he had previously been assistant general manager at the New Crest theatre club at Solihull, Birmingham, for 14 months. Prior to that he held administrative posts at several entertainment centres, to include the Golden Garter night club at Manchester and The Talk of the Town in London. Thereby he not surprisingly got to know many showbiz people, all of whom had been invited to come to the Ye Olde Swan for a drink. Married, his 20 year old wife of 15 months, Lynne, had been an airline ground hostess, and originally hailed from Manchester. Under the direction of the Chief Architect Mr. T. Brown, the alterations had been designed by the Architects' Department of Watney Mann (Midlands) Ltd., with Mr. W. Curran of The Square, Earls Barton, as the main contractor. Then in 1978, and now under the ownership of Hamilton Taverns, came other renovations to include the old beer cellar being made part of the main room on a lower level. Apart from a small area covered by quarry tiles the whole was carpeted 'in a warm golden brown,' and the hosts Bob and Jan Fletcher were particularly proud of The Carvery. Another 'update' was the installation by Cherry Leisure (UK) Ltd. of video games; a pronounced contrast to the pub's former times, such as 1962, when the Swan took the 'Fetch-it' domino medal from the previous winners,' 'The Wharf' at Great Linford.

HENRY FERRYMAN BOWLES

Henry Ferryman Bowles was born in 1858 on December 19th, baptised in 1859 on February 8th at Jesus Chapel, Enfield. He was the son of Henry Carrington Bowles Bowles (it is double Bowles!) of Myddelton House, Enfield, and his Irish born wife Cornelia (nee Kingdom). In April 1861 he was resident with his parents and his 11 month old brother, John, at Myddelton House, Enfield, where by 1871 the family, with their domestic staff, included his parents and his siblings John, and now also Edward, and a sister, Cornelia. (Both John and Cornelia died of consumption in 1887. Edward, who never married, became a gardening expert, writing several books on the subject, and becoming vice president of the Royal Horticultural Society). In 1874 Henry began his education at Harrow. There he entered Mr. Bertrand Nigel Bosworth Smith's house in Peterborough Hill, with Mr. J. Stogden as his form master, and on leaving in 1876 he went to Jesus College, Cambridge.

In other pursuits, dated 1878 August 7th it was announced in the London Gazette that he was to be a 2nd Lt. in the King's Own Royal (Tower Hamlets) Militia. Then on September 25th 1880 came an update that he was now to be a Lieutenant. Meanwhile, and whilst living at Myddelton House, in his ongoing education he was now a law student, and in 1881 gained a BA. That year the Tower Hamlets Militia became the 7th Battalion of the Rifle Brigade (The Prince Consort's Own) and in 1882 dated February 8th he was elevated from Lieutenant to Captain. The following year he was called to the Bar, Inner Temple, and in 1884 was awarded an MA.

Then with Mr. S. Ricardo as his best man in 1889 at St. Peter's Church, Pimlico, on Thursday, January 24th he married 22 year old Florence 'Dolly' Broughton. As the London address of her father, John Lambert Broughton (also of Almington Hall), she was resident at 43, Eaton Square, and with Lady Folkestone amongst the many distinguished guests it would be at Folkestone that the honeymoon was partly to be spent. Previously on the night of Tuesday, January 22nd a torchlight procession with flags and a band had proceeded from the Conservative Club in Enfield to Myddelton House, there to present Henry with a wedding present. Also an address to himself and his bride signed by some 80 members of the Club and the local Conservative Party. In fact as one of the original members of the Middlesex County Council, it would be that year that he was unanimously chosen to represent Enfield West and defend the parliamentary seat. This he won, with riding on horseback his chosen means of travelling to Parliament. (As for more modern matters he was the first man to tap out a radio message from the House of Commons.)

In 1890 on February 20th a daughter, Wilma Mary Garnault Bowles, was born, baptised at Jesus Church, Forty Hill, Enfield, on April 8th. Also in 1890, when resident at 27, Chester Square, Belgravia, he was initiated into the Bard of Avon Lodge of Freemasons, and would subsequently become a member of several other Lodges. Henry was now an MP, JP, and barrister at law, and in 1891 with the household attended by an extensive staff he was living at Myddelton House with his parents, his brother Edward, and, as a granddaughter to his father, Cornelia. In 1892 he was re-elected to Parliament, whilst in business matters in 1894 dated January 17th it was announced in the London Gazette; 'the partnership between Henry Ferryman Bowles, formerly of 1, Cloisters Temple, London, but now of 27, Chester-square, London, SW, and Frederick Ritter, formerly of Cloisters aforesaid, but now of 8, King's Bench-walk, Temple, London, and George Brooks, of Enfield, Middlesex, Printer, carrying on business as Newspaper Proprietors, and Newspaper and General Printers and Publishers, at Enfield, Middlesex, under the style or firm of Brooks and Co., and of Myers, Brooks, and Co., has been dissolved by mutual consent, this being from June 24th 1893.' (In depth details of his business activities are not relevant to this book, but much archive material is available from the library and other sources at Enfield.)

At the General Election in 1895 he was again elected to Parliament, and that year his father purchased Forty Hall, Enfield, where the following year Henry and Florence came to live with their daughter Wilma. In May 1899 Henry transferred to the 1st Volunteer Battalion of the Middlesex Regiment, whilst in political matters in 1900 he was again elected to Parliament. Then in 1903 as Lieutenant Colonel he retired from the command of the 1st Volunteer Battalion of the Middlesex Regiment, and in August 1904 was appointed Honorary Colonel. From its early days he had been a motoring enthusiast, and from appointment in 1905 as the first president of the Middlesex County Automobile Club he retained this position until his death. At the General Election in 1906 he lost his Parliamentary seat, and in 1908 in business activities notice was given that regarding 'T.I. Syndicate Limited' from being a creditor of the Company, he had presented a petition on February 7th for its winding up by the High Court of Justice. This would be heard before the Court on February 25th. Also in 1908, when the Volunteers were reorganised as the Territorial Force he was appointed Honorary Colonel of the successor, the 7th Battalion Middlesex Regiment. In further elevation in the next year after 20 years as a councillor he was elevated to the position of county alderman.

In 1913 at St. Andrew's Church, Enfield, on June 11th his daughter, Wilma Mary Garnault Bowles, of Forty Hall, married 28 year old Eustace Parker, a clergyman's son of (as was stated on the marriage certificate) Malpas Hall, Chester. A son, Ralph Derek, was born in 1914 on March 20th but sadly died on March 23rd. Then in 1915 on December 18th a son, Derek Henry, was born, and in 1917 on December 4th a daughter, Daphne Wilma (d1995). During WW1 Henry served as county commandant for volunteer units in Middlesex, and also during WW1 in 1918 he would be one of the executors when, on February 1st, his father died at Myddelton House. For many years the deceased had been Governor of the New River Company and left effects of £373,486. The other executors were Henry's brother Edward Augustus, and his son in law Eustace Parker, with Henry by the terms of the will acquiring all his late father's real estate in Middlesex and Hertfordshire.

Also that year dated May 8th he was made Deputy Lieutenant of the County of Middlesex. At the end of WW1 with the rank of Colonel he retired from military service but maintained his political career, being returned to Parliament in the 1918 General Election, held on December 14th. By Royal Licence in 1920 on August 14th his son in law, Eustace, changed his name to Eustace Parker Bowles, and the 'Royal' association of the name remains to this day!

That month Henry and his wife embarked on a tour of Canada, and after their return to England, in July 1921 he unveiled the roadside war memorial at Woughton. In the next year at the General Election he retired from Parliament, and in July 1926 for political and public services was created baronet 'of Enfield in the County of Middlesex.' In further accolades in 1928 he was appointed Lord High Sheriff of Middlesex. However that year also brought sadness, for on October 10th his daughter Wilma, of Far Croft, Market Drayton, Shropshire, died at the Bedford Hotel, Brighton. At Woughton, as the principal owner of land and property in the parish, and patron of the living, Henry came to open a church fete in 1934 on Saturday, August 4th. The event was held on the rectory lawn, and he used the occasion to announce that due to his absence from the village he could no longer devote the care and attention to his local interests that he wished. Therefore he had decided to hand his property, houses and land to his god daughter and niece Miss G. Wetherall.[28]

In 1935 his wife, Lady Florence, who had been heavily involved in the newly established girl guide movement, died, and in 1936 Henry retired from the Council and also as a JP. However he still maintained an interest in Woughton, and in 1937 on Saturday, May 8th planted a Coronation tree, one of the 28 planted in a field belonging to Wilfred Shirley and recreationally used by the village.

Bowles Place at Woughton

200

Also to the village children he distributed golden replicas of the anointing spoon which, since the time of Edward 1st, had been used to anoint Kings of England. In retirement, at the outbreak of WW2 he was living at Forty Hall with his grandson Derek, who was now a farmer and also a 2nd Lt. in the Royal Horse Guards reserve of officers. Among the domestic staff was a butler and also a chauffeur, Alan Pearman. In 1943 having suffered a stroke the previous day he died on October 14th at Enfield War Memorial Hospital. He was 84 and the baronetcy then became extinct on his death.

Throughout his eventful life he had held office at Enfield and London in at least 30 organisations, including Fellow of the Royal Sciety of Arts, London Zoo, and the Royal Horticultural Society. With effects totalling £237,014 probate was granted to Derek Henry Parker Bowles and his wife Ann, and Daphne Wilma Kenyon Heber Percy and her husband Algernon George William Heber Percy DSO, a lieutenant colonel in the Army. Derek inherited Forty Hall and the family continued to live there until 1951, when the estate was sold to Enfield UDC and the house converted into a local museum. As for Woughton, the family association is recalled in the naming of Bowles Place, built as a new housing estate of Newport Pagnell RDC. Eventually to comprise six houses and five bungalows this was opened in 1965 on March 18th by Sir Henry's grandson (the patron of the living) Mr. Derek Parker Bowles who, being resident at Newbury was a Steward of the Race Course.

FARMING

"The Corporation said it was poor agricultural land, but it wasn't. We used to raise some of the best beef in the county. It was good land." Such was the comment of a local farmer, Mr. Clarke, at the loss of the agricultural acres for the development of Milton Keynes. In further emphasis the Silverton herd of Shorthorn dairy cattle of Mr. Shirley was renowned for its quality, winning many awards at prestigious shows. At the first mention of a new city, from memories of the crisis of food production during WW2 many local farmers were appalled at the idea. A vigorous action group was started, but perhaps many of a cynical inclination, including the then MP, Robert Maxwell, knew, despite a condescending veneer of 'public meetings,' and 'inquiries,' that it would be a foregone conclusion. And so it proved to be. Thus the fields that existed for centuries are now no more, and in this brief timeline are recalled some of the farms and the farming families of that bygone age.

1878

On Friday, October 25th on the premises of Rectory Farm an auction took place of farm stock, grass keeping etc. This was by the direction of John Chapman, who was leaving the farm on Lady day next.

1879

In February, Rectory Farm was advertised to let: 200 acres in nearly equal parts of grass and arable, including river meadow with a house and premises. 'To be let on a lease or yearly tenancy. Apply to Mr. Wigley, Land Agent, Winslow, or at the Rectory.'

1880

On Thursday, October 14th the annual meeting of the National Agricultural Labourers' Union took place. Having been voted to the chair Mr. Haywood, assistant secretary, put the resolution; "That this meeting pledges itself to petition Parliament to abolish the old antiquated Land Laws, and to enfranchise the labourer." For seconding the same he then called upon Mr. Joseph Arch, who gave a speech in favour of the resolution. Preceded by a tea the meeting proved neither very large nor enthusiastic, although the cause was making some progress in the district.

1883

Joseph Arch paid a visit to Woughton on Monday, May 7th. Having been engaged for the occasion, the Wavendon Brass Band arrived in full dress uniform at Walton at 1.30pm, and, via Simpson, reached Woughton at about 2.30. Henry Watson of the Old Swan had provided a sumptuous tea for 'a goodly number,' and in the meantime came the arrival of Joseph Arch. After tea the band paraded the village and then returned to the paddock adjoining the Old Swan where, 'to their continuous lively airs,' dancing was indulged on the greensward. At 7.30pm Joseph Arch came forward, and receiving a hearty welcome mounted the platform and gave an eloquent address on the social state of the labourer. Also the readjustment of the land system, saying that when you look upon the labourer tilling the ground from morning till night you look upon one of England's greatest sons. He spoke in total for two hours, and at the conclusion invited the gathering to join the Union, as "union is strength." Receiving acclamation a vote of thanks was proposed and carried.

1889

On Thursday, October 17th, due to Edward Augustus Lines relinquishing Green Farm at Michaelmas the whole of the livestock was auctioned on the premises by Mr. George Wigley. Also the household furniture and effects; 'The Horses are excellent, and thoroughly sustain Mr. Lines' well deserved reputation. The Implements are numerous, in good condition, and by established makers.'

(Green Farm was opposite Apple Tree Cottage, and as recalled in 1982 by one resident, Miss King; "The farmhouse fell down just like that, one Sunday afternoon. It was a very still day, no wind. The house had been empty about two or three years and then two years later one of the barns fell down in exactly the same way."

1890

In June at a meeting of the village labourers and the Newport Pagnell Rural Sanitary Authority it was stated that Mr. Whitworth was prepared to let an arable field of some 11 acres for allotments. This was provided that proper compensation was paid to Mr. Sharman for tenant right. For this he required about £30, with the cost of measuring out the ground and other expenses estimated at about £7 10s. When the labourers said they couldn't pay it was promised by the Rev. F. Field, the rector, to try and raise the money among the land owners of the parish. He duly met with success, the contributors being Mrs. Levi, £10; W.J. Levi, £10; H.C.B. Bowles, £7 10s; W. Whitworth £5; the Rev. Field £5.

1892

On Wednesday, August 31st, at the meeting of the Newport Pagnell Board of Guardians an undated letter from the Allotment Holders of Woughton was received;

"To the Sanitary Authority, Newport Pagnell. Gentlemen - We

the undersigned, being the Allotment Holders in the parish of Woughton, beg to ask your kind consideration in reference to a barn or some kind of shed wherein to thresh our corn. Last year it was a great loss to us, through the wet; a lot of our corn was spoiled, and it might be so again this year. We beg of you to take this into your kind consideration, and remain your obedient servants."

However at the meeting it was stated that no funds were available for such a purpose, and it was hardly for the Authority to provide such accommodation. Also it was impossible to charge it on the rates. Some guardians considered that local farmers might allow them to use their sheds, but it was remarked that a good feeling did not exist between the farmers and the men. As for the cost, a shed would be about £55 and even a temporary one about £15. The matter would be considered at the next meeting.

1894

In October at the meeting of the Newport Pagnell Board of Guardians Sanitary Authority the situation regarding the Woughton allotments was reported by Mr. J.C. Coales. He said the working had been carried out very satisfactorily. When some three years ago the matter came before the Authority it had been thought the venture wouldn't prove successful, especially as the land had been in a very bad state. However the holders had worked it into a creditable condition, and regarding finance there were no arrears. The rent was fully paid up and a loss had only occurred through one man of about £2.

1905

On Thursday, June 15th at the Swan Hotel, Fenny Stratford, by direction of the trustees of George Horwood an auction was held of Bleak Hall, a grass farm of 80 acres with a farmhouse and homestead. Situated off the Watling Street, and 'approached by a wide lane, or direct into one of the fields off the lane at the entrance,' this was presently let to Thomas Fountain at £48pa; 'It is a Property well worth attention, as it is capable of much improvement, and will be Sold practically Without Reserve.'

1911

By the direction of Mr. E. Dolden, who was leaving the neighbourhood, at Bleak Hall Farm on Monday, September 11th an auction was held of farm animals and implements, two ricks of hay, and a quantity of household furniture.

1921

At Green Farm, occupied by Mr. J.L. Shirley, the well known breeder and judge of Shorthorn dairy cattle, and head of the firm of Shirley and Son, corn merchants, Bletchley, a serious fire broke out between noon and 1pm on Saturday, May 14th. Causing much damage it seemed to have started in the farmyard and then quickly spread to the farm buildings. Bletchley fire brigade were called but before their arrival all the crops, farm implements etc. had been destroyed. However the house was fortunately untouched and the livestock saved. Colonel Bowles was the owner of the property.

In the aftermath of the fire at Green Farm, Mr. J.L. Shirley decided to dispense with his entire herd of cows. This was due to insufficient accommodation to winter them at his Stony Stratford farm, and the sale would be conducted by Messrs. Thornton and Co. at Brick Kiln Farm, Stony Stratford, at 1.30pm on Thursday, September 22nd. 15 of the nearly 60 head had won honours at local shows including 'Darling,' the winner of two firsts in 1920. Also 'Bess,' a 1st prize winner in a pair cow class at the London Dairy Show in October 1921. Also included in the sale were a number of bulls.

1922

At Green Farm a son was born to Mr. and Mrs. Charles Clarkson on July 22nd. Mr. Clarkson was son of Mr. W. Clarkson of W. Clarkson and Sons, Council Contractors, Vauxhall and South Norwood. Mrs. Clarkson was daughter of the late Mr. A.E. Gains of A.E. Gains and Sons.

1925

At Old Wolverton in January the funeral was conducted of the late Mr. Lawrence Jefferey Shirley. The family mourners included Mr. J.L. Shirley and Mr. A. Shirley, sons, and Messrs. Lawrence and Wifred Shirley, Bletchley, grandsons. On the coffin was the inscription 'Lawrence Jefferey, died December 31st, 1924, aged 79 years.' His widow, Mrs. Elizabeth Mary Shirley, had died at St. Olaves, Stony Stratford, on January 6th aged 77. She was the daughter of the late Mr. J. Gough of Maidsmoreton, Buckingham, who for over 40 years had been chairman of the Buckingham Board of Guardians.

In March commenced the beginnings of an allotment and cottage garden horticultural society for the parishes of Woughton, Great and Little Woolstone, Simpson, Walton and Milton Keynes. Saturday, August 22nd had been decided upon to hold a show, with Captain B. Hudson, the President, placing Woughton House at the disposal of the committee, and taking an active part in the preliminary arrangement. Those giving, or having given, financial support included Canon Whittaker, Rev. H.W. Smith, Rev. J.T. Lawson, Rev. G. Hawkes Field, and Captain G. Bowyer MP. £25 was already in hand, with the secretarial duties shared by Mr. J. Hughes and Mr. C. Mansfield, both of Woughton.

In June the old Forge, having been out of use for some time, was taken over for a workshop and yard by Messrs. G. Faulkner & Son, Builders, Decorators and Undertakers. They carried on the largest jobbing business in the Bletchley district, and orders could be left at the Forge at any time.

As 'a holiday not to be missed', in the grounds of Woughton Park, lent by the President, Captain B. Hudson, of Woughton House, the first annual show of the Woughton and District Horticultural Society was held on Saturday, August 22nd. Mr. J. Hughes, landlord of the village pub, was the honorary secretary of the Society, and being landlord of the village pub he had applied at Bletchley Petty Sessions for an extension of one hour. Normally the pub closed at 10pm and the application was granted since the Cross Keys and the Barge at Woolstones both opened until 10.30pm. With admission 1s for adults and 6d for children (after 5.30pm half price), the Show was opened at 11am by Col. H.F. Bowles, of Forty Hall, Enfield, and with about 350 entries the occasion included classes for flowers, fruit, vegetables and honey. Prizes were also offered for the best cultivated allotments or cottage gardens, and 'You must see the Grand Display of Roses by Messrs. Ramsbottom and Co.' Amongst the many attractions were various sports, and with a £7 prize a mixed doubles lawn tennis tournament. Luncheons and teas were available, with the Newport Pagnell Prize Band obliging for dancing on the lawn.

1926

By direction of the administrator of the late Mrs. Warr, an auction was held at Old Rectory Farm on Tuesday, September 21st of farming stock, implements etc.

1930

In June a fine of 5s was imposed on Charles Clarkson of Green Farm for having allowed four cattle to stray at Great Woolstone.

In June a Dairy Shorthorn bull bred by Mr. J.L. Shirley of, Silverton, Woughton, was awarded the championship of the Dairy Shorthorn section, and judged to be the best dairy bull, in the Show at South Africa, Queenstown. Exported by Messrs. John Thornton and Co., the bull was exhibited by Mr. T.C. Goosen of Haslop Manor, Waverley, Cape Province, for whom it had been selected at Mr. Shirley's sale at Woughton in 1928 on November 8th.

1932

At his residence of Silverton, Woughton, at around 8pm on Thursday, April 28th the death occurred of John Lawrence Shirley. Ten days previous to his death he caught a severe chill and succumbed to pneumonia. For the past 2 years and 4 months he had received special treatment for a serious illness at a nursing home in Ringwood, Hants. Having made a good recovery he had returned home a few months ago and, in a limited way, resumed management of the farm and took an active interest in the cattle feeding cake business at Bletchley. For many years his chief study had been milk production, and well known as a breeder and exhibitor of Shorthorn dairy cattle several of his specimens were exported to America, South Africa, Cyprus and the Falkland Islands. His Silverton herd had secured over 90 awards at the London Dairy Show, and in 1922 the five animals exhibited won five 1st prizes, two seconds and a third. For a long while he had been the Dairy Farmers' Association representative on the World's Dairy Congress, and in other capacities had been a member of the Council of the Shorthorn Society, a member of the Milk Publicity Council, and represented the Dairy Farmers' Association on the governing body of University College, Reading. For a few years he was a member of the Government Advisory Committee on the milk question, and during WW2 was appointed as chairman of the North London Area Feeding Stuffs Committee. Also he had served on the

London Counties' Area Milk Committee, was a past president of the Bletchley branch of the NFU, which he helped to form, and had served as president of the Bletchley Fat Stock and the Bletchley Market Committees. At all the important shows he was well known as a judge; at the Royal three times, and also at the Royal Counties, the Bath and West, and the Royal Lancashire. He twice judged in Ireland, but due to his official position on the society always refused invitations to judge at the London Dairy Show. His death bereaved a widow, two sons and a daughter

On Wednesday, September 14th by order of the executors of the late Mr. J.L. Shirley an auction was held at Silverton, Woughton, of the whole of the live and dead farming stock. Also the agricultural machinery and implements, the sale of which opened the proceedings at 11am. The farm stock was comprised of the famous herd of dairy shorthorns - of about 96 head of pedigree and non pedigree dairy cows and heifers, maiden heifers and bulls - 7 cart horses, 474 sheep and lambs, and 170 pigs. Lunch was provided at tickets of 2s 6d each, returnable to purchasers of £5 upwards.

On September 28th a new private company was registered of 'J.L. Shirley and Son, Ltd.'. With capital of £5,000 in £1 shares the stated objects were 'To adopt an agreement with L.E. Shirley, J.W. Shirley, Ellen M. Shirley, Ethel J. Shirley, and G.F. Shirley, to develop and turn to account the business of a cattle food specialist and cattle and meal merchant comprised therein, and to carry on the business of manufacturers of and dealers in feeding and fattening preparations, artificial manures and fertilisers, seed crushers, oil extractors, corn, grain, flour and oil merchants, millers, bakers, chemists and soap boilers, etc.' The directors were L.E. Shirley, Silverton, Woughton, Bletchley, and J.W. Shirley, Silverton, Woughton, Bletchley, cattle food specialists; 'Qualification: £200. Remuneration: as fixed by the company.'

On November 24th John Wilfred Shirley was elected as chairman of the Bletchley Branch of the NFU. Son of the late Mr. J.L. Shirley, he had been a member for about five years and a farmer for ten years. He and his brother, Mr. L.E. Shirley, were directors in the business of 'J.L. Shirley and Son Ltd .cattle food specialists,' which had been built up by their father.

1935

At St. Andrew's Church, Enfield, on Tuesday, October 1st the marriage took place of John Wilfred Shirley, of Woughton, and Miss Gladys Constance Wetherall, of London. She was the only daughter of the late Ernest Wetherall and Mrs. Festing of Bulls Cross, Waltham Cross, London, and being choral the service was conducted by her uncle the Rev. Granville Cooper, and the Rev. J.W. Daisley. Her cousin, Miss Daphne Parker Bowles, was bridesmaid, and Gerald Shirley, the groom's brother, best man. The bride was given away by Col. Sir Henry Bowles, who together with his wife hosted a reception at Forty Hall. The honeymoon would be spent motor touring in Scotland.

1936

The funeral took place at Woughton on Friday, February 28th of Tom King, of Rectory Farm. He came to Woughton 22 years ago and married the eldest daughter of the late Mr. and Mrs. Warr, who at that time were the tenants of the farm. A member of the Bletchley branch of the NFU, he carried on the farm following the death of Mrs. Warr. The funeral was conducted by the Rev. Lean, with the floral tributes to include those from his widow and children.

1941

Pear Tree Farm, of J.W. Shirley, was designated in January as one of the centres arranged by Bucks War Agricultural Committee for the demonstration of grasslands improvement by surface treatment.

1945

On Thursday, July 19th an auction was conducted of the freehold Rectory Farm by Wigley and Johnson at the Conservative Club, Bletchley, at 3.30pm. Forming part of the glebe lands of the Rectory and church, and with an extent of about 188 acres, this, with the approval and consent of the Ecclesiastical Commissioners, was on the instructions of the rector, the Rev. C.A.M. Roberts. Formerly the Rectory, the brick built farmhouse included an entrance hall, dining, drawing and morning rooms, kitchen, scullery, larder, five bedrooms and a bathroom. The interest also comprised a large garden and orchard with a range of buildings adjoining the drive. Also a cottage near to the farm buildings, having a sitting room, kitchen, scullery and two bedrooms. The purchaser was Mr. F. Clarkson, of Great Woolstone, for £4,100.

1948

In January all persons having claims against the estate of John Clarkson, deceased, late of Green Farm, were asked to send in particulars.

1954

By direction of the executors of the late Mr. C. Rothery, an auction at Bleak Hall Farm of the agricultural implements was held on Thursday, April 22nd.

1959

On the night of Sunday, August 16th at the Seven Gables Nursing Home, Adstock, the death occurred of Mrs. Louisa Constance Festing, aged 88. Two months ago she had fallen down and broken her hip in the dining room of her home, North Cottage, at Woughton. She was taken first to Royal Bucks Hospital, and for the last two weeks had been at Seven Gables. In her younger days she had been a competent chess player, and entered many London championships. She was aunt to General Sir Francis Festing, the present CIGS, and had lived in North Bucks for the last 21 years. Her death bereaved an only child, Mrs. Wilfred Shirley, of Peartree Farm, Woughton. The funeral took place at Brookwood, Surrey.

1965

In January it was reported that an estate of nearly 400 acres at Woughton had been bought by Mr. J.W. Shirley of Pear Tree Farm, Woughton. As tenant he had farmed nearly all the estate, and included in the sale was Pear Tree Farmhouse and buildings, Frenches Farmhouse, Bridge House and nine cottages.

1971

Milton Keynes Development Corporation having bought the property, on Friday, December 3rd Mr. and Mrs. Shirley and their daughter, Diana, who was born at Woughton, moved from Pear Tree Farm to live at Newton Blossomville. A memorable occasion, but for Diana also memorable was her recent experience of being on a hijacked plane! On behalf of her firm, Rankin and Kuhu, who were large Caribbean tour operators, she was travelling between Port of Spain, Trinidad, with a companion when some 12 minutes after take off a hijacker demanded to be taken to Cuba. When told by the captain there wasn't sufficient fuel he instead settled for Canada, and recalling the episode Diana said; "While we were wondering what was going to happen we realised that the plane had turned round and was heading back to Port of Spain. The captain had agreed to the hijacker's demands, but the stewardess was made to take off her clothes to stop her escaping! On arrival back at Port of Spain the hijacker was inveigled off the plane and taken away by the police. The whole operation took about four hours, and it was extremely frightening as we didn't know what the hijacker would do next. ... He had a kitchen knife at the stewardess's throat all the time. But I was terrified that he might also have a bomb planted in the aircraft."

In January 1977 Woughton residents wanted to know why they still had no allotments, despite having been allocated a field. Months of discussion between Milton Keynes Borough Council and Milton Keynes Development Corporation had yet to produce a hand over date. Called 'The Patch,' the area of land offered by MKDC was on a lease to the council. However since a meeting in August nothing had been resolved, with the Woughton Allotment Association blaming the unwillingness of the council to finance the project. Rachel Hogg of the association said, "The council are the black sheep in this matter. The financial responsibility is theirs and the corporation are trying to persuade them to supply the money." Some people in the Woughton area had been on the waiting list for three years, and currently the demand stood at 200. Originally the association had 111 members but after 18 months of waiting this had shrunk to about 25. Estimating The Patch could be divided into 400 plots, a resident of Tinkers Bridge, 68 year old Frederick Brady, said that many were pensioners wanting an allotment for gardening and as a supplement to their pensions. A spokesman for the council said "Discussions are continuing."

Woughton War Memorials.

WARTIME

A WARTIME MANHUNT

Since the end of May 1941 Buckinghamshire police had been looking for a suspicious man who seemed to be impersonating an army officer. Civilians he had spoken to said he was about 5ft 8in tall with a dark complexion, dark hair, going bald on top, and moustache. Then on June 2nd a man answering this description was seen at Weedon, Northants., dressed in officer's battledress with a peaked cap, but without shoulder pips or gaiters. He was not wearing the arm colour-patches of any identifiable unit and disappeared again before he could be apprehended. Then on the evening of Saturday, June 14th police constable Snarey when motorcycling between Newport Pagnell and Bletchley saw a man wearing the uniform of a Scottish regiment hiding in a ditch. The constable stopped and dismounted to speak to him but the man opened fire. PC Snarey returned the shot and despite a bullet narrowly missing his ear chased the man through hedges and across fields. However the fugitive escaped by wading through the River Ouzel and vanishing in the long grass on the other side. PC Snarey got a message through to War Reserve Constable W. Shouler of Woughton who immediately phoned Bletchley Police headquarters. A widespread search began and the following day carrying a light raincoat and a haversack the uniformed 'officer' was reportedly seen twice, first near Little Woolstone and then at Ravenstone, some 10 miles from Newport Pagnell. The hunt for the suspect had been going on for over a fortnight and was now extended to cover a hundred square miles in the counties of Bucks and parts of Oxfordshire, Berkshire, Hertfordshire and Surrey. Armed police, Home Guards, and military units were all deployed, and all towns, villages and hamlets in the area were closely watched. Roads, lanes and country footpaths and field gates were guarded, and military lorries armed with machine guns patrolled along with police cars. Vehicles on the Great North Road and other important routes were stopped on Sunday with drivers and passengers having to produce their identity cards. They were questioned as to whether they had given any one a lift, and were warned not to do so.

During the heightened alert a girl passenger in a car was wounded, when a member of the Home Guard fired when the vehicle failed to stop. She was Miss Jane Strittles aged 20, the eldest daughter of Mr. and Mrs. G. Sprittles of, 4 West View, New Bradwell. Soon after midnight she and Miss Daphne Eldred of Spencer Street, New Bradwell, were returning from a dance at St. Martin's Hall, Bletchley, in the rear of a car driven by Reg Jackson of 16, Wood Street, New Bradwell. Having been stopped twice to show their identity cards, on passing through Loughton the driver failed to notice another instruction to stop and the Home Guard fired, with the bullet striking Miss Strittles just below the shoulder blade. She passed into a dead faint and with the car pulled up on the verge the occupants got her onto the side and bandaged the wound as best they could. She was then driven to Stony Stratford where after attention by Dr. Douglas Bull she was conveyed by the Wolverton Works ambulance to Northampton Hospital.

Regarding those who served in the First World War much information is variously available on the internet, primarily 'Lives of the First World War,' and 'Roll of Honour.'

In the book 'Village Memories' by Ouida Rice are included the following recollections from those who experienced life in Woughton during WW2.

Mr. Garratt

"The General at Woughton House he was so keen on the Home Guard and so was his brother, Mr. Oswold. The General used to drill us in Woughton Park near the cricket pavilion. We used to practice attacking Milton Keynes, we used to climb the church tower and then Mr. Oswald used to order breakfast for us at the Swan and we used to have fried eggs. I remember one night we had been up to the railway, up the old lane and just as we got back there were German bombers around and all at once they let a bomb drop and it came down the other side of Cranfield, it shook the place and it lit everything up. There weren't any bombs in Woughton, but they were very near. One dropped in an allotment field near Great Linford. It made a thirty foot crater, but no one was hurt."

Mrs. Sinfield

"At school we used to knit for the troops, even the youngest children had to knit. There would be khaki wool for the soldiers, dark blue wool for the sailors and airforce blue for the airforce. The children would knit gloves, mittens, even pullovers."

Mrs. Sinfield

"One of the derelict cottages near Appletree Cottage was used as a cookhouse. There was a ginger haired cook down there who used to cook for the troops."

Mrs. Sinfield, regarding the evacuees.

"They didn't like the village life. ... They were queer to us, really queer. They spoke queer and their ways were queer. They went back to London as quick as they could."

ROADS & RESIDENTIAL

1877

Tenders were invited for the erection of cottages at Woughton in August. These would be received by the rector and churchwardens, from whom particulars could be obtained on personal application.

On Wednesday, November 7th at Newport Pagnell Petty Sessions a charge was brought against Mr. J.E. Whiting, of Castlethorpe, of having used a steam engine on the highway which did not consume its own smoke. The offence had occurred at Newport Pagnell on October 16th, with it being stated that sparks had started a fire at Woughton. The case was adjourned pending scientific evidence regarding the construction of the engine.

1880

On Thursday, August 12th at the Swan Hotel, Fenny Stratford, an auction was conducted by Mr. Wigley of several lots of property situate at Fenny Stratford, Bletchley and Woughton. Of the Woughton property Lot 1, comprising two cottages and a dwelling house, plus about an acre of land, went to Mr. Powell for £240 on behalf of Major Levi.

On September 27th, at the meeting of the Sanitary Authority of the Newport Pagnell Board of Guardians, it was reported by Mr. Branson that 'great complaints' had been received about the scarcity of water at Woughton, which had long been regarded as 'bad.' On examining the pump, which stood on property belonging to Mr. Bowles, who owned a number of cottages in the parish, he found it to be out of repair, and Mr. Bowles would be written to regarding the matter. In consequence a letter would be received from Mr. Bowles stating that his property in the village had caused him great expense. However he had now obtained an estimate for the pump repair. It was decided to communicate with the property owners in Woughton reminding them that since the village had no water supply a public supply was much needed.

On Wednesday, October 25th at the meeting of the Sanitary Authority of the Newport Pagnell Board of Guardians a letter was read from Mr. W. Whitworth. He was a property owner in the village and stated in his communication that he would assent to any plan by the Authority of obtaining a water supply. Mr. Levi attended the meeting and said there were only two resident landowners - himself and Mr. Field. The non resident owners were equally concerned in the question, although unless compelled certain landowners would not think of paying anything. For this reason, and because the canal and the railway ran through the village, the matter would be better met by a rate. Therefore he thought they should call a meeting and gauge the feeling of the parish about it, if the Authority agreed. The most favourable and economic means would be to have the mains extended from Simpson. The well belonged to the Authority, so it didn't matter if Fenny Stratford raised any objections!

In the village schoolroom on Friday, November 3rd a well attended meeting of ratepayers was held to consider the scarcity of good water, and also the best means to remedy the situation. The gathering had been called by the rector, the churchwardens and overseers, and to provide information Mr. Branson, surveyor to the Newport Pagnell authority, attended with his son. The rector, the Reverend Field, presided, and after explaining the need for something to be done Mr. W.J. Levi gave an account of his visit to the Board of Guardians. He said that whilst the Sanitary Authority had the power to provide a parish water supply they thought it only courteous that the matter should be discussed by the Woughton residents first. Hence the meeting. Mr. Branson then explained the proposal to extend the Fenny Stratford scheme as far as Woughton, the work necessary and the cost, and it was duly resolved:

(1) That the Rural Sanitary Authority be respectfully requested by this meeting to use their powers for supplying the parish with water by continuing the pipes from Simpson, so that the parish might be supplied from the new reservoirs at Great Brickhill. This was carried unanimously.

(2) That the cost be paid by a loan on security of the rates repayable (with interest) in 30 years.

(3) That the labourers of the parish be employed, and that the Local Government Board be urged to use all expedition in arranging the preliminaries, for the sake of men out of work, who otherwise would have a hard winter before them.

(4) That the chairman forward these resolutions to the Sanitary Authority.

A vote of thanks to the chairman and Mr. Branson ended the meeting.

On November 8th at a meeting of the Newport Pagnell Rural Sanitary Authority it was decided to grant the petition of the ratepayers, with the clerk instructed to communicate immediately with the Local Government Board.

1894

By February much progress had been made in providing Woughton with a water supply. For several weeks 12 otherwise unemployed local men had been digging the trenches and laying the pipes from the mains at Simpson. In March a temporary pipe was erected opposite the Swan where water could be drunk, and by May all the houses in the village except one had availed themselves of having the supply laid on.

1905

On Tuesday, June 13th at a meeting of Fenny Stratford Urban Council the surveyor reported that the meter at Woughton showed a consumption of about 5 gallons of water per head of population. The clerk, Mr. Best, explained that by a payment agreement entered into by the Rural Council and the Urban Council the parishes of Walton and Woughton were entitled to a daily supply of 3,288 gallons.

1911

On September 2nd two of Woughton's oldest residents, Mr. and Mrs. John Pursell, celebrated their diamond wedding. John was 82 and his wife 3 years younger. They had married in the parish church, and except for 3 years at Woolstone had lived in the village all their lives. They remembered times when water had to be collected from the ditches. For the past 24 years their home had been a small cottage on the main road. A son, aged 40, was now a Metropolitan police officer. For over 20 years Mr. Pursell had worked for the Levi family and remembered the previous owner, Mr. Head, and also the disastrous fire there.

1913

In September a comment on the road conditions; "If you drive along the Simpson road after a storm you get a shower bath every few yards!"

1924

In March, since so many of their young people wanted to get married the villagers petitioned the District Council to build some cottages for them to live in.

1927

In March applications for the construction of four cottages at Woughton, put in by the parish council, were referred to the local authority's Housing Committee.

1937

On Tuesday, April 20th at the council offices in Newport Pagnell an inquiry was conducted for the Ministry of Health by Mr. F. Seabrooke, HM Inspector. This regarded an application by the council for consent to borrow £8,850, namely for a water supply for the villages of Woughton, Willen, Emberton, Sherington, Weston Underwood, and Ravenstone. The chairman, Col. J.P. Wyness, said two enquiries had already been held, at the second of which the council applied to borrow £60,919 for their comprehensive water supply scheme. This supplementary estimate of £8,850 was to provide an extension to Woughton, now under the management of Bletchley Urban Council. Since it was at the end of the latter's system the water pressure was poor and the mains needed renewing. If the supply was instead taken from Bow Brickhill the pressure would be excellent and the quality improved. Afterwards the Inspector made a tour of the villages.

1946

In August, of the tenders received to build 8 council houses at Woughton that of Messrs. T.H. Bird and Son, of Old Bradwell, was the lowest at £8,664 5s 6d. When submitted to the meeting of Newport Pagnell Rural District Council this was accepted.

1948

By May the building of the council houses at Woughton was nearly complete, and was marked on Rogation Day by a special open air church service. It had been a custom at Woughton for some years to hold the second part of the evening service in the open, and so after Evensong the congregation, reciting the Litany, walked in procession from the church to the open space in front of the houses. There special prayers were offered asking for God's blessing first on the fields, allotments, gardens and orchards, and on the new houses, their occupants, and on those involved in the construction. Due to the unfavourable weather the concluding part of the service was held in the front room of one of the houses by kind permission of the builder, Mr. Bird. Visitors welcomed at the ceremony were Col. J. Williams, chairman of Newport Pagnell RDC Housing Committee, and the Rev. C.A. Wheeler, Rural Dean of Bletchley.

1954

For many years Miss Annie Jane Saunders had been housekeeper in the village for George Alfred Bidwell. Then with George aged 87 the couple were married on Wednesday, May 26th, and on their return from honeymoon were heartily welcomed by friends and neighbours. Prior to his retirement Mr. Bidwell had been employed for some 50 years by the Clarkson family, both at Vauxhall, where the Clarkson's had a road haulage business, and at the Woolstone farm.

1960

Newport Pagnell RDC decide to build 4 houses and 2 bungalows at Woughton.

1965

On Thursday, March 18th the first stage of Bowles Place was opened, built in conjunction with the village sewerage scheme. Eventually the estate would comprise six houses and five bungalows, with the layout to include the bungalows being built around a small square such as, since most of the tenants would be retired, to provide a quiet and sheltered environment. The new estate would include a car park and eight garages. At the opening six houses and one bungalow had been completed, with one of each open for inspection. The weekly rent for a bungalow was 21s 4d, and the houses, having two bedrooms, 27s a week. The first tenants of the new development were Mr. and Mrs. Cecil Willett who, having previously lived at Shenley, moved into No. 6, Bowles Place. As for their impressions, 84 year old Mrs. Willett said "It's very nice indeed here, but it seems a lot quieter than Shenley."

1975

In the first week of March, Milton Keynes Borough Council were recommended to make a £2,000 grant towards improving the village hall. Despite being very dilapidated the venue was still very much the centre of community life, being used by the Brownies, and the parish and parochial church councils. Also for a whist drive, and it was likely that the Women's Insitute and a new Guide Company might also want to use the facility. However there was a possibility that a new centre might be built in the area due to the new city, and Councillor Cecil Bowden (Labour, Bletchley) said the spending of £4,000 on the project might be abortive; "If you give a specific grant to one village I am worried about the outcry from the other 47." However in making the plea at the council's recreation committee meeting Councillor Tom Young (Conservative, Woughton) said "If you haven't got a village hall your village is dead. A village hall, be it very simple, is an absolute must." The members decided to recommend the council's finance committee to make a £2,000 grant for improvements. A grant of £500 from the former Newport Rural

Council had already been pledged.

The arrival of the new city has caused much new residential development, and also a re-organising of the local administration;
"Woughton Community Council was Woughton on the Green Parish Council but following a local government boundary review the area along with Passmore was removed to form a new Council called Old Woughton Parish Council "which causes much confusion.""

SHOPS AND THE POST OFFICE

THE VILLAGE POST OFFICE

By 1907 a sub post office had been opened in the village by Mrs. Anne Gazeley. There were two collections, one at 11.25am and one at 5.50pm, cleared by the churchyard wall letter box. By local memory it was accommodated in one of the cottages on the road to the Woolstones, later called Fairview, and expanding into a village shop moved to Cairn Cottage, near the Swan. Here it was run by Mrs. Sibley and had the only telephone in the village. However in 1966 in January it was announced that the post office and village stores would

Cairn Cottage and Post Box

close on the 31st of that month. Whilst it was the official office for Great Woolstone and Little Woolstone most residents preferred to go to Bletchley, which was proving too much competition for the owners of the stores Mr. and Mrs. Robbie Pyke, who had worked the post office side for the past three years. The GPO had advertised in the three villages for several months but nobody had come forward and the head postmaster, Mr. A.C. McBurnie, said, "At the moment the office is open for only half of each day and has not been doing very much business. As no one has come forward to take it on, I'm afraid the residents will have to go to Simpson, about one mile away, or into Bletchley."

CLARA & THE CLINCH'S

In 1899 it seems there was only one shopkeeper in the village - a Miss Clara Clinch. Who was she, and what was her family story? So rather than just confine a brief mention to history this section details her family story, and how several members would come to have an association with Woughton.

At Ducklington, Oxfordshire, on November 1st in 1831 James Hosier, a labourer, born at Aston, Oxon., married Mary Jones. She was resident in the parish of Hardwick, and in 1841 they were living in North Street, Aston, with (ages as per census) their children William, 9, Hannah, 6, and Ann, 3. Also recorded is John Hosier, aged 80. In fact Hannah (Hannah Maria, sometimes written as Anna, as per her baptism entry) was baptised at Bampton in 1835 on January 25th. As for Ann, she was born at Aston, baptised in 1838 on July 15th. In 1851 the family were resident in the hamlet of Aston & Cote, Bampton, and in 1854 at the parish church of Bampton on November 20th Ann, being stated as a 'minor,' from being aged 16, married a widowed innkeeper, Thomas Clinch. Born in 1827 he was a native of Aston where a daughter, Clara Selina Clinch, was born to the couple, baptised on March 3rd 1856. That year on December 25th the marriage took place at Shefford of Ann's sister, Hannah, and George Daniels. Born at Buckland, Berks., he was the son of a blacksmith, and present at the ceremony were Hannah's parents,

Thomas and Ann Clinch. George was an agricultural labourer although by 1861 he had become a police constable, resident at Bull Hill, Chadlington, with his wife Hannah Maria and 5 year old niece Clara Selina Clinch. Meanwhile, with Thomas noted in 1857 as an innkeeper, Clara's parents were keeping a grocery shop at Aston. Also resident was their daughter, Louisa, baptised in the 'chapel' of Aston in 1857 on July 5th, and, his father now in occupation as a baker, their son James William, baptised at Aston in 1859 on August 28th.

In 1871 George and Hannah were living at Great Marlow. George was continuing as a police constable, Hannah was now a dressmaker, and their children were Georgina Maria, born at Chadlington in 1864 on December 15th; of the same age Emma Elizabeth, born at Chadlington; and Mary Ann, 3, born at High Wycombe. Also Louisa Hannah (Harriett), born at Great Marlow but baptised at Aston in 1871 on April 16th. His wife having died in 1862, Clara's father, Thomas, was now living at Toll House, Headington, as a toll collector with his daughter Louisa, who was also a toll collector, and son James William.

As for Clara Selina Clinch, in 1881 together with her cousin Georgina she was working in the household at Walton Street, Aylesbury, of a retired farmer, John Fowler - Clara as a cook, and Georgina as a servant. Meanwhile in 1881 Georgina's parents were now at Ellesborough, Butlers Cross, with their children Louisa Hannah (Harriett), Mary Ann, and now daughter Annie Clara, age 4, born at Denton. Also resident was Mary Daniels aged 27, the unmarried sister of George. As for Thomas Clinch, in 1881 he was now at Aston & Cote as an agricultural labourer, as was his unmarried daughter Louisa. Also resident was his grandson George, age 5, born at Sutton, Berks.

Perhaps on retirement from the police it seems that George and Hannah came to live at Woughton, where Hannah died in 1886 and George in 1887 on January 19th. Their fourth daughter, Louisa Hannah (Harriett), remained at Woughton, and in 1891 was an assistant teacher living with her cousin Clara Selina Clinch, who was now a grocer in the village.

As for Louisa's sisters, Georgina and Emma, they were living in Brooksbank Street, Elland, working in the woollen industry. In 1894 on July 10th James William Clinch, Clara's brother, of St. Peter's parish Brighton, married Nellie Tulitt, born in 1870 on September 21st at Redhill, Surrey. She was 'temporary resident in Woughton parish,' whilst at least in 1891 James was lodging at Brighton as a milk carrier. Clara was still a shopkeeper at Woughton but in 1899 at St. Mary's Church, Woughton, on June 6th Louisa Hannah married George Alliban. Born in 1858 at Depwade, Norfolk, to Thomas Alliban and his wife Elizabeth (nee Rix), he had been a farmer in Canada, but when now settled at Woughton he became a road worker. In 1900 a daughter, Dorothy May, was born on May and in 1901 the family were lodging in Chapel Lane, Woughton, with a member, or members, of the Clinch family.

However Clara, in occupation on her own account as a grocer, was living with her 4 year old nephew Cecil Thomas Clinch. He was the son of James and Nellie and although born at Brighton had been baptised in 1897 at Woughton. In fact the family were now living in the village, 'on the Green,' with James working as a gardener, resident with his wife Nellie and their children Archibald Arthur, age 5, born at Brighton, Walter age 9 months, born at Brighton, and Doris Lilian, born at Brighton in 1898 on July 7th. (She died at Northampton in 1916.) Tragically it seems James became afflicted with issues of mental health and having been admitted to an asylum at Aylesbury died in 1902 on April 10th. Then in 1907 as his third wife Frederick Eaton aged 52, born at Simpson, a wood sawyer, married James' widow, Nellie. Thus in 1911 at Woughton the family comprised Nellie and Frederick with Frederick's son Herbert John Eaton, aged 13, an agricultural labourer, two of Frederick's step children, and, as an addition of his latest marriage, Irene Eaton, age 2, born at Woughton in 1908 on April 25th. (She died in 1964).

Elsewhere with all being employed in the woollen industry Georgina Maria Daniels and her sister Emma Elizabeth Daniels were living at 16, Brooksbank Street, Elland, Yorkshire, with Cecil Thomas Clinch, their 14 year old cousin. By 1911 Louisa, George and Dorothy May (d1972) had moved to 13, Turnpike Street, Elland, Yorks. George was employed as a coal porter with a gas company, and it was that year that with her occupation now as a 'cook domestic' Clara went to visit them. George Alliban died aged 67 and by 1929

Clara was living in Brooksbank Street, Elland, being resident there in 1930 with Cecil Thomas Clinch. She died in 1932 and was buried on March 23rd. Louisa, the widow of George Alliban, died in 1938 on December 23rd. Probate was granted to her daughter, Dorothy, who in 1939 employed as a printer's shorthand typist was resident at 13, Turnpike Street, Elland, with her aunt Georgina Maria Daniels, 'incapacitated.' It seems her cousin, Cecil Thomas Clinch, had inherited the afflictions of his late father, James, for as a 'woollen feeder' he was now accommodated at Storthes Hall Mental Hospital at Kirkburton, Yorks. (He died in 1954.) As for Nellie, the widow of Frederick Eaton, who had died at Woughton in 1927, she was resident at Wembley, and died at Hendon in 1944.

RANDOM REMINISCE

"Out of the window of Apple Tree Cottage an old lady used to sell lace and bobbins and pins, little toffee apples and bags of sherbert."

"Mr. Stevens, the baker in Simpson, used to deliver bread every day. If he didn't have enough change on his van and owed us even a farthing, he never forgot and always brought us the change the next day. We had a horse and cart that used to take milk into Bletchley so we could always get a lift into Fenny. Otherwise people walked or went on bicycles and of course we never locked our doors."

ENDNOTES

1 The story of the club is told in the North Bucks Times edition of February 3rd 1971.

2 The life stories of Frederick's several children is not within the realm of this book. However, Mr. Michael Day, a direct descendant of Frederick, has investigated much of the detail which, by private contact, is available on the Ancestry website.

3 Suggested further reading: 'A Lady's Escape from Gwalior, & Life in the Fort of Agra During the Mutiny of 1857,' written by R.M. Coopland and published in 1859.

Another Simpson connection was Mrs. Helen Wynter, the mother of a rector of Simpson. She was the daughter of Lieutenant General Thomas Wynter, a veteran of the Indian Mutiny, and was born at Agra.

4 Stephen was ordained deacon in 1879 and priest in 1880. He was curate of Beckingham, Lincs., from 1879-81, vicar of Temple Brier, Grantham, Lincs, 1881-83, warden of St. Anne's, Bede Houses, Lincoln, 1883-84, vicar of New Basford, Notts, 1884-88, and vicar of Dunston, Lincs., from 1888-1907.

5 The Mission Room had been built in Bletchley Road, Bletchley, in 1886 by the Rev. Alfred Barrow. Able to accommodate 200 it replaced a small parish hall at the rear of the Vicarage at Fenny Stratford, included as part of an extension in 1884.

6 Of 27, South Drive, Ruislip, Middx., Edward died in April 1967, having been vicar of All Hallows London Wall and Assistant Secretary for the Care of Churches since 1961. Educated at Reading School, where he was captain and an athlete, he went to Reading University and after training at Bishops College, Cheshunt, was ordained deacon in 1938 and priest in 1939. He spent his first 15 years in the diocese of Blackburn, being sacrist at Blackburn Cathedral for 2 years. Afterwards for 8 years he became vicar of Walton le Dale, then moving to London on appointment as rector of Hedgerley, near Slough. In literary realms he wrote The Anglicanism of William Laud. Probate was granted to his widow.

7 Details of the chapel at Simpson, including the closure and the sale of the building, are held in the Bucks Archives ref. AR 84/2003.

An obituary of the chapel founder, Thomas Matthews, is contained in the North Bucks Times issue of April 30th 1898.

The story of Methodism, and the chapel's construction by a builder from Bow Brickhill, is contained in the North Bucks Flying Post issue of November 21st 1890.

8 Robert Stevens was born at Great Brickhill in 1828 and after attending the village school was apprenticed in Fenny Stratford in 1844. In 1848 he went to live with a Mr. Tompkins at Heath and Reach, and there began his lifelong involvement with the Wesleyan faith, commencing to preach in Bletchley in 1852. Having lived in Fenny Stratford High Street for several years he left in 1869 to live at Bow Brickhill, until moving in 1876 to Simpson. There he had purchased the Old Bakehouse in 1873 and not only continued the bakery but also divided the house into two parts. In public life he was elected overseer and would be a member of the Woughton and Simpson School Board for 21 years. He died in 1903 and

a memorial service was held at the Wesleyan Chapel, Fenny Stratford on Sunday, November 29th.

9 The inscribed timepiece and the locket were supplied by Mr. Durran of Fenny Stratford.

10 World War One

These extracts from the school log books were researched by Kit and Dorothy Welchman for their publication *One Pair of Cuffs and a Stocking and a Half,* with proceeds for the Simpson County Combined School Fund.

1914

December 22nd

"I, John Cullom, terminated my engagement as headmaster of this school."

1915

March 18th

"Re cheap food campaign week. Mrs. Badger has consented to give demonstrations therein the school house."

March 26th

"The cheap food cookery demonstrations appear to have been quite a success."

June 1st

"Hoisted the flag in memory of the Glorious first of June and gave a brief description of Admiral Lord Howe's great naval victory."

June 3rd

"Hoisted the flag for the King's birthday."

June 22nd

"Today being the anniversary of King George V's coronation the Union Jack was hoisted."

July 1st

"I gave a lesson on thrift and the new war loan this afternoon."

August 9th

"Received today 2 framed photographs of H.M. King Edward VII and H.M. King George V and a new map of the world showing the British Empire."

1916

May 25th

"… received set of various leaflets and covering letter. A lesson was given on War Savings and the leaflets distributed as requested."

August

Re. wartime cookery demonstrations: "11 girls and 9 boys have taken part. They have all been keenly interested and I think the after result will be beneficial. Portions of the cooked food were sent into every household represented by the school."

1917

Empire Day

"Empire day was observed by hoisting and saluting the Union Jack and a 'lecturette' on the privileges, advantages and duties of membership of the British Empire, from the master."

July 2nd

"It has been decided to form a Woughton and Simpson School Savings Association to be affiliated to the Bletchley Local Central Committee. This association is to be open to all residents of the two villages, as well as the scholars of the school.

September 24th

"The school closed this afternoon for blackberry picking in accordance with instructions."

November 2nd

"Altogether 724lbs of blackberries have been gathered and sent away in accordance with instructions, and about 12cwt of chestnuts."

November 28th

"… the senior scholars were taken to the picture palace for a 'lantern lecture' entitled 'War on Land' arranged by the local War Savings Committee."

December 31st

"… the war savings association now numbers 81 members who have since last August purchased 100 savings certificates at a cost of £77 10s 0d."

1918

November 5th

"25 present this morning, 26 in the afternoon. I have not yet had any medical notification of influenza but 14 or 15 children are said to have it." "2.50pm - I have just received a telegram from the education secretary as follows: 'Close school until 18th. Instruct Miss Mould supply Wavendon forthwith."

After the war in 1920 on July 16th is recorded a trip to Southend on Sea. "In addition to the ordinary attractions most of the children sailed round the two big German liners 'Konigen Louise' and 'Friedland' recently surrendered to the British Govt. and now anchored midway between Southend and Sheerness. The children were orderly and well behaved throughout the trip and undoubtedly derived great educational benefit from it."

11 Born at Simpson in 1879 on December 21st, Eneas Percy Bottomley Bates was baptised in 1880 on May 16th. He attended Hull Grammar School, and in July 1896 was successful in the First Division of the London University Matriculation Examination results. He gained a BA (Hons) and then an MA. His teacher training was at St. John's Training College, Battersea, SW., and from 1900-1902 he was Assistant Master at 'London School Board.' Then Craven Street H.E.

School, Hull 1902-3, head master East Riding PT Centre 1903-5, and English Master, Hull Municipal Technical College, Park Street, Hull, 1905. In 1908 on December 29th at Holy Trinity Church, Hull, he married Henrietta Annie Wood, elder daughter of David and Sarah Wood. They were resident at Collingwood House, Morrill Street, Hull, and the newly weds would make their home at 48, Morrill Street. Eneas later became headmaster of the School of Commerce, assistant organiser of evening schools and evening classes. and acting head of the Technical College. Then in 1925 he became principal of the College. In 1933 he was still resident at 48, Morrill Street, Hull. He could have retired in 1942 but due to a shortage of teachers he stayed on, eventually asking to retire as Principal of the Technical College on August 31st 1944. For some considerable time he had lived at St. John's Croft, St. John's Road, Driffield, and in retirement continued as churchwarden of St. John's Church, becoming in 1946 one of the candidates for election to the Urban Council. Resident at 24, St. John's Road, Driffield, he died in 1964 on December 12th.

12 Information, although not within the realm of this book, regarding 'Songs of the West,' and the Rev. Sabine Baring-Gould - of which there was until recently an appreciation society - is nowadays available on the Internet.

13 Peter Barnes of the village of Simpson (Milton Keynes) has studied the career of Edmund, and with his kind permission this extract is included; "Around the time of their marriage 'Frank Pemberton' joined Sabine Baring-Gould's touring company, performing the show 'Songs of the West' which was based on songs from Baring-Gould's book of folk songs of that name. In 1894 Frank/Edmund acted as director for the company. In the following year he took over running the show completely and they were to tour versions of it around the country for the next decade - and even toured in the USA."

14 The local education authority acquired the premises in 1906 and the infants dept was closed in 1907, followed by the boys in 1916, and the girls in 1922. All traces of Day Street were removed in the 1950s/1960s redevelopment in the area.

15 The Thomas Gray Primary School was one of the first council run primary schools in Slough, built by the Stoke Poges School Board in 1895.

16 In March 1940 he married Ivy Jane Wilsher (1917-2001) and died in October 1976 of 5, Leon Avenue.

17 Since that was written, the site of a shrunken medieval village at Woughton has been investigated, the details of which are told on the information boards on the site.

18 As described in 'A Guide to the Historic Buildings of Milton Keynes,' published in 1986 by Milton Keynes Development Corporation with research carried out by Paul Woodfield. This, together with an earlier version, was an invaluable and carefully undertaken survey of the historic buildings of the villages to become part of the New City.

19 For her marriage to the Rev. John Benthall of Willen, see the Woolstones & Willen book in this series.

20 It seems that she had interests in wood carving, and in December 1892 regarding a small sale of articles carved by the Woughton boys' carving class, held

in the village schoolroom behind the church at 2pm, she made known she would be pleased 'to see anyone who will come and give the boys a little encouragement in their work.' In fact this seemed an annual occurrence, since in 1893 another sale of articles, 'of a variety suitable for Christmas presents,' carved by the Village Carving Class, was held in the school on the afternoon of Tuesday, December 5th. The items included photo frames, oak tea trays, bread trenchers, tables etc., and also a number of boxes and frames carved in Cedar wood from the English Lakes. In spite of widespread influenza many people came along, with the incentive of tea at Woughton House. Over £22 was taken and once the cost of the wood was deducted £13 2s 1½d was distributed among the members of the Class, according to the work they had done. Then in 1894 on Monday, January 15th the members of the Carving Class showed their appreciation of the services of their teacher, Mrs. W.J. Levi, by the gift of an illuminated address. This was presented by the rector and had been carved by Miss Graves, one of the pupils.

21 The Morgan Brothers

Successive to that of Edward Halse and Son, of some 50 years standing, in 1852 from a family of Welsh entrepreneurs William Vaughan Morgan, 1826-1892, acquired a hardware business in London. In 1855 with the firm then becoming Morgan Brothers he was joined by his five brothers, one of whom, Septimus Vaughan Morgan (1832-1913) married Ellen Sarah Simkin in 1870. She had been born in 1845 and of their marriage two children were born - Ethel Vaughan Morgan, in 1871, and Gwyn Vaughan Morgan, in 1872. Whilst the initial intent had been to enhance their interests in hardware and druggist's sundries, it was due to the ensuing success, plus the hope of complementing aspects of their factoring business, that in 1859 the brothers established the journal of 'The Chemist & Druggist.' Also 'The Ironmonger,' and subsequently in 1861 'The Grocer,' and in 1863 'The British Trade Journal.' In 1898 the business was joined by Penry Vaughan Morgan and, as the son of Septimus, Gwyn Vaughan Morgan. In 1913 Septimus, of 37, Harrington Gardens, South Kensington, and 42, Cannon Street, London, died on December 2nd. Probate was granted to his offspring Ethel Vaughan Morgan and Gwyn Vaughan Morgan, with the effects totalling £325,223 14s 8d. Then when William Morgan died in 1916 Edward, as the last of the original brothers, took charge. However that year 'so far as Edward Vaughan Morgan is concerned' came the 'Dissolution of the Partnership between Edward Vaughan Morgan, Gwyn Vaughan Morgan, and Penry Vaughan Morgan, carrying on business as Newspaper Proprietors at 42, Cannon Street, city of London, under the style of Morgan Brothers.' In consequence 'under the style' of Morgan Brothers the business was continued by Gwyn Vaughan Morgan and Penry Vaughan Morgan, and after WW1 became Morgan Brothers (Publishers) Ltd. In 1929 on May 1st the amalgamation took place of 'The Engineer Ltd.,' of 33, Norfolk Street, Strand WC, (they being proprietors of 'The Engineer', founded in 1856) with Morgan Brothers (Publishers) Ltd. of 42, Cannon Street, London, proprietors of 'The Ironmonger', and 'The Chemist and Druggist.' The amalgamation took the form of a new company which, with a nominal capital of £500,000 in £1 shares, was to be called Morgan Brothers (Publishers), Ltd., 'which will acquire the three journals from their present proprietors.' The registered offices would be at 42, Cannon Street, but were transferred as an emergency measure prior to the outbreak of WW2 to Bath, where the printing was carried out by The Pitman Press. In January 1946 the office accommodation then returned to London. As for 'The Ironmonger,' the journal came to an end in the later 1960s, with the firm soon absorbed by conglomerates of rival publishing.

22 Austin Uvedale Morgan Hudson

Austin was born in 1897 on February 6th. He was educated at Eton and Sandhurst, being commissioned in WW1 in the Royal Berkshire Regiment. He subsequently transferred to the Guards Machine Gun Regiment, and after the war with the rank of Captain was placed on the reserve in 1920. That year he became a director of Morgan Brothers (Publishers) Ltd., and at the 1922 General Election became Conservative MP for Islington East. He lost this seat the following year but in 1924 took Hackney North from the Liberals. In June 1940 amongst others he was appointed by the King to be Commissioner 'for executing the office of Lord High Admiral of the United Kingdom.' In 1942 he was made a baronet and in 1943 gained election as Senior Warden of the Worshipful Company of Ironmongers, becoming Master of the Company the following year. At the Labour party's landslide victory in 1945 he lost his Parliamentary seat, but in April 1948 was made vice chairman of Morgan Brothers (Publishers) Ltd. Two years later he returned to Parliament as MP for the new Lewisham North. This he duly held until his death on November 29th 1956, having been made Chairman of Morgan Brothers (Publishers) Ltd. just a few months before.

23 Apparently when resident at Birstal, Yorkshire, John Foster purchased an estate at Marston Moretaine at the end of the 18th century. Later he was resident at Brickhill House, Bedford, and when he died in 1831 he left the estate to his eldest daughter Margaret, wife from 1836 of the Rev. Maurice Farrell, who was noted as the owner in 1837 and 1840. Margaret was also left the Shelton estate, and after her marriage Maurice is named as the owner of the house in 1838 and 1842. The farm homestead was leased, plus some 255 acres, to a tenant farmer Thomas Bennett. In 1863 the Rev Farrell is recorded as owner of the estate. At Upper Shelton in 1850 the Exhibition pub was purchased by the Reverend, who in 1864 gave it to his son Maurice Foster Farrell of Brownlow Street Middx. In 1878 he leased it to Charles Wells, a brewer, for 14 years at £14pa. Presumably following Maurice's tragic death from drowning the freehold was then bought by Charles Wells.

24 Edward was extremely wealthy, with a personal estate amounting to around £2,000:

The will of Edward Islip Sibley, farmer and grazier of Cogenhoe - made 1791 September 7th, proved 1793 October 12th.

The will was made when the testator was 'weak of body' and includes the following bequests:

To his wife Sarah and daughter Elizabeth Sibley all his real and personal estate. This was for the life of Sarah and charged with provision for the maintenance of his son John, 'a lunatic.'

After the death of Sarah, Elizabeth was to receive all the household furniture, beds, bedding, chairs, glasses, china, silver, pewter, brass, copper, brewing vessels, tubs, barrels.

After the death of Sarah the real estate and remaining personal estate was to be equally divided between his daughter Mary Coles, wife of Joseph Coles, farmer and grazier of Denton; his daughter Sarah Collier, wife of Thomas Collier, farmer of Little Houghton; and his daughter Elizabeth Sibley.

The above bequest of the real estate was charged with the provision for his son John for life.

His wife Sarah, and daughter Elizabeth Sibley as executrices.

25 In June 1792, in the parish of Cogenhoe the most substantial single landholder was Edward Sibley, and then in June 1793 John Chapman.

26 Deeds relating to the newly built George, at Tickford End, Newport Pagnell, mention William Yates and Charles Redden to John Chapman of Woughton, dated 1836 April 7th and 8th. (Bucks Archives D254/5/11.)

27 The will of John Chapman yeoman 'formerly of Cogenhoe, late of Wollaston,' made 1831 June 21st, proved 1837 March 11th.

This includes the following bequests:

To his sister Mary Chapman, all personal estate, including monies and securities. This bequest was for the life of Mary, and after her death was to be equally divided between his 5 children - ie.

Elizabeth Terrell bapt. 1800 Dec. 21st, wife of Samuel Terrell, blacksmith of Wellingborough.

Stephen Chapman bapt. 1803 Apr. 17th.

Ann Boyson, bapt. 1805 Mar. 21st, wife of Thomas Boyson, innkeeper of Wollaston.

Martha Chapman bapt. 1808 Aug. 7th.

Jane Chapman bapt. 1811 Sep. 8th.

His sister Mary to be executrix.

(The five children who were beneficiaries of the will were all children of John Chapman's marriage in 1800 to Sarah Norton.)

28   Baptised on May 3rd, Grace Constance Wetherall had been born in 1900 to Ernest Victor Albert Wetherall and his wife Louise Constance (nee Cooper.) The family were resident at Hill Crest, Addlestone, but following Ernest's death by 1911 Louise and Gladys were living at 42, Woodfield Road, Ealing. Then in 1913 on June 14th at the church of St. Stephen, Westminster, Louise married Morton Henry Festing. Morton died in 1917 and by 1934 Louise - now as Louise Constance Festing - and Gladys were resident at 3, Myddleton House, Enfield. In 1935 on October 1st at St. Andrew's Church, Enfield, Gladys, who had been District Commissioner for the East Division of the Enfield Girl Guides Association since 1925, married John Wilfred Shirley, a farmer, aged 30, of Woughton. She was given away by her guardian, Col. Henry Ferryman Bowles, with the service conducted by her uncle, the Rev. Granville Cooper, and the Rev. J. Daisley. A reception was given by Col. Bowles and his wife at Forty Hall, and the honeymoon would be a motoring tour of Scotland. The newly weds made Pear Tree Farm their home at Woughton, to where by 1939 Louise had also moved, resident at North Cottage. This was still her address when she died in 1959 on August 17th. As for

Gladys, she died in 1963 on October 5th, with probate granted to her husband.